Agony
in the
Garden

Agony
in the
Garden

SEX, LIES, AND REDEMPTION FROM
THE TROUBLED HEART OF THE
AMERICAN CATHOLIC CHURCH

John van der Zee

THUNDER'S MOUTH PRESS/NATION BOOKS
NEW YORK

AGONY IN THE GARDEN: Sex, Lies, and Redemption from the
Troubled Heart of the American Catholic Church

Copyright © 2002 John van der Zee

Published by
Thunder's Mouth Press/Nation Books
161 William St., 16th Floor
New York, NY 10038

Nation Books is a co-publishing venture of the Nation Institute
and Avalon Publishing Group Incorporated.

Library of Congress Control Number: 2002113815

ISBN 1-56025-471-8

9 8 7 6 5 4 3 2 1

Book design by Paul Paddock
Printed in the United States of America
Distributed by Publishers Group West

A portion of this book appeared, in slightly different form, in *salon.com*

Introduction

*A*gony in the Garden could serve as the template for the series of scandals that struck the Roman Catholic Church in the early years of the twenty-first century and continues up to the present moment.

The Church, which met the great political challenge of the twentieth century, Communism, but failed to meet its most significant moral challenge, the Holocaust, now faces an adversary more threatening to its interests than either: the Church's own internal demoralization.

What the seductions and force of totalitarian ideologies and the lingering horror of the revelation of ecclesiastical indifference to the existence of the death camps didn't accomplish, the institutional Church, in its refusal to confront openly the consequences of clergy sexual abuse and its prolonged and systematic cover-up, is doing to itself.

The still unfolding story of priest sexual abuse in Boston, California, Florida, Canada, Ireland, Austria, France, Australia, Poland, and elsewhere, compounded by hierarchical obfuscation, is damning in both the universality of its occurrence and the uniformity of official response to what is always forced exposure: denial and insistence on blind faith.

The bishops and cardinals and the Holy See—precisely the people who should insist on the primacy of truth and the insistence upon justice—have turned away from enduring values in the short-term interest of image preservation and the maintenance of position and influence. In the process, they have lost both.

By turning away from its own people when its counsel and comforts were needed most, the Church has betrayed its own ideals, undercut its moral authority, and told its members what in effect is most damaging to any organization: that ultimately, we are on our own.

As the scandal spreads, diocese by diocese, country by country, it has become clear that the greater evil is not the individual instances of priest sexual abuse, cruelly exploitative as many of them are. It is the systematic and patterned cover-up, the lies and evasions, the denial of empathy and haste to move on, the unexamined transfer of offenders and negotiated silence of victims, the blocked investigations and sealed records, the shared techniques of attorney hardball and litigious rationalization, the corporate cowering behind legal and public relations counsel, that have turned the Church into a giant copying machine, churning out repeat traumatic situations parish by parish, for decades. And it is responding now with formulaic expressions of shock, personal sorrow, and promises to impose stricter screening of candidates.

These tactics, effective as they may be in the short run, only deepen the long-term consequences of what continues to be revealed. By extending distraction and draining resources they undercut the Church's vital functions of teaching, counseling, and the administration of the sacraments. And by failing even to discuss the root issues—mandatory celibacy, the restoration of married priests, the ordination of women—they guarantee that this problem will continue to manifest itself, perhaps in altered forms such as increased alcohol or drug abuse by priests, or in clerical embezzlement. The cover-up has become an exercise in antinomy, preserving faith by destroying its original Greek meaning, trust.

This lack of limits or, a bedrock acceptance of responsibility or, some sense of where the buck stops has produced draconian suggestions such as the statement from a Vatican spokesman presenting the possibility that the ordination of all homosexual priests might be voided. Doing so would be a further draining of an already shrunken talent pool. This failure to provide firm footing, combined with the length and depth of the cover-up, means that there will inevitably be a purge of some kind that will result in more than one case of an able priest, who maybe once had a lapse and made a pass at a kid, having his career destroyed. This may be the most poignant tragedy of this whole sad business.

In the parishes where these incidents have been made public, the reaction of the parishioners is similar to that of the victims: shock, anger, resentment combined with wonder if they or their actions have brought this upon themselves. This concern—radiating outward through empty assurances that the abuses are all in the past, that we must forgive and forget—both broadens and deepens concern without a firm boundary of faced truth. Were these people in cahoots? Is there a conspiracy, a priestly sexual Comintern, some system of mutual understanding and tradeoffs within the priesthood that renders the rest of us outsiders? If so, what does this mean for the future of an inclusive, universal, Catholic Church?

The requests to move forward and let bygones be bygones are an insult to people who have been taught that true contrition is a required condition for the forgiveness of sin. The truth is that the hierarchy of the Catholic Church needs to go to Confession. Not some blanket agreement to forgive and forget, but the whole process: an examination of conscience, followed by an enumeration of sins and a promise to do penance and to amend—which

Introduction

means change—one's life. Every Catholic, practicing or lapsed, knows this process. And it is exactly what is missing from every official statement, press release, and bishop's or cardinal's message concerning this sad series of scandals. Nothing less will do, because it will not resonate among people who have been trained by Catholic priests and religious and lay teachers to expect better.

The machinery for effecting this ecclesiastical clearing of conscience already exists. It is there in the Councils that have altered the structure of the Church in response to previous crises and in the statements like those of the American bishops on peace and nuclear weapons. The smug assumption that the Church has survived for 2,000 years by remaining adamant does not withstand serious investigation. It is the Church's capacity to change, while keeping its abiding teachings intact, that has allowed its survival.

It has been observed elsewhere that the Catholic Church, in its penchant for silence and secrecy and top-down management style, resembles a modern corporation. If so, it's one whose operations are in trouble—declining attendance, shrinking recruitment, recurring sexual and financial scandal, selling off property to pay for legal settlements. Maybe it's time to consider a new business model, say, the Church of its first thousand years: a generally thriving enterprise employing both celibate and married priests, with laity who had a say in its operations and popes who were subject to criticism and sometimes dismissal by lay-summoned Church Councils.

What we have come to is an almost complete reversal of the centuries when it was the clergy who were the Latin-speaking elite and the rubes in the pews who were confined to the vernacular. Now, in almost any Catholic congregation you will find men and women who not only have better administrative ability and executive experience than the pastor, but who are better educated. The cargo carried by the vessel of Christendom has shifted, and the ship must be trimmed to reflect it.

What is crucial here is that lay Catholics with influence—that is, people with money, the people whom the hierarchy turns to first when it needs help—must use their clout. They must refuse to seed the fund drives or bail out the lagging raffles unless concessions are made in return: reconsideration of mandatory celibacy, reinstatement of priests who have married, consideration of the ordination of women. Wealthy Catholics must resist the blandishments of the hierarchy and bond instead with their fellow Catholics in the pews. This is where the leverage can be applied to greatest effect. The Catholic Church in the United States is reputedly the Vatican's cash cow. And it is simply good business to make sure you get what you pay for.

It may be that these changes—ending mandatory celibacy, reinstating married priests, ordaining women—are too sweeping and simplistic to correct the abuses within the Church. What is certain, however, is that the refusal even to discuss them guarantees that the worst of the present wrongs will continue and perhaps manifest themselves in other ways.

If the institutional Church continues its increasingly revealed practices of concealing evidence, transferring guilty offenders and buying the silence of victims, contaminating both the Church and the legal system, it will be forcing individuals to choose between being good Catholics and being good Americans. That is a contest the Church can't win.

The question needs to be asked: from a purely utilitarian point of view, is the Catholic Church worth saving in America? Are its consoling functions not met by the assurances of the Constitution and the Bill of Rights? Is its teaching function not better filled by secular institutions? Is its penchant for silence and secrecy, for top-down management by a distant, foreign-based authority not a threat to democratic institutions?

The need for spiritual expression inevitably seems to find, in those places where formal faith has been suppressed or abolished, truly grotesque substitutes such as giant photographs of political figures, a theologically empty restoration of tribal folklore, an embrace of extreme nationalism, or of money. As the poet Aram Saroyan has pointed out, the United States is a country without a culture. We have an economy instead. As Americans, Catholic and non-Catholic alike, we need the tempering of all the seasoned, mature spiritual influences we can get to oppose the ultimately despairing embrace of the money culture. Among other benefits, spiritual influences represent the accumulated learning from mistakes by others we can profit from, which is much less painful than making them ourselves. Also, the money culture is powerful. In its relentless practicality, its denial of the value of spiritual concerns, it is pervasive even though it eventually leaves us abandoned. We need strong, spiritually based organizations to oppose it if only to maintain equilibrium and give the breathing room against some prevailing orthodoxy—whether economic, political, or religious—that each of us needs to survive.

The institutional Church, particularly the Curia, cannot initiate the changes that the restored health of an American Catholicism requires. They are too removed from the pain of necessity to do what needs to be done. Instead the process needs to proceed at the pastoral level among the priests in the parishes, the nuns in the hospitals and schools, and the laity in the pews where, out of necessity, it has already begun. Where doctrinal intolerance—denying sacraments to the divorced and remarried, condemning people for practicing birth control, excommunicating those associated with abortion—has already become a matter of individual conscience. In a sense we have come full circle, back to Jesus who was essentially a layperson opposing, from the call of his own conscience and the realities of the day-to-day world, an entrenched and dogmatic priesthood.

It is both a problem for the Church, and an opportunity, for those who are willing to name the pain. One of them is Monsignor

Clement Connolly, pastor of Holy Family Parish in South
Pasadena, California. In a Sunday homily to his congregation,
Monsignor Connolly observed that "This is a good time for the
Church. Bad for the image perhaps, but good for the Church. It is
a passage of purification."

In his thirty-eight years as a priest, Connolly told his parishioners, according to *The National Catholic Reporter*, he had never
"felt the power and challenge that is abroad today in life. It is a
time of painful suffering, but it is necessary to face it, to own it and
to share it. Purification is always painful. It always takes courage. It
always takes faith. That's what lies before us."

Amen.

Prologue

This story began for me with a phone call in the late dusk of a summer evening: my old friend Lucky was on the horn again, yammering about one of the two subjects which had come to obsess him, the Irish Republican Army and pedophile priests in the Catholic Church.

Always jittery, radiating nervous energy, he had edged over into a full-time manic state these last few months, not sleeping, not eating, drinking heavily, getting into one scrape after another including an arrest for illegal possession of a concealed firearm after an altercation in a hotel disco. For the last five months, he had been calling me every day—as many as six calls in a single day—at times argumentative and abusive, at others maudlin and apologetic.

"I have a plan I want to try on you," he told me now, "to see if you can find any flaws in it. And moral considerations don't count."

Our conversations, over these months, had taken on some of the flavor of a moral and ethical debate. In his increasing obsession with the IRA and pedophile priests, he had become convinced that violence was both justified and necessary against the opponents of the one and the practitioners of the other. At one time a nationally recognized CPA, he had been spending enormous amounts of energy badgering his old friends to donate money to The Cause, providing funds for weapons through San Francisco's network of barstool revolutionaries. Just about everyone had turned him down in his efforts to act out his first obsession. Now he was concentrating on his second.

"As you know, I have a gun. It's only a pellet gun, which I have the legal right to own. But it's powerful enough to kill someone at close range, say ten feet. Here's what I intend to do. I'm going to take a plane to San Diego, and I'm going to put the gun in my checked baggage. Know why?"

Lucky had always considered himself just a little smarter than everybody else. It had been a major source of his problems.

"No, I don't."

"There's no baggage check in intrastate flights. In San Diego, I'm going to rent a car, which I'm going to drive across the border to Ensenada. I've located Kevin Dugan there, and I'm going to kill him."

"Don't do it."

"I told you, moral considerations don't count. Do you see any flaw in this plan so far?"

"No."

"I'll dispose of the gun in Mexico. Then I'll drive back to San Diego, where I'll pick up another gun. I used to live there, so it's easy to do. Then, in San Diego, I'm going to locate and kill Nicholas Topfer."

Kevin Dugan was a former classmate of ours, a Catholic priest and a convicted pedophile. Nicholas Topfer, another pedophile priest, had been the cause of a record civil judgment against the Catholic Church in another state and was now supposedly living in San Diego.

Lucky sounded calm, rational, a criminal mastermind addressing his hopelessly befuddled stooge. "Do you know how I'm going to get his address?"

"No."

"I'm going to call the California State Directory of Convicted Sex Offenders. And I'm going to give them your name and phone number."

"Don't do this."

"Can you see any flaw in this plan? Moral considerations don't count."

"Don't do it. Don't leave your kids with this."

He hung up on me. When I called him back, there was no answer. He'd said he was about to leave for the San Francisco airport. For better or worse, he was on his way.

He'll fuck up, I told myself, get lost or get busted or killed. He's wacko, no real danger to anyone but himself. As for the pedophiles, I didn't care if they lived or died; my concern was for Lucky and his family, with whom I'd been in touch ever since his trouble with the gun. Plus I felt responsible for having planted the seed of this obsession in the fevered jungle of his mind.

For months we had been arguing, as lapsed Catholics, about our problems with the Church, to which I had recently returned and Lucky had maintained an off-again, on-again relationship with over the years. My problem had to do with pedophile priests in the Church in general and Kevin Dugan as a living instance of that problem.

It had been nearly thirty years since Dugan, a high-school classmate of ours, and a college classmate also of Lucky's, had been charged with molesting two young boys who had been left in his care at a parish rectory. Another classmate, one of the cops who investigated the case, had told me that Dugan had pleaded *nolo contendere*, been convicted, and been granted probation on condition that he never be allowed around children again. Six months later, Father Dugan turned up at the policeman's church, assigned to the parish, which had both Christian Doctrine classes and a grade school. There was no warning or explanation; the conditions of his probation had been ignored.

Over the years since, there had been at least a half-dozen known instances of molestation associated with Dugan, including one with the son of a deceased prominent political figure following the funeral at which Dugan had officiated, and another that amounted to a near-rape. There were currently molestation settlements in the diocese where I live concerning Dugan approaching a half-million dollars. At the time Lucky and I were talking, Dugan was supposedly in Mexico, where he was rector of an orphanage.

I don't know whether Lucky had ever been molested as a boy, but the rank injustice of such a series of unprosecuted criminal acts definitely hit him at some profound level. With each civil suit and most often a financial settlement by the Church in exchange for an agreement of silence, Lucky's sense of injury and indignation had snowballed until he had convinced himself that since neither the Church nor the civil authorities would deal with this plague effectively, some sort of vigilante action on his part was called for. He would be a kind of Catholic kamikaze, an avenger, who through murder would force the pedophiles in the Church to answer for or at least restrain their crimes. Maybe a thwarted attempt would be enough to satisfy this need in him for vengeance and present him with limits beyond which he could not go. I could not bring myself, at this point, to turn him in.

His mission failed; something went wrong in San Diego. In the extravagant behavior associated with people in a manic state, he hired a cab and paid the driver $2,000 to drive him the more than 500 miles back to Northern California. The obstacles in his path, however, only further provoked him to travel it. Less than a week later, he was back on the phone with another plan. His family were trying to get him to return to Texas, where he could be entered into treatment, and he had agreed to go, but with a hidden agenda: he would switch tickets and carry out his previous plan.

I called his family. They had been through this before. A ticket would be paid for, and he would either cash it in or use it to head to some other destination. They asked if I would take him to the airport and make sure he got on the right plane and I said I would. I called Lucky and offered to take him to the airport, but I insisted that there be no gun. He agreed, but said there was to be a change of plan. Now he was going by train on Amtrak.

"Know why?" He was in his criminal mastermind mode.

"No."

"No weapons check."

He was out to con me, but at least there was the possibility of getting him help. Also, I had a guilty conscience for bringing up the issue of pedophile priests and Kevin Dugan in the first place. I told him I would pick him up and drive him to the Amtrak station.

Minutes later, another friend and classmate called, a lawyer who had also been in touch with Lucky's family. I told him what I'd agreed to do, and he said, "You can't do that. He'll never make it." The lawyer said he'd make some phone calls and asked me to stop by his office on the way to Lucky's apartment. I got in my car and headed south, wondering how on earth I'd got myself into this.

When I reached the lawyer's office, he had been trying unsuccessfully to contact a psychiatrist in order to arrange Lucky's immediate commitment. I told him about the death threats.

"We have to call the cops," he said. "This is prior knowledge of an attempted felony."

I told him I had misgivings. "He has a gun. It's not a real gun, but it looks just like one. He's so paranoid I'm afraid if they go in there, he'll pull it out and they'll shoot him."

The lawyer, thinking strategy while I was still on tactics, pondered this. "Okay, here's what we'll do. There's a strip mall near his apartment. We'll have the cops meet us there. I'll wait there with them while you go to pick Lucky up. Tell him you dropped me off to make a phone call, and that you're going to stop and pick me up on the way back. When you get back with him, the cops will grab him."

"Jesus."

"What's wrong?"

"We're setting him up."

"It has to be done."

We headed in my car to the strip mall, reminiscing on the way that there was a time we would have been trying to spring Lucky loose from the cops rather than turn him over. We were, among other things, betraying our longest loyalties to our own younger selves.

There were two patrol cars at the mall, two pair of county sheriff's deputies. The lawyer explained to the sergeant in charge what was happening, then I detailed the death threats to him while he took notes. A deputy briefed me about what to do: roll the car windows down; if the person is resisting or giving you trouble, flash the headlights; if there's physical resistance or a fight, get out of the car, but make sure you grab the keys.

When I was alone, starting the car, the sergeant in charge came over to the window. "You realize that you are entering a situation where there is a man with a gun, and you understand and accept the possible consequences of this situation?"

He was halfway through it before I realized it was a waiver absolving the department of liability in case I got shot.

I agreed. I'd come this far; there was no point in turning back now. With the car windows down, I headed out of the strip mall parking lot. How *had* I ever got myself into this?

John van der Zee

+ + +

The Catholic priesthood, another former classmate, 15 years a
Jesuit, once told me, is in many ways a prolonged adolescence.
"You have a job, from which you won't be fired, a roof over your
head, three meals, and no wife and kids to support. For some
priests, there's even an allowance." There is also a kind of adolescent absence of consequences. If a priest gets into trouble with
drinking or drugs, money or sex, the matter is traditionally handled privately, discreetly, to avoid giving scandal and protect reputations. There is—or has been—in effect a separate system like the
juvenile justice system that insulates offenders from the full adult
consequences of their acts. Again, as with adolescents, there is the
assumption that any messes will be left to others to clean up, with
the perpetrators permitted to retain the purity of their amateur
standing and even a certain air of moral superiority. I was where I
was right now because I was trying to clean up one of those messes.

For nearly thirty years, Lucky and I and many of the Catholic
men and women we grew up with had lived with the knowledge of
a serious wrong—maybe *the* most serious kind of wrong, the
destruction of children's innocence—being euphemized and
hidden and denied by our Church. Part of this was the knowledge
that no other organization, whether governmental, educational,
business, or military, could have permitted this situation to have
continued for so long unaddressed. The fact that the consequences
of these acts were not dealt with by the Church does not mean that
they disappeared. They were simply, as in adolescent behavior, left
to others to deal with: the victims and their families in the more
serious case of molestation; people who unwittingly find themselves physically at risk in lesser situations such as mine. Did the
Church have any idea of the resentment, the rage sometimes bordering on the urge to murder that simmered among people who
had to assume adult responsibilities for men they were expected to
address as Father? This was part of The World, that inferior place

where people dirtied themselves in jobs where you could be laid off or fired, in maintaining relationships and being there for children, in earning the money that paid the parish bills, provided the parochial school tuition, and filled the Sunday collection envelopes. People who pretty much lived by the rules that priests, in a pinch, could be exempted from. It was this resentment, compressed into a rage by repeated Church denial, that had set Lucky on his mad mission and had engendered the guilt or responsibility toward friendships formed in Catholic school that made the lawyer and me try to stop him.

At Lucky's apartment, a radio was blasting rock 'n' roll oldies at such a high volume nobody could have heard the bell. I thumped my fist on the door: no answer. Through the window, I could see into the kitchen, where a pair of bottles, gin and vermouth, were displayed atop the refrigerator, elevated and gleaming like objects of veneration. I tried the handle: the door was unlocked. I went inside, calling his name before I entered each spacious, unfurnished room. I found the radio in the bathroom and turned it off. He was in the bedroom, tapped out and snoring on a bare mattress, a fresh livid cut on the front of his bald dome. I spoke and then yelled his name until he woke up.

He came back from some deep vengeance fog, a teenage world like the one we'd shared of beefs and not taking shit from anyone. The cut on his head, he explained, came from some row he'd had that morning with local kids; a man in his sixties, for God's sake. I told him I'd come to take him to the train and explained how we had to stop at the mall and pick up the lawyer. Confident he was outthinking me, he assured me he wasn't bringing his gun and told me I could check his backpack if I wanted. I said I would, and did.

He turned the radio back on before we left. "Makes people think there's somebody home," he said, always scheming. *Great for the neighbors,* I thought but didn't say, harboring a scheme of my own.

"You guys are the greatest friends, to do this for me," he said as my heart sank, driving him to where the cops were waiting to take him into custody.

We headed into the strip mall where the lawyer stood, waiting. I stopped the car next to him; Lucky got out and embraced him. Two cops stepped up and slipped the cuffs on him. Lucky knew immediately what was happening. "Here we go again," he said.

Two days later he called me from the locked mental ward of a local hospital. His voice was subdued; he was probably medicated. "I just wanted to thank you guys for what you did."

I yelled at him. "It's okay to be pissed off! I'd be pissed if somebody did that to me."

No, no, we had done the right thing; he was grateful. And in truth it seemed as if the storm that had been raging in his brain had passed, for at least as long as he remained in therapy and took his medication. And in time, though the storms continued to come and go, the need for that particular form of vengeance seemed to have passed. He grew distracted or had somehow moved on. But the question remained: why did it have to come to this? Not just for my friend Lucky, but for the children these priests had molested after their pathology was known, and even, God help us, for the priests themselves. Why had their acts and condition not been addressed effectively years before? Why had these legally adult men repeatedly been granted adolescent absence from the consequences of their acts?

There is a price to be paid for secrecy and silence in the preservation of reputations. Gaining power in darkness, it is a price that is paid with interest by people innocent of the original injurious acts. To talk about these things and to bring them to public discussion is, as the Church says, to give scandal; but there are worse things than giving scandal. Ignoring agony for one; standing by while lives are broken, for another.

Prologue

This, then is my bias, the passion behind what follows, set down with the skills and in fidelity to the values I was originally taught by priests and nuns.

Agony
in the
Garden

I t was in the spring of 1996 that the fabric of the black curtain began coming apart.

St. Mary of the Angels was an old, cramped stucco church in the heart of the redwood region town of Ukiah, California. For years, the Catholic parishioners had been contributing money through special collections, fundraising events, and regular pledges for the construction of a new church. It was planned to be bright and sun-splashed, as Ukiah's climate is in summer, with a rich natural wood interior reflecting the great forest extending westward to the Pacific and north toward Canada. The woods were the reason for Ukiah's existence, both the source of the raw material that fed its mills and pulping plants and the flashpoint for environmentalist action against the logging of the world's last remaining stands of old-growth redwood forest. The two faiths, the tree and the cross, had combined recently when the diocesan bishop, George Patrick Ziemann, the area's most influential religious figure, had announced his support for a moratorium on old-growth logging. It suggested a promising reconciliation of New Age consciousness with Old World reason and logic, a convergence of conscience that might forestall further confrontation with its implicit and sometimes explicit violence.

Bishop Pat, as the unpretentious Ziemann was known to Catholics of his sprawling diocese, geographically the largest in California, was an enthusiastic supporter of a new church for the Ukiah parish. He went so far as to suggest that the traditional requirement of 60 percent parish financing before any construction could be approved might in this case be waived. It was a promising initiative, a constructive mirror image of his efforts to bring peace to the redwoods. His unofficial official endorsement, hastening the day of a tangible start on the new church, had stimulated increased donations on the part of the members of St. Mary of the Angels' congregation. The only problem was that some of this money—along with other money from parish collections—was disappearing. The pastor, Father Hans Ruygt, had grown concerned enough about it to contact Fred Keplinger, Ukiah's chief of police.

"The thefts went back months and months," Keplinger recalled nearly three years later, "and a member of the church office staff was suspected. I called the Department of Justice, and got hidden cameras installed, watching the parish safe."

Keplinger is a man in his forties, wearing sweats and a baseball cap and carrying a cane. Diagnosed as having multiple sclerosis, he is on disability leave from his job as police chief.

"Nothing happened on the cameras. Then the office employee who had been suspected of taking the money left. The thefts stopped for a while."

Before long, money began sporadically disappearing again. Collections, both cash and bank bags containing cash and checks, were being put in a safety deposit box. "We felt something was happening at the box," Keplinger says, "so we did a sting."

The parish office changed to numbering the bank bags and

logged out the numbers to the individual priest and mass so they could be traced.

Then an unusual opportunity to confirm such a trace presented itself. There was a pair of women in the parish who had pledged regular donations to St. Mary's building fund and maintained them faithfully. "They were old-time friends, who most people thought were sisters. They dressed alike, went everywhere together, and they donated the identical amount to the building fund every Sunday."

When the two women received an annual statement of their donations from the parish for tax purposes and the statement didn't square with their own records, they brought it to the attention of the parish office. "I don't know if they were dunned or not," Keplinger said, "but it established a pattern, a clear record of funds missing after masses said by one particular priest."

The priest, the Rev. Jorge Hume Salas, a native of Costa Rica, had been ordained in an elaborate ceremony by Bishop Ziemann in 1993. In part of what was considered Bishop Pat's outreach policy to the area's large and often neglected Latino community, Hume Salas was made a priest without graduating from a seminary, after serving fifteen months as a deacon.

The missing donations were traced to Hume Salas's Sunday afternoon masses. That same evening, Keplinger sent Detective Mariano Guzman down to the church rectory. Guzman found that Hume was removing bank bags from the safe, breaking a seal, and removing cash. The remaining money was put into a bank bag that could be freshly sealed and returned to the safe. Detective Guzman had found both opened and changed bags in Hume Salas's possession. He had also overheard Salas admitting to Father Hans, his pastor, that he had taken the money.

The identified missing money amounted to some $1,200, though the total thefts were later estimated as high as $10,000.

"Father Hans, a good man, honest and kind, had confided in his fellow priest, Salas, about the hidden cameras, so nothing had happened then," recalled Keplinger. "The suspected employee, a woman, had left, and everyone had pointed the finger at her. When this happened, Salas was in the room at the time. He said nothing."

At one point, the parish safe had been passed out the window to a buddy of Salas, a man who had been living with him at the rectory.

"Detective Guzman was ready to make an arrest that night. But Bishop Ziemann called Father Hans, the pastor, and asked him to intervene."

The bishop told the pastor that he would come to Ukiah, some sixty miles from the diocese's chancery office, to address the matter personally.

"We thought the world of Bishop Pat," Keplinger recalled. "My son had worked for him for two years. He was the head of the youth group here." A meeting was held at the church rectory. "In the meeting, the bishop was very demanding. 'This is the way it's going to be.' He got very belligerent. It was a side of him I'd never seen before."

Ziemann was adamant about not prosecuting. "He assured us that Hume Salas was going to be in menial jobs in the future," Keplinger said. "That he would never be around money again. He said that church records were not going to be made available. And that the overheard confession was one priest to another, so that it was therefore under the seal of confession.

"He ordered Father Hans, the pastor, from the room. Then he castigated him for calling the police. Hans was trying to do the honorable thing, but priests make a pledge of obedience to their bishop.

"Josie Vargas, a Latina lady, was in that meeting. Everyone in the room wanted Jorge prosecuted. When I play it back in my mind, I feel like an ass, just sitting there. Josie said that there were rumors in the Mexican community that Jorge was molesting young men. It was the first I'd heard of it. I was dumbfounded. I told the bishop, 'If one kid has been molested, all bets are off.' Ziemann said he'd never heard there was such a thing."

The bishop insisted there was insufficient evidence to proceed with the case, and it was obvious that the Church was not going to press charges. "At the meeting, Ziemann said, 'There is not a victim here, because I'll pay back the money myself.'"

"I had spent a lot of manpower and resources on this case," said Keplinger. "If this had been a business where there had been this kind of embezzlement, I'd have said, 'Fuck you! I'll subpoena all of you!'"

But this was Bishop Pat. The Church. Keplinger's own parish.

"The case was gone. It's the only time I ever allowed my religion to get in the way of my job. When I got home, I told my wife about what had happened at the meeting. She said—she's Italian— 'Listen, either that guy has something on Ziemann, or Ziemann is sleeping with him.' I said, 'Oh no! Not Bishop Pat!' We almost got into a fight about it.

"She told me, 'You must be the most naïve police chief in America.'"

Josie Vargas was not the only woman at St. Mary of the Angels who'd had serious reservations about Jorge Hume Salas. Sister Jane Kelly, a sixty-six-year-old nun, who'd spent twenty-six years in the Santa Rosa Diocese, had been concerned about Hume Salas's character and qualifications since 1992, when he'd first been assigned to the parish and where she was expected to oversee his religious instruction.

"There was no precedent for the training of a nonseminary student," Sister Kelly recalled. "I was pressured into it. No one set a course of study for Jorge. There had been no background check on him, and his English was poor." She was never sure how much

Agony in the Garden

Hume Salas understood during their weekly meetings to discuss his spiritual journey. "He taught himself to say Mass by practicing in his room."

He also, Sister Kelly says, invited young Latino men to visit him in his room and occasionally to stay overnight.

Sister Kelly is a tough mother hen who is tender in her solicitude toward her chicks. Over the years, she had acquired a growing sense of outrage over instances of priestly sexual abuse involving minors, some of whom were her former students, and the diocese's repeated failure to deal with them.

As a deacon, Hume Salas received, in addition to his room and board, a monthly stipend of $350. Yet he was somehow supporting a youth soccer program that included uniforms and trophies.

Sister Kelly expressed her concerns about Hume Salas through the appropriate diocesan channels and got nowhere. Within the church's male hierarchy, she was viewed as a troublemaker, something of a zealot.

"The ministry is job security," she observed. "Anything that alters it, threatens it. When laypersons were allowed to administer the Eucharist, priests here objected: 'Then what will *we* do?' I told them, 'You can go watch football on TV.'"

In Ukiah, she was both outspoken and cause-conscious. "Sister Jane has been active in social causes in this county for years," observed Fred Keplinger. "Served on the Human Rights Commission. Plowshares, the Community Dining Room that offers food services as well as health and psychiatric counseling to the poor and homeless, that's her deal.

"A few years back, there was a Shadow Painting of Hiroshima memorial. In memory of the atomic bomb being dropped on Hiroshima, the shadow painting of a person, like the one left on a wall at Hiroshima, would be painted around town. Sister Jane was involved in the demonstration. I scolded her, 'I know what you are doing. If I catch you I'm going to arrest you just like anyone else.'

"I'm in my second marriage. My first was annulled. When the annulment went through, there was some question whether I could receive Communion. I guess I'm an old-fashioned Catholic, so at first I was very reluctant to go forward at Mass and take the Host. One Sunday I did. When I returned to my pew, I felt someone poke me in the back. It was Sister Jane. 'Freddy,' she said, 'if you didn't go up to receive Communion, I was going to bring a Host back for you.'

"I just love that woman."

There were two objective reasons, or maybe rationalizations, for ordaining Hume Salas: the diocese was desperately short of priests, and he was a Latino. "There was a big growth in the Latino population and few Mexican clergy," explained Monsignor John O'Hare, a thirty-five-year veteran of the Diocese. "Vocations had declined, the Diocese grew desperate for ordained men. Ziemann would scoop up anybody."

It was in July of 1992, only days after Ziemann's appointment to the Santa Rosa Diocese, that Jorge Raul Hume Salas wrote his letter of introduction to the new bishop. Hume had come to the diocese's chancery office in the city of Santa Rosa on the recommendation of the Rev. Jesse Galaz, director of vocations for the Archdiocese of Los Angeles. Though Ziemann had been an associate bishop in the Los Angeles Diocese, there appears to be no evidence that the two men were previously acquainted. A slight, prematurely balding man with close-cropped graying black hair, an engaging smile and a trim beard, the 35-year-old Hume Salas stated in his curriculum vitae that he had completed eight semesters at the Universidad Intercontinental in Mexico City, a term of study he had exaggerated. Other items of his personal and academic history he had significantly omitted. Nevertheless, the Rev. Xavier Ochoa, the Santa Rosa Diocese's Director of Hispanic Vocations, was impressed enough with Hume Salas during interviews over several days that he recommended that the young Costa Rican be sent to a parish where he could get instruction in spiritual matters as well as American culture.

"I believe he is an unsophisticated person," Ochoa wrote, "with a profound maturity acquired from a base of suffering and confrontation with the harsh reality of life." Ochoa proposed that if Hume got a favorable review, he might be ordained as a deacon within a year on the way to eventually becoming a priest.

The course of study for a Catholic priest in the United States customarily varies from between a minimum of six years for a diocesan priest to as many as twelve years for some orders, such as the Jesuits. Jorge Hume Salas was ordained a priest after fifteen months despite protests from the designated overseer of his spiritual instruction.

"Shortly before Jorge's ordination," Sister Kelly recalled, "Bishop Ziemann came to the parish in Ukiah. He asked me if I still thought he [Hume Salas] was a pathological liar. 'If you say so,' he told me, 'we won't ordain him.' The invitations to the ordination had already been sent out. 'Don't put that on me,' I told him. He could have used that for an out: told Hume Salas, 'I can't ordain you. There are objections.' "

In November of 1993, in a major signifying event for Ukiah's Latino community that included a mini-fiesta in a local city park, Jorge Hume Salas was ordained a priest by Bishop George Patrick Ziemann in a rite that included a pledge of obedience to the bishop. Hume Salas was fulfilling his lifelong ambition to administer the sacraments. Legally. He celebrated by acquiring, in short order, a new TV, a personal computer, and a new car with vanity plates.

There is a practice, somewhere between a tradition and a policy, in the Catholic Church of sending priests who have got themselves in trouble with sex or alcohol, money, or drugs off to rural areas. "The avoidance of scandal," says the therapist and former Benedictine priest Richard Sipe, "is the primary goal when the sexual activity of a priest comes to the attention of authority." Standard solutions usually involve sending the priest away—entering him in a therapeutic program of some kind or on a religious retreat (sometimes a combination of the two) or even dispatching him to a mental hospital. When this treatment period is completed, the priest is often reassigned, ideally to a less stressful, bucolic area where, removed from the previous sources of his temptations, Father is able to begin his priestly life over. Get a fresh start. Unfortunately, as part of this clean-slate procedure, and in keeping with the Church's tradition of the forgiveness of sin, transfers of troubled priests were customarily made without informing either the parishioners of the new church or its pastor of the nature of the priest's past difficulties. The practice, however well-intended, in effect involved the Church in covering up serious priestly offenses.

The Diocese of Santa Rosa, shaped like a bulging snake and winding its way northward some 300 miles through country, much of which is steep and wooded, was in many ways an ideal locale for a priest to put some distance between himself and his past. Because of the sprawling length of the diocese, the scattered numbers of its population, and the remoteness of many of its communities, there was little or no communication among its forty-five parishes. Church gossip tended not to spread, or to do so slowly. There was no dominant regional TV station to intensify bad news. A priest, it seemed, really might rebuild his life, out of the heat and light of public attention, if he wasn't overwhelmed by isolation.

As a result of this combination of policy and circumstances, the diocese had been jolted during the 1980s and early 1990s by a succession of sexual incidents about which the pastors and their parishioners were usually the *last* to know.

At St. Mary of the Angels things reached their nadir when a county judge called the parish office, warning that if a visiting priest announced for the upcoming St. Francis of Assisi blessing of the animals were to actually officiate at the ceremony not one of the judge's children would set foot in the parish school again. The priest, the judge explained, had appeared before him in court only days before, charged with being drunk on a local town's main street where he had propositioned men, women, and children to perform oral sex on him. The pastor of St. Mary's, Father Hans, had been completely blindsided, informed neither of the priest's troubled history nor of his recent arrest. The priest had been given another fresh start, but at what thought of consequences? At whose expense?

The staff of the parish grew particularly sensitive to priestly misconduct and the potential harm of ecclesiastical cover-ups. "We've had three bishops in a row," Sister Jane summarized, "who've cared more about the reputation of priests than the lives of children."

2

For Sister Jane Kelly, a woman who had spent a quarter of a century teaching, counseling, and organizing essential services for people in the Santa Rosa Diocese without realistic hope of her own ordination, the elevation of Jorge Hume Salas to the priesthood could not help but come as a personal blow. A man with questionable credentials, little English, and fifteen months of cursory spiritual training now outranked her in the eyes of most parishioners and of her Church. More significantly, as a priest he was—through his ministry of the sacraments—part of an apostolic tradition leading, over nearly two millennia, back to Jesus.

That women, in particular Mary Magdalene, were an important part of that original teaching, Sister Jane would be among the first to remind people, quoting from a gospel attributed to Magdalene that was excluded when the Gospels were sorted, in the fifteenth century, into their present New Testament form.

"In the gospel, Mary is asked by one of the disciples, 'Why does Jesus love you the most?' Her reply is, 'Because I love *him* the most.'"

The story of Mary Magdalene, one of the more prominent

instances of the Church's inequity toward women, was an important consolation to Sister Jane with its suggestion of being part of a greater love and bearing a deeper message. Combined with her own childhood upbringing, it gave her the passion and conviction to say "I just can't stand injustice," and make you believe it.

Oakland, California, where Jane Kelly was born in 1931, is just across San Francisco Bay from its more glamorous sister city and bears a relationship to San Francisco much like Brooklyn does to Manhattan. San Francisco is white-collar, service-and-professional, racially cosmopolitan, and at least superficially sophisticated; Oakland is blue- or no-collar, industrial, at times racially polarized, and visceral. Oakland was the birthplace of and remains the headquarters for both the Black Panther Party and the Hell's Angels.

In the years of Sister Kelly's childhood, Oakland was a political fiefdom run by the Knowland family, owners and publishers of *The Oakland Tribune*. The *Tribune's* publisher, Joseph Knowland, a power in California Republican politics, had sponsored the political rise of Alameda County's racket-busting District Attorney Earl Warren only to have Warren turn out to be, to the Knowland family's great disappointment, a liberal as Chief Justice of the Supreme Court.

Knowland's son, William, a large man with a rain-barrel voice and a face like a clenched fist, proved more in the family tradition, serving in the U.S. Senate most notably as the last enthusiastic advocate of the Nationalist Chinese Generalissimo Chiang Kai-shek. William Knowland later made a heavy-handed attempt to run for the California governorship, which had the effect of turning it over for the first time in twenty years to the Democrats under Pat Brown. His political career at an end, Bill Knowland eventually took his own life at the family's summer home on the Russian River, in the heart of the Diocese of Santa Rosa.

World War II brought an influx of black workers to Oakland to staff the yards building Liberty Ships for Henry Kaiser, the Oakland

Army Terminal, the Alameda Naval Air Station and related war industries, leaving postwar Oakland a socioeconomically divided city. West Oakland, or the flats, the low-lying area sloping toward the bay, was overwhelmingly black and largely poor, while the wooded view highlands to the east were white and affluent. The city's combination of a large black population governed by an over-whelmingly white power structure caused it to be dubbed by *Ramparts* magazine "The northernmost Southern town in America."

The organ of the white power structure in Oakland and of the Knowland family was *The Oakland Tribune*. And Jane Kelly's father worked for the *Tribune*.

Oakland was also a city with a strong Catholic tradition. The Sisters of the Holy Names, which ran grade schools throughout the Bay Area, had their headquarters in Oakland on the campus of The College of The Holy Names. Catholic Charities were particularly strong in Oakland, working effectively across racial lines. In the 1960s, the city, an important military induction and embarkation point, was the center of Bay Area antiwar protests involving both Catholic and non-Catholic elements. Combined with the activities of the Black Panthers, the Maoist Progressive Labor Party, and the drug culture (the city was tagged "Cokeland" by young blacks in the 1970s), Oakland had become the crucible of Northern California social and political concern: elements tested or recombined here tended to be exportable elsewhere.

For Sister Jane Kelly, this legacy of urban social awareness, personal moral concern, and parental affinity for the press was to be of increasing significance in her own life as well as that of her Church.

Following Jorge Hume Salas's ordination as a priest, there continued to be disturbing rumors about him, particularly from among the members of Ukiah's Latino community. Parishioners of St. Mary of the Angels complained to Sister Jane that Hume was demanding a minimum payment for himself of $20 for the performance of baptisms and weddings, income that he failed to report to the parish. The boys' soccer team which he had supported as a deacon was now abandoned. And there were reports of inappropriate behavior involving teenage Latino boys. The draining of funds from parish collections came as no great surprise to Sister Jane, nor did the fact of Hume Salas being caught red-handed as a result of the Ukiah Police Department's sting.

Hume Salas claimed that the money he had been taking had been used for the benefit of the poor in Mexico and Costa Rica, but could produce no donation statements or receipts. In keeping with Church practice, he was removed from the parish. Following consultations with a therapist in the city of Santa Rosa, Hume Salas was notified by Bishop Ziemann that he was being sent to St. Michael's Community in St. Louis, Missouri, a treatment center for Catholic priests, for further evaluation. The reasons given him at this time were the thefts and the allegations of sexual misbehavior with several young Latino men of St. Mary's parish.

On June 27, 1996, according to Jorge Hume Salas, he received a telephone call from Bishop Ziemann, who told him to come to the bishop's residence on a quiet cul-de-sac in an affluent Santa Rosa residential area and pick up his plane ticket.

When Salas arrived at Ziemann's house, the bishop, Hume Salas later told a police investigator, asked him how he was feeling. Salas told Ziemann he was very depressed to the point that he was easily moved to tears. Salas then said that Ziemann embraced him and began to caress his face. Salas, who stands five foot seven and weighs about 150 pounds, asked the bishop, over six feet tall and weighing more than 200 pounds, what he was doing. Ziemann was then touching his chest, stomach, and legs. Salas again asked the bishop what he was doing. Ziemann told him he should have an open mind; he assured Salas that he was comforting him. According to

Salas, the bishop then unbuttoned Salas's shirt. He touched his chest, the side of his neck, and began kissing him on the face and neck. Ziemann then told Salas to remove his shirt and unzipped Salas's pants. Salas said that Ziemann then masturbated him, and he, in turn, masturbated Ziemann. During this incident, Ziemann asked Salas to suck his nipples. Ziemann also asked Salas to orally copulate him. Salas said he refused, and that the bishop orally copulated *him*. Salas then returned the act.

Afterward, Salas asked Ziemann why he had done what he had done, and Ziemann repeated that he should keep an open mind. Upon leaving the bishop's residence, Salas said, he felt "very disillusioned with everything."

Whatever Jorge Hume Salas's previous history, his bishop's sexual assumptiveness on this occasion left Salas, in his telling of it, stunned. He was in an emotionally depressed state, resident of a country largely foreign to him, about to be dispatched to a distant area where he knew no one, and pledged to spiritual and moral obedience to a superior who had just had sex with him. It was not the kind of casual flirtation that might cause an instant rebound in a person's self-esteem.

Following Father Jorge's removal from St. Mary's parish, rumors continued to circulate about him regarding inappropriate behavior with young Latino men. There was also concern among the clergy that, like other problem priests, he might, following a treatment period, simply be recycled into another uninformed parish. Disappointed at the diocese's failure to prosecute Hume Salas, Sister Kelly, in August of 1996, wrote a letter to Bishop Ziemann asking that Salas be required to make public restitution for his thefts, which she estimated to be at least $10,000. "Bishop," her letter said, "I believe that Jorge is a pathological liar and was ordained under false pretenses." She received no reply to her letter.

While Jorge Hume Salas was in treatment in St. Louis, Bishop

Agony in the Garden

Ziemann made regular calls to the secretary at St. Michael's to get progress reports on how Salas was doing. Toward the close of his treatment program, the secretary told Salas that Ziemann had left a message that he would be arriving the day before Salas's final evaluation. At that time, the bishop would take Salas out to dinner and talk with him. The secretary added that Salas should be very happy that his bishop cared that much about him; she didn't know of any other bishop who had ever taken out priests who were at St. Michael's.

On July 11, Salas went with the chauffeur from St. Michael's to the St. Louis airport, where they picked up Bishop Ziemann and took him to the Best Western Hotel in the Kirkwood area of St. Louis. Salas later related to a police investigator that Ziemann asked him to go to his room with him and that Salas declined, saying he would wait in the lobby since they were going to go to dinner. Ziemann, Salas said, insisted that Salas come up to his room. The driver said that he would be back for Salas at around 9:00 P.M., but Ziemann advised that since he and Salas had a lot to talk about, the driver should return later.

Ziemann again told Salas to come up to his room. Salas said no and admitted he was afraid of the bishop. He told the police investigator that Ziemann asked him up to the room several times, and Salas repeatedly said no. Finally Ziemann, upset at Salas's refusal, raised his voice, at which time Salas agreed to go.

Once they were in Ziemann's room, the bishop asked Salas how things were going and how he felt. Salas, he later related, said that he was depressed. He didn't like staying at St. Michael's; it was difficult for him there since he didn't have any friends and his English was limited. He asked Ziemann if he was going to keep him there. The bishop said that depended on the evaluation Salas would be getting on the following day. Salas recalled that he sat on the bed, and that Ziemann started touching him. According to Salas, Ziemann then undressed him completely and they had sex.

Afterwards, Salas asked Ziemann about going to dinner. Ziemann said yes, they were going to dinner, and took Salas to the hotel restaurant where they ate quickly, because it was almost time for Salas to get picked up and returned to St. Michael's. After the meal, while Ziemann was paying the check, he took $80 from his wallet and slipped it into Salas's pants pocket. When Salas asked him what it was for, the bishop said he should buy something for himself. Salas felt extremely bad over the whole ordeal—he said that he felt, in fact, like a prostitute. On the way back to St. Michael's, Salas said, he wept.

The following day, Bishop Ziemann arrived at St. Michael's early for the evaluation. Salas stated that several other priests saw Ziemann arrive and greet him. Ziemann said he wanted to meet with Salas in private; they were led into a large room. Father Michael Foley, the director of St. Michael's Community, was present in the room at the time. According to Salas, as part of his treatment he had made known to Father Mike that he had had sexual relations with Ziemann. In the room, Ziemann and Father Mike had a conversation. Salas recalled Ziemann telling Father Mike that he and Salas were brothers. Ziemann then pointed to his bishop's ring and said, "But I am the Bishop," indicating, Salas said, his authority over Salas.

After the evaluation, which according to Hume Salas documented that he was heterosexual and not homosexual, Ziemann requested a copy of the report and was told he could have one. When it was explained that Hume Salas would be given a copy too, Ziemann questioned why. According to Salas, one of the first paragraphs of the report indicated that whenever Salas was to meet with Ziemann there should be a third party present.

When the evaluation was completed, Ziemann asked to meet with Salas in a private room, which Salas consented to do. In the room, Ziemann began hugging and caressing Salas. According to Salas, Ziemann kissed and masturbated him in this private room.

Agony in the Garden

Afterwards, Salas asked if he was free to leave St. Michael's. Ziemann said, "Okay, you may leave." He told Salas to make airline arrangements and the two men left on separate flights.

On his return to California, Hume Salas, who had been removed from St. Mary's parish in Ukiah, was without a place to live. At first, he slept in his car in Santa Rosa or stayed with friends who would put him up for a day or two at a time. Eventually he found an apartment in Santa Rosa, which he shared with a roommate. The roommate was not a priest, just a single male friend who eventually left, Salas pointed out, and returned to Mexico where he got married.

While he was living in this apartment, his living expenses paid for by the Diocese, Hume Salas continued to be asked by Ziemann for sexual favors. Since Salas didn't have a telephone, the bishop outfitted him with a pager, on which he would beep him at any time and summon him to the bishop's residence. At first, Salas was told to park his car in front of the bishop's residence; in time, he was instructed to park around the corner, and enter by the back door. In the rear of the residence there was an adjoining but separate office/apartment area with a bedroom.

The procedure became routine. Salas would enter the residence through the rear, would walk about fifteen steps, and there would be the bishop, in his office, sitting in his rocking chair. Salas would sit on the bishop's sofa. After a few questions, Ziemann would join him. Salas later claimed that every time he met with Ziemann, the same thing occurred. He would tell the bishop that he did not want to do this with him and Ziemann would assure him that this would be the last time.

Ziemann told him, said Salas, that the bishop was the only friend Salas had and that if the information about the thefts and reported sexual misconduct in Ukiah were made public, it would ruin Salas's reputation. "Look at everything I have done for you," the bishop reportedly told the priest. "Do you feel like I care for you?"

The nature of the sexual encounters advanced to penetration. Salas, as the saying goes, would kick off, and Ziemann would receive. Salas, defensive about his own sexual orientation, asked Ziemann several times if he was homosexual; the bishop questioned why he was being asked this and, according to Salas, admitted that yes, he was gay.

Salas claimed that he always told Ziemann that he felt bad about doing these things, but that Ziemann insisted he had to do it, that this was only between the two of them, and that "they were brothers."

Jorge Hume Salas now found himself in the control of a man to whom he owed his home, his food, his clothing, his freedom from prosecution, his pledged obedience, and his hopes for a career in the priesthood. In a word, everything. It was a debt the bishop was not at all reluctant in claiming.

This relationship with—or servicing of—Ziemann continued through the remainder of 1996 and 1997.

In January of 1997, Hume Salas called Gloria Enguidanos, a friend and a psychologist who had been doing counseling alongside Hume Salas with a Santa Rosa Latino AIDS group. She gave him her last appointment of the day, and they met at her office around six P.M. Enguidanos later stated that Jorge told her a "very long story that was also very disturbing to her." He told her that he had been forced to have sex with the bishop. As he told her about the arrangement and the circumstances, he wept. He asked her if she could be his therapist. She said she couldn't because they were friends, and instead referred Hume Salas to a therapist who occupied a neighboring office, Dr. Jay Judin. The three of them then met. Over a period of two hours, Hume Salas unburdened himself in Spanish to Dr. Judin. Though admittedly nervous about the gravity of what was involved, Dr. Judin agreed to help, and Hume Salas began seeing him regularly.

Agony in the Garden

Enguidanos would still see Jorge occasionally around the office when he was waiting for his appointment with Dr. Judin; or he would call her to talk briefly on the phone. She was aware that he was on some sort of medication, and said she felt that he was depressed.

The last time she saw Hume Salas, he was in his car outside her office. He had just finished a session with Dr. Judin and he looked, she recalled "pretty bad." He told her that this was getting to him and that he wasn't sure how much more he could take. She was concerned that he might do away with himself, and was torn between her feelings for him as a friend and her responsibilities as a therapist. Overall, she felt that he was a victim and had been used.

"True love," declares *Christ Among Us*, a modern presentation of the Catholic faith for adults, "means that we respect the one we love, especially in the use of the power of sex." If we truly love, the Church teaches, "we do not ever want to treat another person as a 'thing,' as the outlet for our passions." In his treatment of Jorge Hume Salas, Bishop Ziemann was violating not only his vows as a priest and his responsibilities as a bishop, but the essence of Catholic teaching about sex as defined and approved by the National Conference of Catholic Bishops.

Along with Ms. Enguidanos, Dr. Judin was concerned about Hume Salas's physical and mental well-being. He referred him to his own family physician and tried to work on Hume Salas's will to say no to the bishop without jeopardizing his career within the Church.

Dr. Judin also felt that, based on the serious nature of the allegations Jorge Hume Salas was making against the bishop, he needed more than physical and psychological assistance. So he referred him to a lawyer.

The Most Reverend Bishop George Patrick Ziemann was more than the Diocese of Santa Rosa's prelate: he was its star. Beginning with his installation as bishop of an already troubled ministry in September of 1992, Ziemann injected a spirit of dynamism, a possibility of positive change within the existing structure that promised to revitalize the Church throughout the diocese, if not beyond.

Issues that had plagued the diocese for years were now addressed aggressively. New ministries were opened, and capable people hired to meet the needs of the Latino community, the homeless, and those with AIDS. New construction projects—churches, schools, social, instructional, and athletic centers, the accumulated hopes of years of parish wish lists—were encouraged from above and quickly approved. Most significantly, the diocese's legacy of priestly sexual abuse was at last met with something other than denial. Lawsuits in negotiation for years were settled. Meetings with plaintiffs' attorneys became less hard-edged and adversarial. Ziemann talked to reporters and met privately with victims, some of whom had never made public allegations. He chose to get directly involved, Ziemann said, "because I've seen it delegated by other bishops and that has not healed."

In what had been the North Coast Counties' religious scandal of the decade, Monsignor Gary Timmons, the diocese's former youth director and founder of St. Michael Youth Camp, had been convicted of child molestation and sentenced in 1996 to eight years in prison. The worst that conceivably could happen had happened, and the diocese had survived. It seemed, with the positive, dynamic Ziemann in charge, that things could only get better.

He seemed to be, ecclesiastically, an ideal choice. He was conservative enough on issues like abortion and celibacy to satisfy the Vatican, yet definitely progressive at the parish level, encouraging local autonomy, the expansion of missions to the needy, the return to the church of Catholics who had divorced and remarried, and the participation of women in the liturgy.

Like the Deity, he seemed to be everywhere, driving himself around his six-county diocese in his white Olds Cutlass, talking on his cell phone, in touch, on top of things, aware, likely to turn up any place.

"He was, in many ways, the best of the four bishops we've had here," recalled the veteran Monsignor John O'Hare. "Very supportive. Very available. He didn't push too hard on the trappings of power. He didn't bring a secretary or a chaplain with him; he'd put his bishop's hat on himself." Ziemann's refreshingly down-to-earth style was not confined to the clergy. "He'd pass out his card, with his private phone number, to anybody. If a group of seventh- and eighth-graders invited him to come and speak to them, he'd come."

"I was teaching an English as a Second Language course," recalled Mary Shea, a Napa community college instructor, "to Latino men, and I wanted them to hear someone who was fluent in Spanish whom they could admire. So I invited Bishop Pat, and he came. He spoke to them in Spanish, he was wonderful, and they thought so much of him they invited him to come back and have lunch with them. And he came."

He seemed, to many Catholics, to be addressing matters—the Timmons case, changes in the liturgy, the sometimes conflicting needs for change and stability within the church—exactly as he should. Generally, people in the area, clergy, and laypersons considered themselves blessed to have a man of such quality, energy, and intelligence at the head of their diocese.

There were dissenters, of course, parishioners who felt that Bishop Pat merely affected concern about parish controversies but rarely used the power of his office to resolve them and parish priests who felt that the bishop, by popping up in their parishes unannounced and handing his personal phone number out to their parishioners, was, in effect, leaving them out of the loop. But the overall feeling was positive, a stimulating sense of forward motion, of a capable hand at the tiller and a clear course in mind. Like the dual nature of his preferred name, Bishop Pat seemed to reconcile the authority of the traditional church with the personal appeal of the new.

To see him preach in those days was to witness a performance as assured, commanding, and professional as that of a nightclub performer or a television talk-show host. These appearances were events, eagerly anticipated and touted by the clergy and staff, that could produce, on a weekday night, a nearly full house at St. Eugene's Cathedral in Santa Rosa.

He worked without props or costume, eschewing even the vestments of Mass for a simple priest's suit of Good Friday black: a tall man in his mid-fifties with a slight paunch, a sensual mouth, and close-cropped thinning gray hair. Instead of shielding himself behind a lectern and a thick volume of Scripture, he strode the church aisle, speaking without a mike, without ever referring to notes, a performer working the room.

A favorite subject was prayer: its efficacy, its spiritual and psychological value, its protean form improvised, formal, solitary, shared, its penetrative power and cumulative force, its linking of the individual soul with the eternal. The lack of embellishment enhanced the message. What Bishop Pat was saying didn't need vestments or candles, music or incense: the words and his conviction, his public act of faith, were enough.

There is an attitude in the Catholic Church that preaching, like gospel music, is something really better left to the more evangelical forms of Christianity. Not much is expected of the homilies at Sunday Mass, which are supposed to serve the larger purpose of union with Christ through the Eucharist. Where expectations are low, there is a tendency simply to go through the motions or deliver an off-the-shelf elaboration on the week's excerpt from Scripture. The fact that due to vocational shortages, so many priests are fresh off the plane from Ireland or the Philippines and therefore culturally clueless, does not help. For Catholics accepting of, maybe requiring, a weekly routine spiritual fix, seeing not just a priest but a bishop who could combine the performing ease of a TV evangelist with the intellectual rigor of Catholic theology could be a powerhouse experience—part Jerry Falwell, part Thomas Aquinas.

As powerful as the effect of Bishop Pat's preaching was on Catholic audiences, both clergy and laypersons, his need for the attention of and bonding with the members of his flock was just as great. He loved what he was doing, being at the center of it all in a dramatic setting, articulating this potent, arresting combination of ancient mystery and immediate concern.

There was a certain Bishop Fulton Sheen hambone quality in Bishop Pat. He had an obvious love of performance combined with a sense of not much patience with detail; a penchant for the bold stroke as opposed to the day to day grind of gradual, lasting change; an instinct for theatrics that may have included a dependence on them, which may have sprung from where and how he was brought up.

George Patrick Ziemann was born in Pasadena, California, on September 13, 1941, one of five children of a gifted and prominent Catholic lawyer, J. Howard Ziemann. A graduate of Santa Clara University in Northern California, with a law degree from Georgetown, J. Howard Ziemann practiced law in Los Angeles and was named dean of the Loyola University Law School. Active in Catholic affairs, he served on the board of the Catholic Hospitals and St. Vincent de Paul. In 1954, he was appointed to the bench by California Governor Goodwin J. Knight and served in the Superior Court of Los Angeles County.

As the son of a judge who was a devout Catholic, George Patrick Ziemann had the experience of growing up in the intimate presence of two kinds of authority, civil and religious, which, while seeming to be in charge of all society, occasionally conflicted with one another. As a judge, J. Howard Ziemann would have been asked to perform civil weddings involving Catholics and was required to grant divorces, sunder families, and establish custody and visitation rights for parents. He would have carried the concerns of his courtroom work home with him, so that his family too had to live with them, day to day. Judge Ziemann was also—as a judge who could preside over murder trials—potentially subject to the moral and ethical quandary of imposing the death penalty, a punishment to which his Church, as of 1978, stood opposed. It was an upbringing that made morality and ethics and the conflicts arising around them a matter not just for Mass on Sunday, but the stuff of everyday life.

Beyond his immediate family, Pat Ziemann was heir on his mother's side to an even more powerful legacy. George Patrick Ziemann's maternal grandfather, Joseph Scott, was, during the first half of the twentieth century, Southern California's most influential Catholic layman. He was born in England, in 1867, the son of a well-to-do Scottish Presbyterian father and an Irish Catholic mother, and though he was the beneficiary of an English university education and a degree in rhetoric, it was his mother's cultural and religious heritage that lay at the core of his character.

Like so many Irishmen of that era, Joseph Scott emigrated to America. Hoping, with his university degree, to embark upon a career in journalism, he arrived in New York in the era of NINA, "No Irish Need Apply," and had to settle, to his great disappointment, for the stock Irish immigrant job of hod carrier.

Through Irish Catholic networking, he found more intellectually congenial work as a teacher and a coach of football, baseball, and handball; but his energies and ambitions were still far from fulfilled. On the advice of a Catholic priest, and accompanied by another priest, Joseph Scott headed west.

In Los Angeles, Scott began, in 1893, reading law in the office of a local judge. The following year he passed the bar. Active in his parish church, he sang bass in the choir, where he met Bertha Ross, a soprano. They married, and she eventually bore him 11 children, seven of whom survived.

With his powerful voice, his Irish Catholic sense of injury, and his Old-Testament-prophet shaggy eyebrows, Scott became an effective courtroom presence and a spokesman for the city's growing Catholic community. Harrison Gray Otis, the self-styled general and powerful publisher of the *Los Angeles Times*, found Scott, one of the rare Irish immigrants who shared Otis's Republican politics, an attractive personality. This friendship ended in 1911 when Scott signed on as co-counsel for two Irish socialists, John and James McNamara, who were charged with bombing the *Los Angeles Times* building.

Scott's co-counsel was Clarence Darrow, the nation's foremost criminal defense lawyer. In a strategy that produced strongly divided feelings within the American labor movement, Darrow and Scott pleaded the McNamara brothers guilty, insuring their conviction but, in Darrow's view, saving their lives. Darrow found himself charged with bribing a juror in the McNamara case, but was acquitted. Scott concentrated on saving the McNamaras' souls: he tried to bring the brothers back to their Catholic faith. His efforts included giving them a prayer book that belonged to a young apprentice who had been killed in the *Times* blast. The book had been given to Scott by the dead man's sister, who was a nun.

Otis, viewing Scott's defense of the McNamaras as a betrayal, began attacking Scott, who was a member of the Los Angeles school board, in *Times* editorials and cartoons. The cartoons regularly depicted Scott, all too accurately, as a hod carrier. The combative Scott endured the abuse for four years until he retired from the school board. Then he sued Otis.

The *Times* had charged that Scott had persuaded a Pasadena woman, against her wishes, to sue her millionaire husband for divorce. Scott sued for libel and won. The paper appealed, and the decision was reversed. The determined Scott pressed for a new trial, which he got and won. The jury awarded Scott $47,000. When Scott returned to his office, there was a congratulatory telegram waiting for him from Hiram Johnson, Governor of California and archenemy of the reactionary Otis. A copy of the check, signed by Otis, hung on the walls of Scott's library ever afterwards.

Scott, whom law and notoriety had made a wealthy man, moved to Pasadena himself, settling with his large family on Orange Grove Boulevard, along the Arroyo Seco, on Pasadena's "millionaire's row." His personal charisma was such that when Harrison Gray Otis died, in 1917, Scott's friendship with Otis's son-in-law, and the new *Times* publisher, Harry Chandler continued. Chandler continually contributed donations for the various Catholic causes that Scott advocated, among them Loyola Law School, where the energetic Scott was dean.

Among Scott's causes was the Irish Republic, whose insurgent leader, Eamon de Valera, wanted by the British Crown, appeared at

Agony in the Garden

a rally Scott organized in Los Angeles' Washington Park in 1919. The rally drew a crowd estimated at 15,000 people.

In 1933, Joseph Breen, public relations man for the Hays Office, the ineffectual production code outfit supposedly overseeing the movie industry, retained Joseph Scott to speak on behalf of the Catholic bishops of America to the most prominent producers in the motion picture business. Acting through Los Angeles Bishop John Cantwell, the bishops, alarmed at what they saw as increasingly explicit sex and violence in movies, instructed Scott to tell the leading industry officials that the American bishops had run out of patience with "a vile industry" that was doing untold harm to the nation's children. Unless the producers recognized the moral significance of entertainment and reformed at once, the bishops would unleash the power of their church against the movies.

Scott, whose courtroom style combined scorching invective with an air of presumed moral superiority, fully rose—or sank—to the occasion. At a meeting in August of 1933, arranged by Breen, of top Hollywood executives, among them Louis B. Mayer, Adolph Zukor, Jack Warner, and Joseph Schenck, Scott launched into a tirade that edged over into an anti-Semitic rant.

Accusing his audience of being "disloyal" Americans, Scott charged them with having been engaged for years in "a conspiracy to debauch the youth of the land." A recent California trial, Scott asserted, had exposed "communistic radicals" as "one hundred percent Jews." Scott went on to warn that the link between "dirty motion pictures" and Jewish radicals who had nothing but contempt for moral distinctions was "serving to build up an enormous case against the Jews in the eyes of the American people."

"Cease your damnable practices," Scott scolded the stunned producers, practices which had brought "disgrace upon the Jews and upon America."

Amazingly, this crowd, which included some notoriously tough cookies—the most prominent of whom were Jewish—took it.

Zukor, the president of Paramount Pictures and the dean of the industry, apologized for the "dirt and filth" that the bishops had found in Paramount's pictures and promised to do his best to keep the studio's product free of this sort of wickedness. The politically conservative Mayer agreed and most of the others fell into line. Only Schenck, then president of RKO, resisted, maintaining that serious films on serious subjects should not be condemned out of hand because of their subject matter. Schenck referred to religious critics of the movies as "narrow-minded and bigoted," and characterized his fellow movie executives as "self-abasing cowards who had allowed a histrionic lawyer to stampede them with anti-Semitic invective."

It was a sensitive time for Jews everywhere. Adolf Hitler, who had taken office as Chancellor of Germany in January, had used the Reichstag fire and attacks on Communists and Jews to consolidate his power and rule by decree. In the United States, the Depression had deepened to what would prove to be its lowest level and people were looking for scapegoats. The movie industry, which had survived the economic bust in better shape than most businesses, would nevertheless be extremely vulnerable to a nationwide boycott by the nation's 20 million Catholics, most of whom were concentrated in big cities.

In the past, pledges on the part of movie executives to reform their industry had been enough; religious reformers were unable to sustain their zeal. Life and the movies rolled on. But this was different. Bishop Cantwell insisted that only "concrete, specific, and immediate" evidence of reforms undertaken would satisfy him that the movie industry was sincere.

In November, Cantwell delivered an address at a gathering of bishops at Catholic University in Washington calling for the need of more forceful action against Hollywood. The bishops then launched a Legion of Decency campaign, calling upon American Catholics to pledge not to attend movies that Catholic officials condemned.

Agony in the Garden

In December, the movie industry capitulated. A Production Code Administration was created with Joseph Breen appointed as director. Breen and his staff were empowered to review and rule upon the content of every Hollywood film, from preliminary script to finished picture. If a movie were denied PCA approval, no mainstream theatre in America would show it. This de facto censorship was the controlling fact of life in the movie industry for the next 30 years.

In 1944, Joseph Scott was once again retained to aim his heavy courtroom artillery in the direction of the movie industry. A young actress named Joan Barry, mother of a baby girl, had sued the man whom she insisted was the girl's father, Charlie Chaplin. Barry and Chaplin had had a relationship during 1942, but Chaplin denied paternity. An attempt to reach a negotiated settlement fizzled when a blood test to which both parties had agreed failed to prove that Chaplin was the child's father. Barry, against her lawyer's advice, insisted on pressing the suit anyway and brought in Joseph Scott to deliver the moral message.

At this time blood tests were rather like lie detector tests—influential in trial negotiations, but inadmissible in court. Also, Chaplin had a notorious history of sexual relationships with much younger women and in June of 1943 while still facing the accusations of Barry had, at 54, married the 18-year-old Oona O'Neill. The lawsuit and the marriage had been the staple of newspaper gossip columns for months. Scott, now in his late seventies, with white hair to complement his bushy eyebrows and booming voice, was more than ever the man to issue a jeremiad against the alluring licentiousness of moviedom. In court, he referred to the five-foot-four Chaplin as a "little runt of a Svengali," "a pestiferous lecherous hound," and a "cheap Cockney cad," who had behaved like a "gray-headed old buzzard."

At one point, Scott held up his client's red-haired baby daughter before the jury and asked them to notice how closely the child resembled Chaplin. The jury, presented with evidence that Barry had stalked Chaplin and that she had also been having an affair with the oil multimillionaire J. Paul Getty, deadlocked seven to four for acquittal. Barry and Scott, however, pressed forward with a new trial that resulted in a nine-to-three vote against Chaplin. The judge thereupon ordered Chaplin to pay Barry a lump sum of $5,000 plus $75 a month in child support until the girl reached 21.

The trial was the beginning of Chaplin's downward career and personal slide in the United States, which ended in 1952 with his leaving the land of his spectacular success and moving to Switzerland.

As reward for his service to his Church and in society on its behalf, Joseph Scott received, during his long lifetime, five papal knighthoods (Knight of St. Gregory, Knight of the Holy Sepulchre, among others), from three different popes. Among lay people, especially Irish-Americans, he was known throughout Southern California as "Mister L.A." When he died in 1958 at the age of 90, his body lay in state in the City Hall rotunda, and a bronze statue of him stands today outside the Los Angeles County Courthouse.

The year after Scott's death, his 18-year-old grandson, George Patrick Ziemann, in certain ways his spiritual heir, entered the seminary. Ziemann seems to have identified strongly with his mother's and grandfather's Irish Catholic heritage. He was never George Ziemann—it was always G. Patrick, and later Father, then Bishop Pat. The Church as the central factor in his life, his guide, faith, and passion, seems to be an extension of his grandfather's intense lifelong commitment. His grandfather had served the Church as fully and successfully as was possible in the secular world: George Patrick would extend the family energy and ambition into the clergy.

At the seminary he entered in 1959—Our Lady of The Angels

Agony in the Garden

in San Fernando, California—he would have been targeted imme-diately as a young man of great promise for advancement within the Church. The son of a prominent judge, grandson of Mister L.A. There and at St. John's Seminary in Camarillo, where he received his B.A. in Philosophy in 1967, and Mt. St. Mary's Col-lege where he was awarded his master's degree, he remained within the corporate structure of the Archdiocese of Los Angeles, which was to some degree the family business.

4

When George Patrick Ziemann entered the seminary, he would have found himself in a world where human sexuality was treated as if it didn't exist. There would have been no semester-length course in how to address one's own sexuality or that of others, and no instruction in how to live a life pledged to celibacy other than a list of prohibitions. Any form of sexual activity, even masturbation, was a sin; sexual thoughts and words connoting sexuality could be occasions of sin. At daily mass and in weekly Confession, he would have been required to ask forgiveness for his own actions, thoughts, and even dreams. In the pursuit of an ideal, he would have been required to deny the most powerful of his natural feelings.

As an 18-year-old boy raised in a Catholic family, educated in parochial schools and committed to a life in the church, it is quite likely that Ziemann had at the time no adult sexual experience. His own sexual orientation was probably unknown to him.

The society he lived, studied, and worked in was all-male. Meals, classes, devotions, and spiritual exercises involved men only. Each day was strictly scheduled and all activities regulated and monitored, so there would have been little chance for a devout and dedicated student to go astray sexually. Celibacy, it was assumed, freed a select number of men from intimate personal attachments for the greater purpose of serving others. It set them apart from other men in what constituted a separate society. It connected them with the saints and martyrs and to the early days of the Church. And it offered the promise of transcendence, of achieving a personal tie with God. Celibacy was a given, the price paid for being admitted to a fellowship where employment was guaranteed as well as the assurance of an overall unified purpose and a certain sense of power and prestige. Any serious questions a seminarian had about his own sexuality or celibacy were simply put on hold. In a world that changed incrementally, over centuries, it seemed that things remained essentially as they had always been.

Though there is a celibate tradition in Christianity dating back through Saint Paul to Jesus himself, the idea of celibacy is not the confident, unbroken continuum that church tradition and teachings suggest. Early Christians, believing in the imminent end of the world, gave little attention to sexual rules and regulations. As the prospect of an immediate Second Coming receded, some thought had to be given to the perpetuation of the species. "The Church," explains Paul Johnson in *A History of Christianity*, "confusedly adopted an uneasy coexistence in which celibacy was praised but matrimony tolerated."

Throughout the larger part of the Christian era, clergy could be either married or celibate. Peter, the first bishop of Rome and considered the founder of the papacy, is believed to have had a wife and two children. A great deal of time and energy were devoted to sorting things out. Though married and celibate clergy served side by side, celibates like Saint Ambrose, the influential fourth-century bishop of Milan, feared the creation of a priestly caste with hereditary bishops. And in fact, three later popes were the sons of previous popes, while nine were the offspring of priests or bishops.

Saint Augustine, a convert from strictly celibate Manicheanism, baptized by Ambrose, envisioned Christianity coming to terms with the world by extending itself throughout society. His thinking, which provided the rationale for the expansion of the Church throughout the Middle Ages, also maintained that all sexual activity except that within marriage for the purpose of procreation is sinful. This is essentially the position on sexuality adhered to by the Church today.

There seems to have been some association between the passionate advocates of celibacy and personal sexual turmoil. Saint Jerome, a fifth-century proponent of strict celibacy, claimed to have been tempted by visions of dancing girls and was accused of cross-dressing. Saint Augustine, the most powerful early celibate apologist, whose sexual struggles are documented in his *Confessions*, as a young man kept a concubine and fathered a son. And Saint Paul, on whose letters the scriptural argument for celibacy is based, is believed to have been, at the time of his conversion, a 40-year-old widower. For these men, celibacy in conjunction with Christianity represented resolution, a means of grappling with pressing personal feelings that also provided an outlet for sexual energies.

For centuries, the celibate idea was the dynamo within the Church, generating a tremendous expansion in evangelism, scholarship, and martyrdom. Men and women, freed from the obligations of spouses or children and with their eyes on a coming world to which the present one was merely prelude, were able to take tremendous risks and sustain enormous burdens in behalf of their faith. This vital, sacrificing, occasionally heroic, otherworldly element of the clergy was complemented and tempered by a more prosaic, stable, pastoral, and perhaps more nurturing married one.

By the late Middle Ages, the power and wealth accumulated by the Church had intensified the differences between married and celibate clergy. The nature of a priest's home and sexual life began to edge over into questions of power and property. Bishops were bequeathing episcopates to their sons in the practice known as simony. The papacy became allied with the aristocracy, and a handful of families came to control who occupied the papal throne. There was also the issue of lay investiture, of bishops being chosen by secular, usually royal, authorities; such appointments often were decided by family ties. These dynastic conflicts strengthened the appeal of strict celibacy as a means of reform. From time to time, various popes and synods tried to enforce clerical celibacy, but these rules were largely ignored.

Finally, in 1139, the Second Lateran Council under Pope Innocent II declared all marriages of priests to be null and void. Any existing marriages had to be severed before a priest could be ordained. There was strong resistance to this law, some of it violent, and clerical behavior did not quickly change. More than a century later, the Synod of Bremen was excommunicating bishops for not upholding the Lateran decisions.

An immediate result of the outlawing of priestly marriage was an increase in priestly concubinage, a practice that continues in many countries into the present day. Though attempts were made in the thirteenth and fourteenth centuries to adopt the Eastern Orthodox practice of maintaining both a married clergy and a celibate one, obligatory celibacy became the ideal if not the universal practice of the Roman Catholic Church.

At the time George Patrick Ziemann was in the seminary, these bedrock issues concerning sexuality, the nature of the priesthood, and the nature of the Church, were undergoing their most severe questioning in 500 years. The Second Vatican Council, called by Pope John XXIII in 1961, had invited clergy, laity, and other Christian faiths to open the door to change in the Catholic Church. There was a new spirit of collegiality. Previously silenced theologians were now heard, tolerance and respect expressed for other beliefs, and hope professed for reconciliation with other Christian denominations. The liturgy was transformed, the vernacular Mass adopted, the priest required to face toward instead of away from the congregation, and lay participation in the sacraments expanded and encouraged. The Church changed more in months than it had in previous centuries.

Pope John had set the Church on a new course of rising expectations. It was an exhilarating time for priests and bishops as well as laity, and the direction he intended to take the Church was clear. When he died, however, in 1963, before the second session of the Council, he had left the Church's authoritarian structure intact. His successor, Paul VI, tried to compromise by allowing the council to continue its work but withdrawing from its consideration two subjects which he reserved for himself. The two withdrawn subjects were clerical celibacy and birth control.

Of all the topics considered at the Council, these were the two that would have profited most from collegial discussion, the expression of a variety of opinions, and a legislated decision. "Both," says Paul Johnson, "concerned sex . . . both tended to divide Catholics from the other Christian churches . . . and both, as it happened, were matters on which the Pope himself found it difficult to make up his mind."

Pope Paul's ruling that mandatory celibacy must stay and that the subject should not be opened was seen by the younger clergy as neither definitive nor just. Combined with his stance in *Humanae Vitae* (1968), opposing all forms of artificial contraception, it created a fundamental split within the consciousness of individual Catholics between espoused belief and individual practice. This was the beginning of the present continuing era of shrinking church attendance, declining vocations, priestly resignations, and scandal.

As a newly ordained priest, assigned in 1967 to St. Matthias Parish in Huntington Park, Ziemann had to be acutely aware of these changes and refusals on the part of the Church. In his pastoral work hearing confessions, providing premarital counseling for mixed Catholic and non-Catholic couples seeking to be married in the Church, or counseling married couples undergoing difficulties, he would have had to interpret the Church's Augustinian teaching in a world transformed by the introduction of the Pill.

Introduced in 1960, the oral contraceptive pill was believed by its discoverer, John Rock, a physician and a devout Catholic, to be entirely consistent with Church teachings concerning birth control. The Pill, Rock maintained, used only natural elements to extend the "safe period," previously considered acceptable as part of the rhythm method endorsed by Pope Pius XII. At last, Rock and many other Catholics believed, there was a rational means of Catholic family planning. But Pope Paul VI, after withdrawing the subject of birth control from consideration by the Council, and ignoring the majority view of his advisory commission, restated in *Humanae Vitae* that "each and every marriage act must remain open to the transmission of life." In effect, he outlawed all artificial means of birth control.

The announcement was disheartening to married Catholics, who responded by dramatically reducing their use of Confession, if not leaving the Church entirely. It had an equally discouraging effect on the clergy, who found their entire credibility on sexual matters challenged, the source of their own assurance in sexual concerns compromised, and the validity of their own sexual sacrifice questioned.

Between 1966 and 1984, according to a report sponsored by the U.S. Catholic Conference, the number of diocesan priests in the United States dropped by 20 percent. Another 20 percent drop was anticipated by 2005.

For Ziemann, a young priest from an educated and worldly successful Catholic family, ordained into a Church whose atmosphere of change he would have found congenial, the closing of the Church door on the issues of birth control and celibacy could only have come as a severe disappointment. In his hearing of confessions, his counseling of betrothed and of married couples, we can assume that, like the majority of priests, he eventually advised people to make their own peace with the rules of the Church as applied to sexual relationships. This is consistent with his later openness and availability as a bishop and with his ambition for advancement within the Church. A hard line in the confessional meant a short line outside the booth, and Father Pat yearned for popularity. Besides, what were the alternatives? Resignation from the priesthood, as so many of his contemporaries, some of the ablest young priests among them, reluctantly decided? Or withdrawal to a monastery? Definitely not Ziemann's style.

There was also, within Church tradition, the *sensus fidelium*: the idea of assent by a significant group of committed Christians being necessary to validate the authenticity of a doctrine. A kind of religious nullification, it had been endorsed by, of all people, Cardinal Josef Ratzinger, later to be the Vatican's hard-line ass-kicker on doctrinal matters. It was conceivable, under canon law, that, since the *sensus fidelium* didn't really exist for *Humanae Vitae*, a priest could counsel Catholics not to obey it in anticipation of corrective change. You could, in good conscience, advise people to make a private sexual peace.

What applied to birth control also applied to celibacy. The refusal to consider both was linked, the product of the same stifled Council, the same closed conditions and conservative mindset. Both were a violation of the intentions of John XXIII in calling Vatican II. As with birth control, an overwhelming majority of the clergy was in favor of a relaxation of the rule of mandatory celibacy. Though it had not been the subject of a recent doctrinal decision, the rule clearly no longer had the *sensus fidelium*. As you counseled others to do, you could make a private peace with Church rules regarding your own sexuality.

There would almost certainly have been homosexually oriented men among the priests and seminarians with whom Ziemann had studied. There has always been a homosexual component to the priesthood; but as with heterosexuals, there would have been strong constraints against any acting out. Any up-front gay behavior would only have surfaced later, after the rise of gay liberation in the world outside. With ordination, however, there was a freedom from the strict supervision and scheduling of seminary life. A significant part of Ziemann's parish duties now involved listening to, contemplating, giving advice about, and passing judgment on other people's sexual problems—yet he was expected to live without human intimacy himself.

In his vacation periods, the student Ziemann had certainly had the opportunity to experiment with his sexual feelings. By the time of his ordination, at the age of 26, he had probably come to terms with his own orientation. As a priest, it was in some ways easier to enter into a relationship with a man than with a woman: nobody raised an eyebrow when two priests went to a movie or out to dinner together. It was not considered unseemly for a group of priests to share a weekend or vacation cabin. At conferences and retreats, a priest who was willing to double up in his accommodations might find himself praised by his pastor for economizing. Most important, the issue of sexuality was linked with that of loneliness, both of which priestly training left essentially unaddressed. The priesthood, recalls one of the thousands of priests who left in the years since Vatican II, "was a good day, but a lonely night."

Richard Sipe, a former Benedictine priest who left the priesthood, married, and became a therapist, has spent more than twenty-five years counseling and interviewing hundreds of seminarians and priests. In his definitive study of celibacy, *A Secret World*, Sipe concludes that celibacy is not a state, but a process, a lifelong journey involving profound struggle, "an honest and sustained attempt to live without direct sexual gratification in order to serve others productively for a spiritual motive."

The impulse and the need extend across cultures and exist in both religious and nonreligious contexts. Celibacy may be the most important source of altruism in human endeavor, and there is a strong nonclerical tradition of it in the United States: Thoreau, Emily Dickinson, Clara Barton, Henry James, Dorothy Day, and (without knowing anything of his personal life) maybe Ralph Nader.

The great exponents of celibacy—Gandhi, Saint Paul, Saint Augustine—all came to it after having had adult sexual relationships. They had arrived at a personal sexual identity and knew what they were giving up. Successful celibacy, says Sipe, involves a dynamic combining following a developmental pattern, internalizing the celibate ideal, and refining and integrating celibate forces. It offers transcendence, a way of being at one with the life beyond life as experienced each day, a promise of "humanness unbounded by sexuality, love beyond loneliness, and sexual identity grounded in real generativity." It is neither easy nor trivial. And as with all things human, the achievement almost always falls short of the ideal.

According to Sipe's estimate, half of all ordained priests are practicing celibacy, though only two percent have attained the pure celibate consciousness he describes. Another eight percent have "consolidated" their celibacy: they have got it together. They are almost there. Of the noncelibate priests, 28 percent have heterosexual relationships, associations, or are experimenting. Ten percent have homosexual behaviors, five percent are problem masturbators, four percent are ephebephiles—involved with adolescent partners—two percent are pedophiles and one percent are transvestites. The figures are inexact and perhaps inappropriate;

few things are more resistant to categorization than human sexuality. Still, it offers some sort of perspective on the overall behavior of priests. What is apparent is that while celibacy is obviously not a way of life for every person, it is also not a way of life for every priest.

For Ziemann, who in 1971 was assigned to the faculty at Mater Dei High School in Santa Ana, the issues of sexuality and changes in the Church remained of constant concern. As a teacher of religion he would have had to explain and live with the Synod of Bishops' rejection that year of the idea that a married priesthood could exist alongside celibate clergy. This meant explaining not only to the students in his classes, but also in his role as counselor to boys considering entering the priesthood, why so many priests, and so often the best ones, were leaving the active ministry.

Mater Dei is, among other things, a jock school, the Notre Dame of Southern California high-school football; and it was here that Zeimann apparently discovered his affinity for and his ability to work with young people. It was his charisma, his gift of grace, the part of his vocation that appealed most to others and seemed to bring out the best in himself. He identified with high school students, listened to them, respected them, learned how to communicate effectively with them on their own terms. In 1993, as bishop of Santa Rosa, he made a 1,000-mile trip to Denver with a busload of teenagers to meet the pope, an assignment that most bishops would have handed off to somebody else.

There is another aspect to this. In 1994, a former student at Our Lady Queen of the Angels Seminary, in Mission Hills, California, claimed in a sworn statement that in 1980 he had complained about priestly sexual abuse to the dean of students—Ziemann— and that Ziemann had ignored his complaints. Is it possible for a priest to have had a genuine concern for the good of high school students and at the same time overlook complaints of sexual abuse against them?

That same year, 1994, at a reconciliation ceremony following the conviction of a Santa Rosa Diocese monsignor for repeated acts of sexual abuse, Ziemann, by then Bishop of Santa Rosa, stated that the monsignor had done what he had "out of love." The statement was incomprehensible and even offensive to the abused boys and girls, now men and women, and to their families. But to a person committed to a vow of celibacy, there is a kind of logic to it.

In return for forsaking what Nikos Kazantzakis termed "the greatest pleasure God has given us on this earth," as well as the possibility of participating in the one miracle accessible to almost all, the birth of a son or daughter, the celibate sees him or herself as an instrument of divine love and a conduit for love unbound by obligation, for all humankind, abstracted, when it is physically manifested, from both himself and the other individual. This does not justify such behavior or explain away the wrong of using another person for one's own sexual purposes. But it does suggest how a person under celibate vows might commit such acts and continue to live with himself. Or how someone struggling with the same vows might sympathize with such a person, even when most others would not. If the Catholic Church never seems to get its stand on sexuality right, there is some consolation in the thought that hardly anybody else does either.

Ziemann's energy and ambition, combined with the intertwined history of his family and that of the Church in Southern California, insured that he would not serve out his career in parish obscurity. From the day he entered the seminary, he would have been someone to watch, a person it would be wise to get to know, a young man on a career path of almost unlimited potential. His family ties—the favors owed for services rendered, the continuing social and ecclesiastical links between his family and the Church—resemble in many ways the dynastic influences of the late Middle Ages. The grandson of Mister L.A, the hammer who had pounded out the Catholic Church's hegemony over the movie industry in what would increasingly seem the high point of Catholic ascendancy in the United States, Ziemann was clearly on as fast a track as there is in the great, lumbering autocracy of the hierarchical Church.

In 1987, at the age of 45, young for the job, he was ordained to the episcopacy and named Auxiliary Bishop of Los Angeles. In addition to serving in the nation's third largest and most dynamically growing Archdiocese, he would have been admitted to the National Conference of Catholic Bishops, the closest thing to a Catholic legislature in the United States. He would be a prince of the Church, one of the youngest, someone to be respected and feared, an administrator largely responsible for overseeing Santa Barbara and Ventura Counties' churches, schools, parish houses, properties, and clergy. His appearance at a parish Confirmation would have been an event, a formal occasion harkening back to the Spanish era: the bishop in peaked crown and embroidered vestments carrying his crozier, the staff symbolizing his shepherdship of his flock, confirmants and their parents kneeling to kiss his ring. All this would have been potent imagery in places still redolent with the names of saints and missions such as Santa Barbara, Santa Paula, Santa Maria, Los Padres National Forest, the islands of San Miguel, Santa Cruz, and Santa Rosa. A jolt of living history in amnesiac modern California. Potent stuff even if you didn't go out of your way to embrace it.

Ziemann would have been the young comer, the welcoming Vatican II window in the Archdiocesan fortress of the right-wing Cardinal John McIntyre. Combining the legal, political, and movie industry operational skills of his family with the ancient ritual and traditional California presence of the Church, he was able to balance a personally progressive style with conservative stands on subjects like abortion and a personal devotion to the rosary.

The press typecast him as someone who was destined for greater things. The *Los Angeles Times*, based on what must have been inside information, identified him as the prospective future Bishop of San Diego. It didn't happen; something went wrong.

In late May of 1992, officers from the Los Angeles Police Department responding to a request to roust loiterers outside a Hollywood Sears store arrested a 36-year-old Catholic priest. The priest was sitting with a young man in a church car belonging to the Simi Valley parish to which he was assigned. In the car, in various bundles, bags, and boxes, was some $10,000 in cash. There were also two matchboxes containing rock cocaine. Several days later, church employees found $50,000 more in the priest's church apartment, some in Sunday Mass collection envelopes and all in small bills or checks payable to the church. A Ventura County judge issued a warrant for the arrest of the priest, who had meanwhile been released on bail provided by his pastor then jumped bail and disappeared.

The matter was kicked up to Ziemann as the Auxiliary Bishop in charge of administration for this region. He made a special trip to the Simi Valley parish to announce the news of the priest's arrest. To the great annoyance of police detectives investigating the case, the Archdiocese ignored LAPD requests to file a criminal complaint against the priest. According to the *Los Angeles Times*, "Auxiliary Bishop G. Patrick Ziemann explained, 'We wanted to hear the priest's side of the story first,' despite the fact the bundles of cash found in his rooms at the church included church collection envelopes—some torn open."

" 'It's a possibility that the money could be his and it's also possible it could be the church's,' said Ziemann, who oversees the archdiocese's churches in Ventura and Santa Barbara counties."

As the Simi Valley parishioners learned more about the priest's arrest and disappearance, Ziemann "stepped in to move the congregation past its worries." Parish records showed that collections had fallen off by about $43,000 a year since the fugitive priest had first arrived there.

Agony in the Garden

"[The parishioners] went through a lot of disbelief," The *Times* quoted the pastor as saying, "they went through anger and then denial, asking for some reason, other than that Father be responsible for what's happening. And then, with the generous help of Bishop Ziemann, [came] acceptance."

Ziemann removed the priest from his post for failing to show up at the church. In a move that was to prefigure later events in Northern California, he personally packed the priest's belongings into boxes, sealed them, and put them in a rented storage shed. There was and still is concern among Ventura County and LAPD law enforcement investigators that, in the process, evidence was removed.

The priest was eventually apprehended at the Mexican border, trying to re-enter the United States, accompanied by an illegal alien. The charges against him eventually were dropped—the drug case because of an insufficient quantity for conviction, and the embezzlement case because the Archdiocese of Los Angeles refused to file a criminal complaint. The priest has long since left the priesthood and the consequences of the embezzlement have been passed on to the parishioners.

A month after this case was settled to the satisfaction of nobody George Patrick Ziemann was installed as Bishop of Santa Rosa. It was a challenging assignment, a big job in a troubled diocese, a place where things needed to be turned around, an impressive responsibility for a man of 51. The Cardinal, now Roger Mahony, stated how much Ziemann would be missed in Los Angeles, how though he hated to lose him, he couldn't stand in the way of Ziemann's opportunity to run his own diocese. It was more than conciliatory, it was flattering. But it wasn't San Diego.

The Diocese over which Bishop Ziemann was to preside was as different from the area where he was born, educated, trained, and seasoned as if he had moved to another state.

Northern California, particularly the western and coastal regions north of San Francisco, is as remote in climate, topography, population density, and culture from the southern part of the state as Maine is from Florida. The difference begins at the shoreline, along an 800-mile coast served by two distinctly different Pacific currents: you can surf off the small, usually rocky beaches of far Northern California, but you'd better wear a wetsuit. The water is so cold, even in summer, that diving through a wave can give you the searing headache you get from eating ice cream too fast.

It rains here, up to a hundred inches a year at Honeydew, near the coast between Fort Bragg and Eureka, or at Cazadero near the mouth of the Russian River, the bulk of it concentrated between November and May. In summer the air stays cool even when the sun is hot, and on the warmest summer days a cotton wall of fog seems to linger a mile or two offshore. Sunshine is not the given, the determinant of wardrobe, diet, décor, and architecture that it is in the south. This is the land of rusting teepee burners, mackinaws, and boots, people wearing ball caps driving pickups with a gun rack in the rear window, heading for a house with a septic system and a propane tank. Moving in from the coast, the terrain is steep and wooded, sheep-grazing hillsides giving way to dense stands of redwood, *sequoia sempervirens*, the world's tallest living things, fringing the sky in waves of valleys and ridges, unbroken woods exuding an air of darkness and mystery, penetrated only by shafts of light, an atmosphere like the lost woods of Europe which the great cathedrals sought to replicate.

Where the redwoods end, the vineyards begin, row upon row of stocks and vines, lining the temperate, snow-free hills and valleys required for *vitis vinifera*, the temperamental grapes vulnerable to frost from which the finest table wines are made. There are valleys here—the Napa Valley, Sonoma, Alexander, Dry Creek, Russian River—names to set the wine buff's taste buds tingling, appellations now recognized as the equal of any in the world, the core of an industry expanding at a rate that suggests that even the highway-divider strips might soon be planted with grapevines.

Wherever you go here, you are in The Garden. Everywhere—redwoods, vineyards, tucked-away marijuana plots, the remaining apple, peach, and prune orchards and grazing grasslands—vegetation is king. In downtown Santa Rosa, the seat of the diocese, stands the home and enshrined botanical workshop of Luther Burbank, America's Genius Gardener. A quote from him, asserting the region's priorities, "I believe that this is chosen place of all the earth where nature is concerned," ran for decades on the masthead of *The Santa Rosa Press Democrat*.

This is the part of California where the Spanish presence runs out. The missions end at Sonoma; soon there are no more *Sans* and *Santas*. No more mission-style architecture and red-tile roofs. The *hidalgos* did not want to farm. The country was too rugged, the

John van der Zee

possibilities of profit too unpromising; the conquistador and padre tide subsided, leaving other cultures unconquered, unconverted, unengulfed. Russian—Fort Ross, the Russian River. Mount St. Helena; Native American—Mount Shasta, Ukiah, Hoopa, Round Valley; Gold Rush-Redneck-Cracker—Eureka, Yreka, Kelseyville, McKinleyville, Red Bluff. It is the country of the Lost Coast, so remote that into the twentieth century, the most direct means of travel between the coastal towns was by sea. Territory so rugged that, for the past five years, since the Northwestern Pacific tracks in the Eel River Canyon were buried by a sliding mountainside, there has been no railroad service.

In such country, dependent on nature yet isolated and sometimes threatened by it, new allegiances are formed, new objects found for spiritual yearning. There is a sacramental aspect to it all, in the wine industry with its celebration of wine lore, the sample sips of vintages, the clearing of the palate with a cracker or a bit of biscuit bearing a certain resemblance to the Eucharist. Among the redwoods, there is a near-druidic veneration of nature, The Goddess, trees (a young woman, originally from Arkansas, spent two years during Ziemann's episcopate, in an anti-logging protest, living in a Mendocino County redwood tree); the pot farmers of Mendocino County, the Napa Valley of marijuana, see themselves, in part, as a persecuted minority, evangelists for an herb with miraculously subversive healing properties. In the quieter canyons on the rancherias and reservations are hogans, blessed by shamans, where Native Americans gather for peyote ceremonies.

In country where the grasp of Western Civilization seems tentative, relaxed, both new and ancient beliefs assert themselves. On an isolated Sonoma County plain halfway between the vineyards and the coast stands the largest Buddhist complex in the United States, partly financed, it is rumored, by Hare Krishna money. On the slopes of Mount Shasta, a 14,000-foot snowcapped inactive volcano, sacred to three Indian tribes, 5,000 New Agers gathered in

Agony in the Garden

1984 to celebrate the Harmonic Convergence. Tucked away in the Anderson Valley of Mendocino County is the former Northern California training center of the Reverend Sun Myung Moon's Unification Church: the Moonies' boot camp. The unruliness, the persistent energy, capacity for renewal, and potential for exponential growth manifest in nature seem matched here by a burgeoning human spiritual hunger.

At night, the illuminated hand of man withdraws, replaced by Hansel-and-Gretel visions of being lost in the woods. Feral pigs, huge and fearless, emerge from the forest to feed on the grapes; coyotes yip and holler, wild turkeys yodel. It is inconceivable that anything standing here could not be converted, without a trace and within a generation, to forest on the one hand or vineyard on the other.

In all these ways, and more, it is tough country for traditional religion.

The Diocese itself was only thirty years old. Extending over six counties, it had been carved out of the larger Archdiocese of San Francisco and the smaller Diocese of Sacramento. The first bishop, Leo Maher, was a mogul, like a nineteenth-century railroad baron; he was personally conservative, but willing to listen. People wanted schools and churches, and he built them. He also built himself a mansion in Santa Rosa's Montecito Heights with a private chapel. He left the Diocese overcommitted to construction and $12 million in debt. The mansion was sold to the cartoonist Charles Schulz. Let go, as it were, for Peanuts.

The diocese began to grow as people moved north from San Francisco and Marin County. With the expanding vineyards came more Mexican workers and a shortage of Latino priests. Vocations generally had declined. The ministry grew desperate for ordained men. Problem priests began to turn up in the Diocese. There were investigations, lawsuits, threats of criminal prosecution.

Ziemann's approach to this challenging set of circumstances

was to go all out. Applying Southern California freeway style to rural Northern California's pickup culture, he cruised up and down his long, thin episcopate, driving himself in a white Olds Cutlass, staying in touch by cell phone, racing from one appointment to another like a political figure in a state of permanent campaign. He appeared at church and community gatherings, came to people's homes for dinner, returned their phone calls, and wrote personal notes to teenagers at Confirmation.

"He did a Confirmation here in Boyes Springs one Sunday at eleven," John O'Hare recalls, "then another in the Napa Valley at one, then a third in Santa Rosa at six." This is comparable, and in many ways similar to, giving three theatrical performances in a single day plus driving yourself between them, in addition to carrying the administrative responsibilities for an entire diocese.

It won him admirers.

"He's the most accessible, hands-on Bishop that I've ever seen," concluded Mark Jones, an attorney and parishioner at St. Eugene's Cathedral in Santa Rosa. "And I've been a Catholic for forty-eight years."

"He's a people's Bishop," agreed Maria Avila, of the Community Organizing Project. "He has a huge heart that you can almost touch."

Driving himself through the long forested, ocean, or vineyard stretches of his diocese, contemplating subjects for homilies, addresses to classes of students or groups of confirmants, Ziemann must have felt the metaphoric power of the gospels made manifest around him. The marriage feast at Cana where Jesus turned water into wine. The parable of the lord of the vineyard and his tenants who wished to steal his land. The chalice of wine, blessed and passed at the Last Supper. And deepest of all, the words of Jesus, defining himself: "I am the vine, you are the branches. I am the good shepherd. Do this in memory of me."

Or, more ominously, Jeremiah: "Woe be unto the pastors that destroy and scatter the sheep of my pasture."

Agony in the Garden

Who Ziemann was—the history, stature, and influence of the family he came from—might not mean anything here. People might not only be unimpressed but hostile to a big-shot L.A. legal and movie tradition. But there were meanings, insights, sudden jolts of congruence available in this sprawling, nature-dominated country. You had to be willing to be vulnerable to them.

The first crisis of Ziemann's episcopate came early, and it came hard.

At the time of his installation as bishop, there were already rumors and complaints concerning one of the diocese's most prominent priests, Monsignor Gary Timmons. A man of considerable energy and ability, active in the diocese for twenty years, Timmons, by his mid-fifties, had acquired a reputation as a take-charge individual, a trouble-shooter, as well as a gifted preacher and counselor. He had been an effective pastor at two parishes and had founded Camp St. Michael, a Catholic youth camp in Mendocino County attended by some 10,000 boys and girls since the 1970s. In addition to operating the camp, Timmons was currently the diocese's youth director. He also kept, in his apartment, a coffin, made to his measurements, which he used as a coffee table.

"We have a weak bench," explains Monsignor John O'Hare, "and here comes Jerry Rice. Timmons was energetic. He got things done. St. Bernard's in Eureka had been hemorrhaging money for years. He got it straightened out. People overlooked clues to his behavior because of the positive aspects of his performance."

In 1992, Donald Hoard, a man in his thirties who had attended Camp St. Michael as a teenager, was watching a television documentary on priestly sexual abuse when he turned to his wife and said: "That happened to me." He explained that Timmons had molested him, as well as a number of other boys at Camp St. Michael, but that he had never reported it because he feared that nobody would believe him. Hoard's wife insisted that her husband, who was then in therapy, tell his therapist what had happened. The therapist, as required by law, wrote letters about the reported abuse to the district attorneys of Mendocino and Sonoma counties, who began an investigation.

Ziemann, who at the time was trying to clean up other molestation charges and had invited abused people to come forward, was publicly promising cooperation in all abuse cases as part of his new, energetic, and compassionate administration. Those who came in were offered therapy if they were willing to agree not to go public with their complaints. It was open-checkbook time: one young man who confused Timmons' name with that of Camp St. Michael, reported that he had been molested by "Father Mike." He got an immediate reply from Bishop Ziemann saying that while Father Mike was no longer in the diocese, they would pay for his therapy anyway. Yet, as more young men claiming they had been molested by Timmons came forward, the bishop refused the Sonoma County DA's request that he make a statement confirming where and when Timmons had been assigned. According to Don Hoard, Donald's father, " there was eventually a list of forty-five kids Timmons had molested. His camp was a smorgasbord. The counselors did nothing to stop it."

Among the children Timmons had molested was the now grown son of Sonoma County Superior Court Judge John J. Gallagher. A lifelong Catholic, Gallagher had at first found it difficult to comprehend that his son had been molested by a priest. In the course of the prosecution's case against Timmons, Judge Gallagher learned that the diocese's first bishop had destroyed unfavorable information in Timmons's personnel file. Also, a priest who had known for years that Timmons was bringing young boys to his room at a parish rectory had done nothing about it. Like many other Catholics, Judge Gallagher came to believe that the coverup was as bad as if not worse than the molestations. His estrangement from the diocese was complete when some of Timmons's victims tried to hand out information fliers outside St.

Eugene's Cathedral. The pastor called the police who ordered the young men to disperse.

Eventually nine boys were willing to testify that they had been molested. The diocese lawyers proposed a settlement offering therapy in exchange for confidentiality. "The other guys were going to go along," says Don Hoard. "Our son Don refused to make a settlement." Timmons, facing indictment on criminal charges, was suspended from his priestly duties and entered a church-conducted therapy program in Chicago. Eventually he was arrested and brought back to California to stand trial.

The case became public in February of 1994. As news of the charges against Timmons appeared in the media, Patrick McBride, a 36-year-old man who worked in the chancery office, went to Bishop Ziemann and offered his support. He too had a history of priestly sexual abuse. In 1976, according to McBride, as a 14-year-old arriving at Camp St. Michael, he had been assigned by Monsignor Timmons to another priest, Father John Rogers. According to McBride, Father John had given him beer and had, eventually, sodomized him. McBride, who had been a good student, but whose grades and life had drastically deteriorated after the incident, had at the urging of his parents reported the incident to Monsignor Thomas Keys, the vicar of the diocese and a family friend. Keys had shown a book with pictures of diocesan priests to McBride, who had identified Rogers from it. Rogers, confronted with the charge, denied it and was sent to a San Francisco hospital for an evaluation. The McBride family was told by Keys that Rogers would be put in a place where he would never interact with kids again.

Patrick McBride eventually went to work in the chancery office, where he felt he had been well-treated. He liked and respected Bishop Pat, and when the arrest of Timmons cast its shadow over the diocese, McBride went to the bishop and offered to tell his story to the press as an example of how as a young man, involved in this same scandal, he had been treated fairly and considerately by the Church. Bishop Pat urged McBride not to expose the matter publicly and warned that the press would crucify him if he did.

As the extent and details of the case against Timmons were revealed at his trial, McBride became curious as to the whereabouts of Father Rogers. He went to Monsignor Keys, who admitted to him that Father Rogers was running the Newman Center at Humboldt State University—still associating with young people. In the atmosphere of heightened tension and increased exposure surrounding the Timmons trial, Ziemann decided to recall Rogers, who still denied any involvement with McBride, and dispatched him to a university in Louveigne, Belgium, while the bishop conducted an investigation of the charges.

As molestation victims continued to give public testimony against Timmons, McBride insisted that Father Rogers face charges. On November 4, 1995, Ziemann ordered Rogers to return home for a further psychiatric evaluation. Nine days later, after a series of agonized phone calls to friends and family, Father Rogers walked into a forest near Louveigne and shot himself to death.

In a last letter to a fellow priest, Rogers quoted a magazine article, saying that "This is a time of tremendous change, and I don't see the institutional Church helping the process too much." He linked the loneliness of celibacy with the need for sharing and the overwhelming depression such circumstances produced.

"When I was ordained [as a Benedictine priest] in 1959," Richard Sipe recalled in an expert report submitted as evidence in a 1993 Dallas pedophilia lawsuit, "I learned that some priests had sex with adults and even minors, and to some degree this behavior was taken for granted by Church authorities." There was, however, no atmosphere of urgency within the Church about addressing these matters. "The secret world of sexual activity, including sexual activity with minors, was known by the Catholic hierarchy, and though considered unfortunate and morally wrong, was accepted as an inevitable and easily forgivable failure of some priests."

There was in this, as in so many things, a sharp distinction between the Church's public and private posture. As early as 1949, the Catholic Church had opened a center in New Mexico for the care of problem priests, including priests who repeatedly had sex with minors. By the late 1960s and early 1970s, a number of Catholic treatment centers had opened specifically for priests and religious. In 1976, the New Mexico center, the Servants of the Paraclete, began what was perhaps the world's first program designed to treat psychosexual disorders, including those involving the sexual abuse of minors. "The fact that preparations for the opening of this program were years in the making," concludes Sipe, "demonstrates widespread knowledge of existing sexual misconduct with minors by Catholic clergy."

At the same time, treatment of the victims of priestly sexual abuse was ignored. "In response to their complaints," Sipe reports, "victims consistently report that they were seen as traitors and disloyal to their church. The victims felt that they were viewed as seducers, seductresses, sinners, or in some cases, opportunists, and treated largely without sympathy."

As late as the early 1990s, a Dallas monsignor was stating publicly that children who got involved sexually with priests were the victims of their parents' inattention, while an archbishop stated that priests who got involved with children were the naïve victims of streetwise youngsters.

Ziemann—trying to reach out and heal people financially with payments for therapy while at the same time maintaining the church's policy of no apology and handling matters of priestly discipline secretly—was a man with a foot in both camps of a badly divided Church. One camp, as defined by Eugene Kennedy in *Tomorrow's Catholics, Yesterday's Church*, represented the Vatican II vision of the church as people of God, embracing a more flexible

moral code; the other remained traditional, anchored in patri-
archy, rules, and obedience. Ziemann's attempt to do both, to be
both, would increase the stress upon him and intensify his weak-
nesses to the great disadvantage of himself and his diocese.

In 1996, Timmons was convicted of felony child molestation in
the case of two of the complaining boys, and was sentenced to
eight years in state prison. Despite the demoralizing nature of the
case's revelations, the bishop's performance generally met with a
positive response. "As far as I can tell," observed a past president of
St. Eugene's parish council, "Bishop Ziemann has dealt with this as
head-on and openly as possible." Others, particularly the victims'
families, were less sanguine.

"When Timmons was arrested," says Don Hoard, "Ziemann
said, 'This is a church of forgiveness, that Timmons was a good
priest, is a good priest, and will be a good priest in the future.'
Even after all the disclosures, by victims at the trial, he never
retracted this."

To the inherent isolation of the priesthood and the homesick-
ness of being in a region remote in almost every respect from the
southern California archdiocese where he had lived his entire life
was added the loneliness of command. As bishop, Ziemann was
everybody's boss, every individual's opportunity to state their case,
plead their cause, make their request. When people looked into his
eyes they sought not the man inside, but their own reflection. They
hoped to measure how they were doing in this human mirror, the
ordained mounting of the Church, illuminated, so they hoped, by
the light of God.

To mend his own divided feelings as well as the broken trust of
the people of his diocese following months of shattering revelations surrounding Monsignor Timmons' arrest and trial and
Rogers's suicide, Bishop Ziemann scheduled an extraordinary
evening healing service. Drawing on his southern California

upbringing and his own penchant for dramatics, Ziemann, in November of 1995, invited the men who had been molested as boys, their families, and any other interested parties in the diocese to a reconciliation ceremony that was adapted from a Spanish penitential rite.

People arriving at what was soon a packed house at St. Eugene's Cathedral in Santa Rosa found themselves entering a dimmed church illuminated only by candles. At the foot of the altar, where the communion rail used to be, was an enormous all-black cross. As people groped their way into the pews and their eyes adjusted to the theatrical darkness, the atmosphere was gradually filled by a choir chanting a dirge: the ancient, potent *Dies Irae*: Days of fire, days of wrath.

As this haunting music played, a very attractive woman appeared at the head of the aisle, dressed in a black velvet gown that reached almost to the floor. Standing straight-backed, the woman began moving down the aisle toward the altar, one ceremonial step at a time, maintaining a posture and a pace suggesting that of a bride at a formal wedding. Behind her, ten to 15 paces back, dressed in black vestments, walking at the same stately pace, came Bishop Ziemann. Every ten feet or so, the bishop would drop to the floor and prostrate himself face-down in the middle of the center aisle, remaining there briefly in a gesture of humility, acknowledgment, and regret. Then he would rise, resume the stately, ceremonial step for another ten paces or so, and prostrate himself again.

For some people in the pews this was a profound demonstration of atonement, an expression of the apology which could not be expressed verbally because of constraints laid down by the diocese's lawyers. "Anybody who comes to me who's not under litigation, I apologize to them," Ziemann was to comment later. To others the ceremony was off-putting in its spookiness, a reminder of Black Masses and the Inquisition.

At the foot of the altar, Ziemann prostrated himself again before the large black cross, beneath which lay two dozen red candles and more than a dozen red roses. Two other priests spoke, then Ziemann stood before the cross to deliver a brief message. He referred to the story of Jesus, the words he used before raising a young girl from the dead. "Fear is useless. What is needed is trust.

"We gather with fear and hurt," Ziemann told the crowd of some three hundred people. "We gather with anger and hope, but we gather because we're family."

"He spoke about reaching out, forgive and forget," Don Hoard recalls. "He spoke about Timmons more than the victims."

The healing ceremony was followed by a reception at the Monsignor Becker Center behind the Cathedral. One of the boys who had been molested by Timmons, Steven Gallagher, was embraced by Bishop Ziemann. "This was the first time in twenty years that I've felt comfortable inside that church," Gallagher said at the time. He considered the service "a start," but observed that on its own it wouldn't change much.

Don Hoard took a more jaundiced view. "Like now we're at a party. Tea and cookies. There was a little fruity priest going around taking pictures. My son's wife, my daughter-in-law, is beautiful. Ziemann was standing with us, telling my son Donald how sorry he is. He has hold of my hand. He referred to my daughter-in-law: 'Hey, he got a good one, didn't he.' It was inappropriate. I felt like belting him right there, but I didn't do it, out of respect for my daughter-in-law. She left the reception in tears.

"I had a feeling of evil from this guy. Ziemann."

The building was the most imposing in the still-expanding industrial park: a sprawling, one-story, pastel-green complex with tinted glass, vertical blinds, and a new Lexus in the reserved CEO parking space out front. Along the handsome aggregate sidewalk and on the benches overlooking the landscaped flower beds and grass strips, lean young men and women talked to cell phones. An Express Mail van waited at the front entrance. Every now and then an aircraft with an overnight delivery logo, FedEx or DHL, loomed overhead, approaching or leaving the Charles Schulz Memorial Airport two blocks away. Like the other new buildings in the park, mostly local or regional headquarters of technical and medical firms, the building looked as if it had been airlifted complete with its occupants from Silicon Valley some hundred miles to the south. It was all so new that in the glassed-in lobby there was no furniture. Instead, on the carpet in the corner, were grouped plaster figures of Mary, Joseph, and the infant Jesus.

This is the Catholic Church? It is, and also, it isn't.

For eleven years, the president and CEO of this firm, The National Scrip Center, now the largest operation of its kind in the United

States, was also the chief financial officer and vicar general of the Diocese of Santa Rosa. In fact, according to the Scrip Center's own information, the whole idea for this spectacularly successful startup was hatched in the chancery office of Monsignor Thomas Keys.

Originally conceived as a desperation measure for a struggling parish in the city of Petaluma, the idea of establishing a continuing fund-raising program for schools, churches, and other nonprofit organizations of all kinds through the sale of scrip was massaged into a major enterprise by Keys.

Using $25,000 seed money supplied by the diocese, with a board of directors appointed by the bishop, Keys in 1988 began to offer to a growing list of nonprofits the opportunity to make money from a comparably expanding list of its supporters' purchases. The original operation worked out of a church rectory, with four women taking orders by hand.

The way it works is that the Scrip Center buys scrip—gift certificates and coupons issued by department stores, supermarkets, and other merchandisers—in such quantities that it gets a discount rate, say seven percent. The Center then sells the scrip, for which it has paid ninety-three cents on the dollar, to the participating nonprofit for ninety-five cents. The participating school or church then sells the scrip to its members, parents, and friends, for the full value, which the buyers can use like cash when they shop at participating markets and stores. The school or church keeps five cents out of every scrip dollar for itself, and the Scrip Center keeps two cents for brokering the transaction. The system allows people to make donations for schools, churches, and other organizations in continuing need of support out of funds they would be spending anyway. It's a painless form of tithing. And it enables participating retail stores to build a core of regular repeat customers who associate the store with local loyalty. The Scrip Center also awards grants and scholarships as funds become available. When to this financial chassis are fastened the designer body of the riches, real or imagined, of the Catholic Church and the fancy interior appointments associated with the Church's tax-exempt status, you have a vehicle capable of traveling almost anywhere. And travel is what the Scrip Center did, moving out of the parish rectory to its own Santa Rosa offices in 1995, then outgrowing those by 1999, when the operation was moved to its 30,000-square-foot, $3 million headquarters in the industrial park. As of the end of 1999, the Scrip Center was doing $450 million worth of business a year. The Center eventually had its own Web site and its offerings include a National Scrip Center Mastercard Program, where even credit-card purchases could be made with scrip.

What this meant, in the era of sanctified dot-com entrepreneurship, was an unquestioned, dynamic ongoing success. What it represents in terms of the values taught by Jesus and supposedly preserved by the Catholic Church was something else again.

Monsignor Keys is a man who seems to have had little difficulty reconciling rendering unto God with rendering unto Caesar. Now in his late fifties, with a pink complexion, a thick head of white hair, rimless glasses, and the soft remnant of a brogue from Derry, the Northern Ireland city where he was born, Keys at one level resembles the stock middle-aged parish priest. Father Tom. Yet at the financial and operational level, he has been an influential figure, "the most consistent leadership presence," says *The Santa Rosa Press Democrat*, "in the Diocese for more than thirty years."

Keys appears to be one of those Irishmen who, like an old pol, combines personal charm with a quick grasp of some of the harsher realities of American life. He also seems to have understood, early on, that the road to advancement within the Church lay not so much through the day-to-day ministry of a parish as with the administration of Church offices and funds. Recruited, following his ordination in Carlo, Ireland, by Santa Rosa Bishop Mark J. Hurley, a man with strong family and emotional ties to

Agony in the Garden

Ireland, Keys arrived in the Santa Rosa Diocese in 1970, hoping, he later told *The Wall Street Journal*, "to be a priest, working directly with parishioners." Instead he was assigned to "special ministry," helping run the Diocese's business affairs. He soon became director of Catholic Charities and the Catholic Youth Organization. He became Bishop Hurley's secretary and returned with the bishop to Ireland where they visited the Maze, the notorious prison where IRA members convicted of violence against the government of Northern Ireland were incarcerated. In 1979, under Hurley, Keys was appointed chancellor of the Diocese, becoming, in effect, office manager of the chancery, the diocesan headquarters.

In addition to assuming these administrative responsibilities, Keys had enrolled in the graduate program at the University of San Francisco, where he earned his master's degree in business administration. It was while Keys was a member of the USF MBA Program that he first learned of the Consolidated Account used by the Greyhound Corporation. Greyhound, fundamentally a bus transportation company, had developed the practice of depositing receivables from its scattered offices into a single bank account which, while allowing people in individual offices to write checks, greatly reduced administrative costs. At the same time, the concentration of funds at a single bank gave the corporation considerable clout in earning interest on its deposits and a more advantageous rate when negotiating loans. Keys was so impressed with Greyhound's cash management program that he wrote his master's thesis on it. He then persuaded Bishop Hurley to adopt a similar overall plan for the funds of the Santa Rosa Diocese with its forty-five different parishes. Activity in the account was originally administered manually, but with the increasing capability of computers, the Consolidated Account came to be monitored electronically, and the account grew increasingly sophisticated.

Each participant in the Consolidated Account would have checks printed which identified the account holder as a particular school or parish. In fact, there was only a single account number at one bank, a bank that identified the diocese as the account holder. For bookkeeping purposes, each participant, and its single or multiple sub-accounts, were assigned identification numbers by the diocese. These I.D. numbers appeared on the participants' checks and on the monthly statements prepared by the Diocese. Eventually, there were more than 200 of these sub-accounts. In addition to tracking the activity of these 200 sub-accounts, the diocese computer program also calculated an interest rate for the participants' daily balances. As a result of the program, the Diocese actually sent monthly interest checks to the participants based on their daily balances within the Consolidated Account.

For the participating schools and churches, writing their own checks with an individual I.D. number and receiving monthly statements and interest checks with the same I.D. number, it was easy to assume that each account was separate, that their funds were not being mingled with those of other parishes. It was equally easy to assume that the funds were being administered by the bank, when in fact the bank recorded only a single account, the diocese's, and the administering was being done by the diocesan office: in effect, by Keys. He was not a licensed financial professional, nor was he a banker. Yet he acted in the capacity of both.

When individual participants abused the Consolidated Account by overdrawing from the fund's pool of money without having the balance to cover their checks, it was Keys who called them to admonish them about, in effect, using other people's money. And when one church, St. Bernard's in Eureka, became overdrawn to the tune of $1.9 million, it was Keys who threw the parish out of the account.

Keys was also involved in investing the diocesan funds, trying to navigate the churchly vehicle between the hazards of risk to the safety of reward, a dicey balancing act usually associated with young men and women working in the heavy traffic of Wall Street financial firms rather than an Irish Catholic monsignor in the bucolic Diocese of Santa Rosa.

There is a certain survival necessity for any organization hoping to function in today's world, to make use of business and corporate skills. It is something else when that organization is a church. The purpose of a corporation is to diffuse responsibility. It begins with finance, the issuing of stock to spread risk and fund expansion, and continues through departmentalization: "That's not my area of responsibility," the delegation of authority and the chain of command. But the essence of the Catholic Church, the source of its enduring influence over individual lives, has been in getting people to accept responsibility, personally, for every aspect of their lives. The phrase *mea culpa*, "through my fault," comes from the *Confiteor*, the traditional Catholic confessional prayer, where it used to be repeated three times, accompanied by a literal beating of the breast. The Catholic Church in Garrison Keillor's Lake Woebegon is named Our Lady of Perpetual Responsibility, an epiphany of recognition for almost any Catholic. Through the 1960s, Catholic schoolgirls were taught that, if a boy came on to them sexually, it was their responsibility for dressing, speaking, or acting in such a manner that they had provoked the boy's attention, thus providing an occasion of sin. *Mea culpa, mea culpa, mea maxima culpa.*

When an organization espousing unlimited responsibility tries to internalize values of organizations dedicated to diffusing it, there has to be a split either within the organization or within the individuals administrating it. A person begins to operate in one aspect of his life entirely split off from the values lived and espoused in another aspect, rationalizing or denying any conflict between the two. This psychical splitting tends to be intensified when the organization operates in an atmosphere of secrecy. If Monsignor Thomas Keys was aware of any profound conflict from being President and CEO of the National Scrip Center, while

serving as Chief Financial Officer and Vicar of the Diocese of Santa
Rosa, he never expressed any serious dissatisfaction with the situation. And if the participants in the Consolidated Account believed
that their funds were each being kept separate and administered by
a bank, Keys seems to have felt no real need to disabuse them of
that notion. He was a busy man with a full plate, a businessman
with a business life as well as a priest with a priestly life.

"National Scrip Center," Keys declared in a letter to *The Wall
Street Journal*, "is my educational ministry and an independent
nonprofit corporation that I have served in an unpaid executive
capacity for ten years. If it were a publicly listed company, based on
growth performance, National Scrip Center would be No.1 on *Inc.
Magazine's* 500 fastest-growing companies list."

"No man can serve two masters," the evangelist Matthew tells
us, "for either he will hate the one and love the other; or else he
will hold to the one, and despise the other."

Monsignor Keys, attempting to serve both God and the money culture, was denying to the people of his diocese and probably to himself the divided nature of what he was doing. By doing so he would
help create a situation for which the schools, the churches, and the
people of the Santa Rosa Diocese would eventually pay dearly.

Keys's worldly skills accelerated his hierarchical advancement. By
the time Bishop Hurley left, in 1987, Keys was vicar general of the
diocese, second in command to the bishop, and empowered to act
in the bishop's name when he was not present. Embodying as he
did through the Consolidated Account the financial administration
of the Diocese as well as, beginning in 1988, the operations of the
expanding Scrip Center, Keys continued as vicar through the administration of the next bishop, John Steinbock. Following Steinbock,
Keys acted as interim bishop during the 10 months it took Pope
John Paul II to name Ziemann as Steinbock's replacement.

It was not his financial acumen alone that enabled Keys to serve

Agony in the Garden

as second-in-command under three successive bishops: he also had to please and not dispute with his reigning prince. The Catholic Church, usually thought of as a monolith, is much more episcopal than most people realize. The bishop of a diocese is legally a Corporation Sole: he is the owner, apart from the schools, of all buildings, land, and investments of the diocese, and he is free to dispose of them as he sees fit. As bishop, he is also free, within certain advisory constraints, to ordain whomever he decides is qualified as a priest, an authority George Patrick Ziemann exercised despite objections in ordaining Jorge Hume Salas. As vicar, Monsignor Keys had to please and satisfy, in succession, three regionally powerful men, distinct personalities who were in direct authority over him, an authority they might well feel was compromised by the fact of someone else having so complete an operational grasp over the financial life of the diocese.

To compensate for his take-charge inclinations, the energetic Keys became the man his bishop could rely upon in handling especially difficult or sensitive matters. If, for example, a man who had as a teenager been sexually abused by a priest and who had moved to a distant state was threatening to go public with his accusations, Keys was the person a bishop would send off to speak sympathetically to the young man, offer a settlement, and—in exchange for an agreement of confidentiality—write a diocesan check. Keys was effective, he was discreet, and he was submissive to ecclesiastical authority, whomever the person in authority might be.

A man of unquestionable energy and considerable ability, Keys also possessed a more broadly negotiable personal asset: charm. He was particularly effective, and charming, among people who shared both his clerical and business interests; that is, Catholics with money.

In 1996 Bob and Barbara Walter, a couple in Sebastopol, California, owners of a promising racehorse named Cavonnier, had the

68

stimulating experience of seeing their three-year-old gelding qualify for the Santa Anita Handicap. Seeing this as an unusual opportunity, the Walters asked their friend, Monsignor Tom Keys, if he would bless Cavonnier before the race. Keys replied that in the course of his career, he had blessed a fishing fleet, farmers' crops, grape growers' vineyards, store openings, and even automobiles. Why not bless a horse? On the day of the race he appeared at the Santa Anita Race Track, where he placed a hand on Cavonnier and intoned a prayer for the success and safety of the horse and his jockey. Cavonnier, a longshot, a "cute, but disrespected entry," won at Santa Anita, thereby both satisfying his owners' faith in the efficacy of prayer and qualifying for the Kentucky Derby.

The Walters, who ran a mom-and-pop as opposed to a full-scale professional stable operation, viewed the Derby as a once-in-a-lifetime opportunity. So they pulled out all the stops. They had CAVONNIER bumper stickers printed, wore their stable colors everywhere, asked their Chinese goddaughter to burn joss sticks, and invited Keys to fly to Louisville with them for the Derby.

In the week leading up to the race, the accessible down-to earth Walters and their horse with its own spiritual groom were human-interest food and drink to reporters from both local and national media. "I just don't want the Pope to get wind of this," Keys confided in a disarming quote, "so he doesn't cut in on any of my action." By race time the odds on Cavonnier, increasingly a sentimental favorite, had dropped from 10 to 1 to 5 to 1.

In a scene out of an old Pat O'Brien movie, Keys, in the paddock, placed his hand on Cavonnier and blessed the horse. "Heavenly Father, please give Cavonnier and Chris McCarron [the jockey] a safe trip today and protect them from all obstacles on the course."

Keys offered McCarron a St. Christopher's medal, but the jockey, having no place to put it and perhaps concerned about making the weight, handed it back.

The race began. Cavonnier started in the pack, was ninth at the first turn, then began to climb; at the quarter he was third, ready to begin his run. At the eighth pole, he began to pull away, passing Unbridled's Song, the favorite, and opening up a three-length lead with a hundred yards to go. Then Grindstone, a horse near the rail, swung wide and began to make his move; the horse closed fast; it was neck and neck at the wire.

"We got it!" *The Santa Rosa Press Democrat* reported a man at the rail shouting. "[He] was jumping up and down and finally grabbed the arm of Santa Rosa Monsignor Thomas Keyes [sic] like the Monsignor was a buddy who had just come back home from six months of sea duty.

" 'And then I could slowly feel his grip loosen and the emotion drain out of (him),' the Monsignor said. 'I could feel his body sag.' "

Cavonnier had lost in a photo-finish, the closest Kentucky Derby race in thirty-seven years.

There is a song about the semilegendary sixteenth-century vicar of the English village of Bray, who, throughout the conflicts of that turbulent era, retains his position no matter what religious or political party—Catholic or Protestant, Stuart, Tudor, or Hanoverian—rules the nation. At the start of each verse, the vicar has adopted a new political and sometimes religious identity. The chorus remains the same:

> And this is law, I will maintain
> Unto my dying day, sir.
> That whatsoever king shall reign,
> I will be Vicar of Bray, sir!

There are, as we shall see, parallels of several kinds between the Vicar of Bray and the Vicar of the Diocese of Santa Rosa.

During 1997, Jorge Hume Salas made several return visits to his native Costa Rica. These trips may have represented an attempt on his part to end his dependent relationship on Bishop Ziemann or to seek some sort of priestly position, based on his *norteamericano* clerical credentials. Either way, the attempts failed. In order for him to retain his INS residency card, he was required to return to the U.S. every two months, using airline tickets paid for by Ziemann. The bishop, aware when Hume would be returning to the Santa Rosa area, would contact the priest and summon him to have sex with him.

As for finding a priestly assignment in Costa Rica, Hume's resume, questionable enough at a distance of some 2,000 miles, was even more suspect when scrutinized closer to home in Central America.

Jorge Hume Salas was born on September 26, 1957, into a poor family in the town of Tucurrique in the province of Cartago, on Costa Rica's central plateau, and neighboring the province of the capital, San Jose. He was the oldest of six children of Marina Elena Salas and Jorge Hume Smith, who worked as a tractor driver.

Agony in the Garden

His educational record was spotty. While he completed elementary school in the area, his secondary education was repeatedly interrupted by the need to work to support his family. Eventually he went to night school, so he could keep the day job required by his family's economic circumstances.

"It was during this time [1976–1980] that I felt the call of God to the priesthood," Hume wrote in his 1992 letter to the newly appointed Bishop Ziemann. "But I could not enter as a student in the seminary as my parents did not have the financial means. I had to dedicate myself to work, and so I had to make a seminary within my family."

Hume's imaginary seminary involved a degree of fantasizing ample enough to expand to the outside world. It was at this time that Hume began acting like a priest, performing certain ecclesiastical duties in Costa Rica for which he was not ordained.

According to Father Carlos Rojas, a priest of the Archdiocese of San Jose, Costa Rica, Jorge Hume Salas presented himself as a priest on many occasions in hospitals in the city of Juan de Dios. To this effectively captive congregation, Hume Salas ministered by hearing confessions, blessing the sick, and offering spiritual guidance. Father Rojas could not say whether Hume Salas had celebrated Mass: he had never seen him do it.

Hume, who left home to attend school in Mexico City in 1980, continued to return to Costa Rica over the years, where he repeatedly got himself in trouble with church authorities. Another Costa Rican priest, Father Ovidio Burgos Acuna, states that Hume, who had been a student for two years in a Costa Rican preparatory seminary but had left, was afterwards passing himself off as a priest. Father Burgos identified Hume Salas from a passport photograph. A third cleric, Father Marco Diego Bonilla, has stated that he has testimonies from priests in other Costa Rican dioceses indicating that Hume Salas had conducted missions, celebrated marriages, and administered the Eucharist, all without being an ordained priest.

From 1980 to 1982, according to Hume's letter to Ziemann, Jorge Hume Salas lived and worked in Mexico City, where he intended to study philosophy. In 1983, he left Mexico for Honduras, where, despite his previous impostures, he obtained entry to the major seminary, Seminario Mayor, in the capital, Tegucigalpa. In what appears to be a pattern suggesting Hume Salas's ability to ingratiate himself with persons in ecclesiastical authority, the Bishop of Comayagua had given Hume a dispensation, granting in a certified document that Hume was "excused from all irregularities that happened during offenses committed against the Church laws." After the seminary's director conducted his own investigation into Hume's background, however, Hume Salas was expelled.

Though the director refused to buy Hume Salas's act, it appears that the Honduran bishop did. In a foretaste of Ziemann's covering up for Hume, the Bishop of Comayagua ordered the school to give Hume an opportunity to take final examinations and admonished the director for expelling Hume for previous violations of church law concerning priestly conduct. In a 1984 letter, the Honduran bishop characterized Hume's impostures as "impeding his receipt of the orders of a priest, but not his studies of theology." The Honduran bishop explained that he had issued his previous dispensation in order not to have problems in the future, and that he did not inform the seminary of his action because Hume's misdeeds were committed by a youth who apparently did not know better.

In Hume's 1992 letter to Ziemann, he made no mention of his studies in Honduras. And in response to the question on his job application asking whether he had applied for admission to a seminary before, he answered "no."

In 1985 and 1986, according to Hume's resume, he attended two colleges in Mexico City, the Universidad La Salle and the Universidad Intercontinental. According to transcripts obtained by *The*

Agony in the Garden

Santa Rosa Press Democrat, most courses were in theology, church history, and biblical studies. "The official Universidad Intercontinental transcript," reported *The Press Democrat*, "differs from a course list submitted by Hume with his application to the Santa Rosa Diocese." Hume's list, which apparently bore an official stamp from the school, showed an additional two dozen courses he claimed to have taken in 1987 and 1988. "However," *The Press Democrat* concluded, "an official at the school's scholastic services department told *The Press Democrat* it has no record of Hume attending the school in 1987 or 1988."

On one of his visits to Costa Rica, Hume Salas identified himself as a Claretian priest who practiced his ministry in a parish in New York. He also claimed to be a member of the Diocese of Newark. According to an official of the Claretian order, Hume was in fact a seminarian of the order, which is headquartered in Chicago, from 1986 to 1990 when he was expelled after being caught acting as a priest during a pilgrimage to the Holy Land.

"The ruse was discovered," reported *The Press Democrat*, "according to Claretian documents, when two women came to a Claretian parish in Chicago asking for Hume and produced photographs of Hume celebrating Mass."

On being kicked out of the Claretian seminary, Hume made his way to Bolivia where he entered his fourth seminary, in La Paz. In 1992, Jorge Hume Salas was expelled yet again from this seminary, ejected for falsifying his resume and for "immoral conduct that included possession of pornographic materials and contraceptive devices."

Jorge Hume Salas, it appears, was a man responding to the call of two vocations: priest and confidence man. Ever resilient, he turned up the same year that he was bounced from the seminary in Bolivia in California, where, in September, he first approached Bishop Ziemann, who ordained him the following year.

The feeling that Hume Salas seems to have elicited in the

people he gulled was not so much conviction as compassion. A slight man with an appealing smile, liquid wounded eyes, and a gentle manner, emotional, given to tears, he is presented repeatedly in people's description of him as a victim, a man put upon, turned out, taken advantage of, more preyed upon than predator. He understood how to make people want to rescue him. Priests, therapists, lawyers, and acquaintances repeatedly stepped in to help him. A Santa Rosa police investigator compared Hume's situation with Ziemann to that of an abused wife. Hume Salas was more than capable of accentuating this impression of vulnerable victimhood. He had doctored his resume, editing out the bad experiences and embroidering the positive ones, and had written an effective letter in his initial approach to Ziemann. And how was it that he spoke only rudimentary English after spending four years with the Chicago-based Claretians?

He repeatedly got caught, yet he kept coming back for more— another shot at the seminary, another attempt at legitimization as a priest. Could this not be seen, in his own mind, as a true vocation, a priestly calling so powerful that it was able to withstand rejection and failure beyond the endurance of most aspiring priests?

Surely it was this vulnerability, this wounded-deer quality that was at the heart of Hume's appeal to George Patrick Ziemann. Here was a person whom Ziemann could protect and shelter, mentor, converse with in Hume's more comfortable Spanish, and initiate into the in-your-face realities of *norteamericano* culture: the living embodiment of Ziemann's commitment to an expanding Latino ministry. From the start, it is clear that Ziemann had convinced himself that what he was doing with and to Jorge Hume Salas was for Salas's own good.

Early on in Ukiah, before the discovery of Hume Salas's thefts, the bishop had taken an interest in him. In the spring of 1996, as part of the Latino Cursillo movement within the Church, Hume had been sent on a retreat to Spain accompanied by another Ukiah man, a Latino businessman. When the two men returned from the retreat, the businessman told people in the Ukiah Latino community that Hume had fondled him and propositioned him to have sex with him. Salas insisted that it was the businessman who had propositioned *him*, and that he, Salas, had indignantly refused, because he was a priest and did not do such things. Nevertheless, the businessman continued to make public statements about the incident and because of them, Hume Salas in July of 1996 received a call from Bishop Ziemann, asking to have a meeting with him.

The bishop drove to Ukiah, where he met with Hume in Hume Salas's residence. Ziemann advised Salas that there had been accusations of a sexual nature made against him. When Salas asked whom the people were making the accusations, Ziemann told him it was various young men whose names the bishop couldn't reveal because the allegations were confidential. According to Salas, he started crying because he couldn't believe the charges that were being made against him and didn't know how the church was going to deal with them. He became, he said, extremely depressed. And he told the bishop that he, Hume Salas, had to drive to Santa Rosa.

The bishop insisted on meeting with Hume Salas later the same evening in Ukiah. Hume had left Ukiah, and driven, at speed, the sixty miles to Santa Rosa. He returned to Ukiah later that night and met with Ziemann again. At this later meeting, Ziemann told Hume that he had followed him into Santa Rosa and back, a round trip of over 100 miles. He said that, based on the way Hume was driving and his depressed state over the sexual allegations that he thought Hume might be intending to commit suicide. This interest may have represented Ziemann's solicitude toward the welfare of the younger Latino priest, in so many ways his protégé. Or, aroused by the sexual charges, Ziemann may have been cruising him. Probably, the bishop himself did not know for sure where one feeling—

compulsion or impulse, protection or seduction—ended and the other began.

At any rate, it was shortly after this when Hume had been dismissed from St. Mary of the Angels and was about to be sent to treatment in St. Louis that the two men's sexual relationship started.

For Ziemann also, there were considerable risks involved in beginning a relationship with another person, one involving the threat of exposure and blackmail. Suppose Hume Salas threatened to publicly reveal their relationship unless Ziemann rewarded him with promotion or money? The bishop was taking a tremendous risk in having sex with the priest. Then again, maybe the danger of exposure, the chance of getting caught, was part of the allure, an exhilarating testing of the limits of the bishop's worldly power. There was still the assuring safeguard of the black curtain, the atmosphere of secrecy and sexual denial prevailing within the Church. No one, especially other priests, really *wanted* to know that a bishop was having sex with a priest. In addition, Hume could not denounce the bishop without serious risk to himself. Whenever Hume protested about being required to service the bishop sexually, which now averaged about twice a week, Ziemann would remind him that he, the bishop, was all that stood between Hume and prosecution for theft, suspension from the priesthood, and possible loss of his INS residency card.

Hume, on his part, despite his vulnerable, wounded-deer persona, was fully capable of scheming in his own behalf. He had, after all, lied successfully to church authorities in at least three countries. For some months now he had been confiding in and receiving advice from both a therapist and an attorney, and it was apparently at the attorney's suggestion that, for Hume's own protection, he surreptitiously collected a semen sample from Ziemann, on tissue paper which Hume kept in a plastic bag. It was also suggested to Hume that it might be to his advantage to secretly tape Bishop Ziemann making one of his repeated apologies, combined with the equally repeated promise that this would be the last time that he would ask Hume to do this.

It is apparent that this was not a love relationship. What then, exactly, was it?

"Sexual maturity," writes Richard Sipe, "is an elusive goal, not necessarily achieved under the most favorable circumstances. But sexuality is relentless, a natural hankering fueled by a persistent animal curiosity." In the priesthood, a monosexual world where friendships and subculture are overwhelmingly male, there has always been a certain homosexual component. Sipe estimates that, projected from all sources, approximately ten to twelve percent of clergy involve themselves in homosexual activity. About half the priests who describe themselves as homosexual "either practice celibacy or have consolidated or achieved celibacy," about the same proportion as those describing themselves as having a heterosexual orientation.

According to Sipe, some three percent of the clergy in his study behave homosexually either episodically due to situational stress or as part of a transitional adjustment reaction. "These men," he observes, "have severe or at least moderate guilt feelings in association with their homosexual activities. They really try to control their behavior, mostly because they see it as a contradiction to the ideal they have set for themselves. They are the first to call themselves hypocritical."

Within this group of priests are some who may or may not be obligatory homosexual. "Their fantasy life is ambiguous, as are their friendships . . . . Their limited sexual play may be heterosexual as well as homosexual. Their immaturity may lead them to occasional homosexual behavior within the context of their friendships; that behavior in turn is confusing . . . as well as spiritually unsettling for them."

It would seem as if George Patrick Ziemann, a man working

under steam-engine stress with a take-charge penchant to control and keep secret even his most fundamental yearnings, would fit into the first part of this sexual category. Jorge Hume Salas, a younger man insisting on his heterosexuality even while engaging in homosexual acts with his bishop, would qualify for the second. Here were two men, sharing sex but not intimacy, each with his own agenda, each unable to move beyond himself in embracing the other. Both were priests needing and using, probably experiencing tremendous feelings of guilt, without coming close to Thomas Aquinas's definition of love: to wish for the good of another.

And yet there remained, in Bishop Ziemann, a certain sense of obligation to Jorge Hume Salas. Hume was, after all a priest, like himself, a person set apart, called by God to a life of celibacy, however imperfectly realized. In return for servicing Ziemann sexually, Hume had never demanded money or gifts or any sort of special treatment. All Hume asked in life was to be allowed to practice his vocation, to function as a priest, and in pursuit of this goal he had certainly undergone his share of trials and humiliations. Wasn't such a man, in keeping with the Catholic tradition of the forgiveness of sin, deserving of another chance? Besides, Ziemann was an administrator, the hierarch in charge of a diocese desperately in need of priests, especially priests with a Spanish-language capability. At some point, considering the continuing influx of Spanish-speaking Catholics into his diocese, couldn't Ziemann's refusal to assign Hume to a parish be considered the waste of a resource?

In the spring of 1997, Ziemann assigned Salas to St. John's Church in the city of Napa, in the heart of the wine country and with a significant Latino element among its congregation. The assignment seemed to have solved two problems at once, and if there was some continuing criticism from people like those at Hume's previous parish in Ukiah, Ziemann's episcopate had racked up enough successes by now to weather it. His personal popularity continued to grow as did the effectiveness of his ministry. The diocese seemed at last to have put behind it the problems of priestly sexual abuse which had dogged it for a decade. Even the lawyer who had represented nearly a dozen molestation victims in suits against the diocese felt that Ziemann represented a significant improvement over previous bishops. New construction, involving some projects which had been delayed for years, was going forward throughout the diocese, including a new church for St. Mary of the Angels, Hume's previous trouble-spot in Ukiah. The Scrip Center, of which Ziemann was chairman, had survived a beef with a rival firm which Monsignor Keys had bought out as well as a threat by the Department of Justice to strip it of its nonprofit status and had reached annual sales of $350 million. The AIDS ministry had added thousands of new members, Catholic Charities had dramatically expanded, and the Church's involvement in Latino activities—led by Ziemann—had intensified.

It was no wonder that this popular bishop, who occasionally suited up in old sweats to run in charity fundraisers, was routinely mentioned as a candidate for much larger jobs within the Church. He was fifty-six, a young comer in the geriatric world of the Catholic hierarchy, and he was proactive, a doer not a caretaker. If a few carping, negative people objected to his reassignment of Jorge Hume Salas to a new parish, well, Bishop Pat had the administrative successes, the churchly rank, and the personal popularity to shrug them off.

I n his state of hubris, inflation, or maybe even infatuation, George Patrick Ziemann had either overlooked or underestimated the indignation, amounting now to rage, that had accumulated among Catholics, laypeople and clergy alike, concerning the Church's treatment of instances of priestly sexual abuse.

The cases that had been settled had all been brought to light through civil action. Not one had been initiated by the Church. In the cases where settlements had been made, out of court, the settlement always included an agreement of secrecy sealing information concerning the actual abuses. In at least one instance, where a priest, accused of repeated molestation, had fled the country, Church authorities had withheld from the police information concerning his whereabouts. While publicly proclaiming willingness to respond to and investigate all cases of alleged molestation, diocesan authorities had been dilatory at best in cooperating with police and governmental authorities. In 1994, a Sonoma County state legislator introduced, in the California State Assembly, a measure extending to parochial schools the legal requirement of teachers, counselors, and administrators to report cases of suspected molestation to the police. The Church opposed it on grounds that it was an intrusion on the separation of church and state. Only through the strenuous efforts of the assemblywoman, a practicing therapist, and the lobbying and committee testimony of the parents of molestation victims, was the measure enacted into law.

Added to this was the frustration involved in bringing alleged priestly molesters before the law at all. The window for initiating prosecution of such cases was narrow. After a year from the time the molestation was reported, the statute of limitations ran out. But victims who had been molested as children had often not realized the seriousness of what was happening to them at the time, and the effects of what had occurred had manifested themselves only years later. It was extremely difficult to work from memory as well as to contact other people who may have been victimized by the same priest and try to get them to come forward, often at the cost of re-traumatizing them through recall of emotionally painful incidents. Attempts to extend the one-year deadline ran the risk of being challenged in court as ex post facto legislation, not applying to incidents occurring years in the past. In all these instances, Church authorities, working through attorneys, took the hardest possible line against the plaintiffs and were in effect dragged into compliance with the law rather than, as people in the business of morality and ethics, leading the way. This was true not only of the Diocese of Santa Rosa, but of the Catholic Church hierarchy in general throughout North America.

According to Richard Sipe, during his research he was told by several different Catholic bishops that, during the 1980s, Pope John Paul II explicitly forbade them to talk about "contraception, abortion, homosexuality, masturbation, a married priesthood or women's ordination to the priesthood other than to defend the Church's official teaching." Sipe recounts an incident at a national meeting of diocesan vocation directors when, during one of the breaks, the conversation turned to the possibility of women's ordination. "A bishop in attendance," says Sipe, "by eyewitness account, red-faced and gasping, shouted out, 'The Pope has forbidden us to talk about this!' "

Reinforcing this attitude was the feeling that bishops and chancery officials did not consider priestly sexual abuse, as unacceptable as they saw it to be, as a matter for civil prosecution. The civil authorities, in this view, had no jurisdiction over the spiritual lives of priests. In general, clerical sexual abuse was regarded as spiritual weakness rather than crime or psychopathology.

For Catholics dealing directly with the human consequences of the secrecy and denial surrounding priestly misconduct, the split between what the pastoral church taught and the institutional church practiced concerning sexual matters had become increasingly difficult to bear. Parish priests and nuns, Catholic police officers, therapists, lawyers, district attorneys and judges, and Catholics in the media found themselves conflicted not only between the teachings of Jesus and the practices of the Church, but between the need to be good Catholics and the requirement to be good citizens.

For Sister Jane Kelly, some of whose former students had been among the victims of priest sexual abuse, and who had witnessed Jorge Hume Salas's apprehension for theft of church funds, it had become apparent that silence and secrecy concerning these offenses not only allowed them to gain power in darkness but guaranteed that they would be repeated, if perhaps in altered form.

In August of 1996, while Hume Salas was undergoing treatment in St. Louis, Sister Kelly, unaware of any sexual relationship between the two men, sent Ziemann a letter which she asked the bishop to include in Hume's personnel file.

"After much prayer and discernment," she wrote the bishop, "I have to speak out what I feel in my heart."

"I know for a fact," Sister Kelly stated, "that Jorge has deliberately and systematically stolen from church collections. That is a criminal act that should be acknowledged and prosecuted in a civil court of law.

"To me, the scandal is not so much that Jorge stole but that he is allowed to escape prosecution and is not required to make *public* restitution for his acts of thievery.

"We teach our young people that they must own up to their mistakes and make restitution to those they have wronged. How do we explain that if you are a priest this is not required? To me that is a double standard."

Sister Kelly went on to recount how, in May of 1996, she had confronted Hume Salas on his lack of accountability regarding the finances of his sacramental programs. This was presumably his charging of fees, to Latino parishioners, for the performance of baptisms and weddings. Hume, she recounted, "grew angry with me and refused to discuss the matter. I then went to Father Hans [the pastor] and shared my concerns about Jorge and money. I once again pointed out that I felt Jorge was making purchases far beyond his income as a priest."

She restated her belief that Hume Salas was "a pathological liar and was ordained under false pretenses." Sister Kelly concluded by expressing her deep sadness concerning the whole issue. "I pray that Jorge will have the courage and integrity to return to St. Mary of the Angels and confess his wrongdoing and make public restitution . . . . As bishop I hope you encourage him to do just that. It would certainly give a clear signal to others that this kind of behavior would not be tolerated."

Sister Kelly sent copies of this letter to, among others, Chief Keplinger and Josie Vargas. She also sent a copy to Jorge Hume Salas. She received no reply. Finally, in January of 1997, she sent a copy of the letter to the Diocese's Priests' Personnel Board. In March, she received a reply from Monsignor James Gaffey, pastor of St. Eugene's Cathedral in Santa Rosa and a member of the board.

"The issue you raise," he explained, "has not come up explicitly in the meetings of the Priests' Personnel Board. The bishop only announced—briefly—a change of assignment" (Hume's assignment to St. John's parish in Napa). "None of us was given any reason. If the matter ever comes up, there is a chance that the bishop will mention the reason for this change. He has been pretty frank with us when an appointment has to be made. Sometimes of course he keeps certain facts to himself perhaps because of some seal of secrecy."

To Sister Jane, this was precisely the source of the problem. Several days later, she wrote another letter to Ziemann.

"I am utterly astonished," she wrote the bishop, "to hear that Jorge Hume has been assigned to a parish . . . . I am still of the opinion that Jorge is a 'con artist,' and will steal again if he has not already done so."

"However," she continued, "the time will come when it cannot be covered up and he will be made to face the consequences." Appointing him to another parish, she charged, was only "perpetuating the real possibility of repeating his scandalous actions."

The fact that a member of a religious order was willing to persevere in this matter despite the indifference or hostility of the Church hierarchy stiffened the resolve of other members of Ukiah's Catholic community. In 1996, while Hume Salas was still at St. Mary of the Angels, the Ukiah businessman who had accompanied him to the Cursillo retreat in Spain, Ramon Mendoza, became the focus of local Latino protest against Father Jorge. After Mendoza had described his experience with Hume Salas in Spain, a number of young Latino men of the parish had come to him, confiding to him how they too had been approached, groped, and propositioned by Father Jorge. Mendoza, angered and upset at this information, went to three other leaders of the Cursillo movement and asked them what he should do. The men, all Latino, quoted a passage from the Bible, saying you must denounce the sin, if not the sinner. They urged him not to be afraid and said they would support and accompany him if necessary in bringing this information to the attention of the bishop.

Mendoza made a tape where the "teenagers talked to the guys." They recounted, in Spanish, their individual and parallel experiences with Hume Salas. The alleged incidents on the tape ranged from sexual groping to masturbation of one man while he was sleeping. In April of 1996, *before* the Ukiah meeting regarding the thefts, Mendoza, accompanied by his wife and three of the Cursillo leaders, brought the tape with them to an evening meeting with Bishop Ziemann at Ziemann's residence. The Latino men told Ziemann that they felt that Father Jorge was approaching teenagers sexually. Initially, it appeared to them that the bishop did not believe what he was hearing. The meeting continued for two hours and included interviews by the bishop of the complaining men. According to the men, they turned over to Ziemann the taped statements. At the meeting's conclusion, the bishop assured the Cursillo men that he was going to take care of the matter. Nothing was ever done.

When Hume was removed from the parish in Ukiah, Mendoza said he felt it was only because of the money he had stolen. The allegations of priestly sexual abuse had been ignored. The news that Hume had been reassigned, and was working out of a church in Napa, left him "totally disgusted with the bishop and with the Catholic Church."

Fred Keplinger, still serving as Ukiah's police chief, received a phone call from the Napa Police Department. One of the police captains there had seen Father Jorge Hume Salas in a pizza parlor with young people, behaving inappropriately, "kids sitting in his lap in a way that seemed strange. Their detective called us. We told him our story, said we'd been told he would never be around money or young men again."

On October 15, 1998, Sister Kelly called Monsignor Keys, the Vicar of the Diocese. "I got his secretary. I said I had sent three letters to the bishop and made two phone calls to him, and I needed to hear from him. I told her it was urgent. He set up a date. We had a meeting, and I took Russ Liebert from the parish council with me."

Sister Jane recounted to Keys the story about the two sisters and the thefts. She showed him copies of the letters she had written to Bishop Ziemann. "Keys feigned interest. Said he was going to take care of it. Thanked me for sharing this information with him. He said there were too many instances of this kind of information being kept secret. He promised to get back to me."

Keys never did.

"I had gone through the process, the way you're supposed to," Sister Kelly recalled. "I had confronted Jorge about his behavior; I had gone to the church, with the letters; I had gone to a meeting and brought another person with me. There was nothing left but to go public."

By the summer of 1998, Ziemann himself had begun to feel pressured to resolve his situation with Hume. After the priest had been reassigned to his new parish, Ziemann continued to summon Hume to his residence to service him sexually. The bishop would call the priest at the parish rectory or beep him on his pager. Once, when Hume Salas protested he had a meeting he had to attend, Ziemann had told him to unlock the door of his residence so that the bishop could come in without ringing the bell. "I need to see you," Ziemann insisted. He rendezvoused with Hume later that night and they had sex. The chances of exposure through this increasingly risky behavior challenged the limits of even George Patrick Ziemann's capacity for denial.

On August 22, 1998, Ziemann and Salas met at the Embassy Suites in the city of Napa. The two men were scheduled to concelebrate Mass together the following day, and Ziemann had summoned Salas to his hotel room. At this meeting, Ziemann told Salas that he was going to be removing him from the Napa parish and that he was going to send him back to Costa Rica as a missionary. Hume Salas, conscious of his dubious clerical reputation in his home country, opposed this move. After a brief discussion, Ziemann told Salas that if he was unwilling to return to Costa Rica, then he would need to leave the priesthood. Salas said that this was extremely difficult for him to do and began weeping. Ziemann insisted that his only two options were to return to Costa Rica as a missionary or leave the priesthood.

Hume Salas told Ziemann that he would need a letter from him for the bishop in Costa Rica, and that he would like another letter for his family in order not to shame them. He was still in tears. At this point, according to Hume Salas, Ziemann approached him and began caressing him. He told Hume that he wanted to have sex with him and Hume said he didn't want to. Ziemann told Salas, according to the priest, that he had to do it, assuring him yet again that this would be the last time.

Hume Salas left the hotel around three A.M. Ziemann did not stay for the Mass the two men were scheduled to concelebrate the following day. Instead, the bishop returned to Santa Rosa.

The next day, *post triste*, stood up by his promised concelebrant, Jorge Hume Salas was depressed. Thief, liar, weeper, con man, sexual plaything, he seemed to have come to the end of the line. If he returned to Costa Rica, he would be free of Bishop Pat's sexual demands, but he would also be beyond the bishop's protection. Bishop Pat's clout might be strong enough to get Hume a position in Costa Rica but, considering the degree of awareness back home of Jorge's previous impostures, how could Ziemann help him keep it? The alternative—resigning from the priesthood—meant giving up all hope of the fulfillment of Hume's lifelong dream. In this state of depression and personal dilemma, Hume felt he needed to talk to someone. So he went to Confession. According to Hume

Salas, during the act of confession he disclosed to three different priests that he had been sexually active with Ziemann. Although this disclosure was made during confession and was therefore under seal, Hume later told an investigating police officer, one or two of the priests made the information known to Ziemann. If this is true, it is a violation of a trust priests are supposed to defend unto death.

A few days later, Ziemann summoned Hume Salas once again to his residence. This time Hume had his own agenda. On the advice of his attorney, Hume had concealed a small tape recorder on himself and taped his conversation with Ziemann without the bishop's knowledge. The meeting took place on September 8, 1998.

To the Spanish-speaking Santa Rosa police detective analyzing the tape, it was clear that Hume Salas was leading the conversation in certain directions to get Ziemann to apologize and to admit that he had coerced him to have sex. Ziemann, the detective felt, was using the police issue to threaten Hume Salas, telling Salas several times that even if he had done nothing wrong, if the police started to get complaints, they would come after him. "It was obvious," the detective observed, "that Salas was not familiar as to how the judicial process works here."

During the conversation, Salas expressed his pain and disappointment at Ziemann's decision to remove him from St. John's Parish. Ziemann justified his decision by recalling the allegations of sexual misconduct in Ukiah, for which police were now after Hume, as well as the thefts of money. Ziemann alluded to other allegations being made at St. John's Parish, saying that priests were against Salas and that people were talking about him. Since it was in his, Ziemann's, best interest to protect Salas, Ziemann felt by sending Salas to Costa Rica as a missionary, Salas could salvage his reputation.

Salas, aware that the conversation was being taped, denied any and all allegations against him. He repeatedly asked for the names of people making complaints or talking about him, asking to meet with the individuals in private so that he might clear up any misunderstanding or ill feelings. Ziemann told Salas that would not happen.

While Salas continued to deny any of the allegations and restated his hope of remaining at St. John's, Ziemann tried to persuade Salas into going to school. He tried to convince Salas that by getting a master's degree and learning something about counseling, he could return to Costa Rica and become a pioneer in the field of therapy there.

"Salas," the detective observed, "continued to try to talk Ziemann into allowing him to remain at St. John's. Ziemann continued to say people were talking and were against Salas, and he was only trying to protect Salas's reputation, in addition to protecting him from the police. Ziemann told Salas numerous times that if the police came after him, there was nothing the bishop could do."

During the conversation, Ziemann said, "You know when we were physically intimate with each other?" Salas said yes. He admitted having sex with the bishop. Ziemann then went on to say, "It has been my fault, and I am sorry for that, I don't think that you wanted to do that." Salas said that he did not want to have sex with the bishop, and Ziemann said, again, "I know, and I apologize for that. We won't do it again."

Salas recalled how every time this happened, Ziemann would tell him that this was the last time, but it continued to go on. "Jorge," Ziemann said, "I did not know I was hurting you." He asked Salas if he accepted his apologies. Salas said he did, but for him, it was too late. "Maybe I'll make it up to you," Ziemann said. "It's too late, Bishop," Salas repeated.

The refusal of the diocesan leadership to hear what Sister Jane Kelly was telling them was not an exception to the attitude of the Catholic Church hierarchy generally. It exemplified it.

The Church does not listen to women. It often chooses not to see them. It castigates woman, through Eve, as the co-conspirator in man's fall. It exalts one woman, Mary, the mother of Jesus, as being "alone of all her kind," free from the taint of Original Sin. Historically it has attempted to deny and regulate the reality of women's own bodies. It was nuns, not priests, who for centuries were required to shroud themselves in habits, often have their heads shaved, and bind their breasts. To a structure where power is interwoven with male celibacy, women represent danger. A threat.

The subjugation of women within the Catholic Church has no basis in scripture or early Christian experience, nor did it develop naturally over time. It was a deliberate construct of the celibate system, justified, according to Richard Sipe, by Augustine's definition of original sin in the fourth and fifth centuries, consolidated by mandatory celibacy in the eleventh and twelfth centuries, and solidified, by the Council of Trent, in the sixteenth century.

"One can trace," says Sipe, "the progressive and massive idealization of the image of virgin/mother and the denigration of lover, wife and sexual equal. The system could not endure or function in its current mode if the place of women within systemic functions were altered."

In 1984, a delegation of thirty-one American Catholic bishops went to Rome to negotiate a liturgical alteration with the Vatican. The alteration: to allow girls to function as altar servers along with boys. Thirty-one bishops to get permission for girl altar boys. The function of power within the Church is so connected with male celibacy that even the presence of girls at the altar and in the sacristy is considered a serious issue, if not a threat. The models for female behavior in the church, the saints of the Catholic calendar, are overwhelmingly virgins, martyrs, and widows, "the sexless, the silent and the dead."

When minor changes like that of girl altar servers finally occur, the overwhelming reaction among parish priests, nuns, and laypeople is one of relief. "Well, of course. Why wasn't this done long ago?" What is true in small sexual matters is also true in large. In studies made under the auspices of the National Conference of Catholic Bishops, the idea of married priests has repeatedly had 70 to 90 percent support among both clergy and laity, as does, to a lesser degree, the ordination of women. Yet the message is never heard in Rome, and in some instances, since the bishops are unwilling to be the bearers of bad news, the message isn't even sent. The blanket prohibition of any discussion of abortion, homosexuality, birth control, celibacy, married priests, or the ordination of women, other than to reiterate the church's official stand on these matters is not an expression of sexual maturity, groundedness, or confidence. It smacks of fear and defensiveness and further undercuts the moral authority it is intended to reinforce.

There is no instance in the gospels of Jesus mandating celibacy for his apostles. What scriptural support exists for the treatment of women as inferiors comes from Paul's letters and is open to question. In Paul's first letter to Timothy, 2:12–14, Paul is quoted as saying: "I am not giving permission for a woman to teach or to tell a man what to do. A woman ought not to speak, because Adam was formed first and Eve afterward, and it was not Adam who was led astray but the woman who was led astray and fell into sin."

This prohibition is repeated in the First Epistle to the Corinthians, 14:34–35: "Women are to remain quiet at meetings . . . they must keep in the background." If they have questions, "they should ask their husbands at home."

This does not seem to square not only with the life and teachings of Jesus, but with Paul himself, who says, in Galatians, 3:28: "Let there be no distinction between Jew and Greek, slave and free, male and female, but all are one in Christ Jesus."

According to a number of scriptural scholars, it doesn't square. "It has long been recognized," says Rev. Jerome O'Connor of the Ecole Biblique, "that these verses are an intrusion . . . inserted after Paul's death to borrow his authority for a view which he would have energetically rejected."

Beyond what Paul said, there is the example of the life he lived. Paul was a proselytizer, an includer, a man who devoted his life to and was eventually martyred for spreading Jesus' message throughout the Mediterranean world. In the process he transformed the followers of Jesus from a minor cult within Judaism to a universal religion, Christianity. He excluded nobody. That was the essence of his life and his message. To maintain otherwise is antinomy.

It was her grounding in scripture and her awareness of the realities of early Christianity that gave Sister Kelly the resolve to contend with the hierarchy of her own diocese. "The bishop is supposed to be a shepherd," she points out. "An animal is in the sheepfold. It is attacking the lambs. The animal is taken out, and put into another sheepfold. What kind of shepherdship is that?"

In addition to her doctrinal awareness, Sister Kelly had an active social conscience. Her years of community activism had given her a certain ease in relating the values of the church to those of the secular world beyond it. She was comfortable in addressing the society at large. Still, by going public, she would be compounding the solitude of her own celibacy by risking ostracism within her Church.

As a newspaper kid, the daughter of an *Oakland Tribune* reporter, Sister Kelly was aware of the effectiveness of print as a medium of reflection, a vehicle for a call to conscience. "Every move I made was going nowhere. So I gave the letters to Mike Gienella." Gienella was the Ukiah bureau chief of *The Santa Rosa Press Democrat.*

"I went to Canada for two weeks," Sister Kelly recalled. "When I had returned there had been no response from the chancery office. So I called Mike Gienella, and discussed with him what we should do."

Gienella, a burly veteran reporter, was a member of St. Mary of the Angels parish. His son had been confirmed, at St. Mary's, by Bishop Ziemann.

"I'd known Sister Jane for years before she came to me with this. She rubbed a lot of conservative local people the wrong way. She served on the City Planning Commission. She was always honest, straightforward, outspoken. This was very hard for her to do. She felt very much alone at first."

Gienella also was uneasy with the information. "We were wary of opening Pandora's Box. At this time, we had no idea that the Bishop might be having a sexual relationship with Jorge or that there was a tape. I took a lot of long walks for about ten days, drank a lot of wine. The lawyers for her order and for the *New York Times* (the parent paper of the *Press Democrat*) were very nervous about libel."

+ + +

"For this lady to do what she did," says Don Hoard, "is mind-boggling. If you don't have a Catholic background, I don't think you can conceive of the courage it took."

"We didn't have that much evidence to go on at first," says Gienella. The Church had refused to press charges in the thefts against Salas, and the young Latinos complaining about him on the tape refused to be identified by name.

"Ramon Mendoza had the tapes of boys molested by Hume," says Sister Kelly. "Ramon called Mike, and agreed to let his name be used. That was the breakthrough."

Sister Kelly contacted her order, the Sisters of The Presentation, headquartered in San Francisco. She sent copies of the letters, and the president of the order conferred with their attorney. Gienella checked with the lawyers for the *New York Times*. "We were cleared for libel," Sister Kelly recalled. "I told our pastor and the staff."

On January 22, 1999, the *Press Democrat* broke the story: UKIAH PRIEST'S MISCONDUCT KEPT UNDER WRAPS BY SR'S ZIEMANN. ACCUSED OF THEFT, SEXUAL ABUSE. In his opening paragraph, Gienella got right to the conflict between Ziemann's stated aims and personal practice:

At a time when he was publicly assuring Catholics he would deal openly with priestly misconduct, Bishop Patrick Ziemann hushed up the case of a Ukiah priest who had admitted stealing money from St. Mary's Church and had been accused by four men of sexually accosting them.

Ziemann acknowledged hearing of the sexual misconduct allegations, the article continued, but defended his treatment "of the Rev. Jorge Hume, who is now a priest in Napa. Ziemann contends full disclosure of such sensitive matters is impossible because of a need to follow church guidelines requiring him to consult with all parties as well as his senior advisors before acting."

Agony in the Garden

In a long feature story, Gienella recounted the church collection thefts in Ukiah, Hume Salas's apprehension for them, and Ziemann's refusal to press charges. He went on to include the allegations of sexual misconduct and quoted Ramon Mendoza, Chief Keplinger, and Sister Kelly. Ziemann, trying to stuff cats back into bags, was quoted as assuring that proper protocols were put in place to prevent any further misconduct on Hume's part while at the same time suggesting the he was contemplating reassigning Hume to a nonparish role.

"I think the concerns will then become moot," Ziemann was reported as concluding. "I had to make a prudential judgement in this case. I believe every decision I've made since has been fair to everyone involved."

The story revived memories of previous diocesan trauma, instances of priestly misconduct and church cover-up, injuries many Catholics thought had healed. Some Catholics flinched at what they saw as an unnecessary reopening of old wounds.

"At first, there were some defensive reactions," Gienella recalled. "People said, 'Don't you think you're going too far? Do you really want to say that?' Ziemann, when I talked to him over the phone, said, 'Mike, you know me.' Yet he knew at the time this stuff [his own sexual involvement, the financial complications] was out there."

At the same time this was happening in California, the Senate was conducting the impeachment trial of President Clinton in Washington, D.C. After nearly nine months of disclosure and speculation, the public had become both inured and receptive to revelations of the sexual misconduct of men in positions of trust and the persistent and repeated attempts to cover it up. Both the novelty and threshold of plausibility had been worn down. There were to be continuing congruencies between the executive in Washington with his attraction toward young women and the bishop in California with his attraction to younger men.

✝ ✝ ✝

On January 26, in the aftermath of the *Press Democrat* article, Jorge Hume Salas was relieved of his duties at St. John's Parish in Napa. Monsignor Thomas Keys, acting as the diocese's vicar general, removed Salas after a complaint had been received from a 19-year-old Napa man that Hume had sexually groped him. Ziemann, attending a church retreat in Bodega Bay, could not be reached for comment. Three days later, the Ukiah police department opened an investigation into the complaints of the four young Latino men who had complained on tape about Hume Salas. This was turning into a flashback of the situation Ziemann had overseen in his previous position in Ventura County.

"As a policeman," says Fred Keplinger, "you look for patterns. I think this was Ziemann's way of life. In Ventura County, there had been earlier incidents of the same kind. Molestations covered up, thefts, embezzlements. There, it was the priest who was paid off."

"Everything had to be forced," says Mike Gienella, pointing to the diocese's reluctance to cooperate with the police, its refusal or unwillingness to address repeated wrongdoing itself. There is a certain Captain Renault quality, after the character played by Claude Rains in the movie *Casablanca*, at the expressions by Church officials being shocked, shocked! at the public revelations of the repeated misbehavior of Jorge Hume Salas. The fact is, their attorneys had been negotiating with Hume Salas's lawyer for months.

In September of 1998, the month after Hume Salas's last sexual assignation with Ziemann, Hume's attorney, Irma Cordova, to whom he had entrusted a plastic bag containing tissue and a towel with the bishop's semen on it and the tape recording of Ziemann's apology, approached the diocese. Cordova contacted the vicar, Ziemann's money guy and man of all work, Monsignor Thomas Keys.

"These were the people right under the bishop," Cordova recalled later. "Father Salas, after two years of the sex, was fed up.

Agony in the Garden

He finally decided that he couldn't keep it to himself. It was destroying him."

Lawyers for both sides, Cordova and attorneys for Ziemann, began meeting on neutral ground to prevent disclosure. "I was so concerned about confidentiality that we didn't meet at my office," Cordova said. "We met at conference rooms that were neither theirs nor mine."

According to Cordova, it was at the urging of the diocese's lawyers that she submitted a settlement demand. The demand included Ziemann's resignation, his enrollment in therapy supervised by someone outside the diocese, an apology by the bishop to Hume Salas, and a ballpark figure for a financial settlement.

The ballpark figure reflected the inflated amounts of the era of sports free agency. It was eight million dollars.

According to Cordova, the amount was chosen at random, but was deliberately big enough to get the diocese's attention. "You can imagine a lowly priest such as my client making accusations against the biggest guy in the diocese, the bishop, how easily that kind of thing gets ignored. We wanted them to take it seriously . . . [show] that it could not be shoved under the carpet."

"Thank God Jorge sued for eight million," Sister Kelly recalled later. "If it had been one million, they'd have settled."

Mike Gienella agrees. "The dumb shit. He would have got his money. And none of this would have come out."

According to Cordova, the talks broke down not because of money, but because the monetary settlement was tied to a demand that Hume Salas quit performing the duties of a priest. "They offered a sizable amount, but this man was going to be hounded and destroyed financially," she stated. "What they were talking about was blackmail."

The negotiations continued until January of 1999, when all demands, including the eight million dollars, were withdrawn after the allegations against Hume Salas were made public.

+ + +

On February 23, the Mendocino County District Attorney's Office rejected the police case against Hume Salas based on the complaint filed by the four Latino men in Ukiah. "Under current law," the deputy district attorney said, "only sexual assault allegations dating back one year can be prosecuted." The incidents in Ukiah had occurred in 1996, outside the time limit. In June, Napa prosecutors dropped their sexual battery case against Hume Salas, saying they weren't satisfied with the credibility of the man who had made the accusations. Salas, unassigned to any parish but still supported financially by the diocese, was still living in Santa Rosa, taking occasional trips to Costa Rica, and conferring regularly with his attorney.

For Ziemann, adept at maintaining appearances, life, on the surface at least, seemed very much business-as-usual. "Ziemann is intelligent, polished, slick," says Mike Gienella. "He may have sensed that, in coming here, he had gone as far as he was going to go in the church. That may have produced an urge to self-destruct, let it all hang out."

Following the disclosure of the diocese's handling of Hume Salas's thefts from St. Mary of the Angels, a group of teenagers in that parish, approaching Confirmation, opposed being confirmed by the bishop. Ziemann came to Ukiah, met with them, and brought about a change of heart. Only one member of the group continued to object to the idea of being confirmed by a man who had condoned collection-basket thefts, and dropped out of the class. Once again, Ziemann's energy and hands-on management style seemed to have triumphed.

The confirmation ceremony, which took place in June, was yet another performance, one more in a series of theatrical reconciliations. It was Ziemann's first appearance before a large parish group in Ukiah since the revelation of Hume's hushed-up parish thefts. Some of the Confirmation candidates were Sister Jane Kelly's former students. The pastor, Father Hans Ruygt, had been scolded by Ziemann for calling in the police.

"The fact that the bishop will be with us makes some parishioners very uncomfortable," Ruygt conceded, "because they are disturbed at the way he has handled certain scandals in the diocese."

To everyone's relief, there were no boos or hisses at Ziemann's ceremonial appearance at St. Mary of the Angels, and nobody walked out. Ziemann afterwards expressed satisfaction with the confirmation Mass and agreed that it seemed to represent a reconciliation of tension between the diocese and the parish.

What neither the parishioners, nor the confirmants, nor the pastor knew was that Ziemann had already submitted his resignation as bishop to the Vatican. In April, the bishop had sent a formal letter to the Pope, requesting to be relieved of his responsibilities as head of the Santa Rosa Diocese; the resignation had not, as yet, been accepted or refused.

"Secrecy and silence are the tools of corruption and dysfunction," says Monsignor John O'Hare. There was the feeling in this diocese, extending outward to the Church at large, that whatever happens is okay, as long as it remains secret.

There are, says Sipe, three elements to the system of secrecy regarding sexual matters within the Catholic Church. The first is denial: the problem doesn't exist or it is unimportant. The second is to encapsulate, seal any problem within the Church, to shield it from public awareness. The third is to define any sexual problem as an "act" isolated from any long-term or relationship problems or any serious flaw within the organization itself. The act is then forgiven and presumably forgotten.

In this system of secrecy, going public is the worst offense. Secrecy, embraced to the degree that it is within the Church, becomes an end in itself. It obliterates accountability, assists denial, and guarantees reoccurrence.

In an increasingly media-conscious and information-accessible world, secrets become harder and harder to keep. The more an organization is based on secrecy, the more it has to lose. "What's happened here is just the tip of the iceberg," says John O'Hare. "There are problems throughout the church over celibacy, the ordination of women, the role of women."

Though traditionally demeaned, ignored or unheard by the church hierarchy, women have for centuries formed the backbone, in more than one sense, of the Catholic Church. It was women who, for centuries, ran the grade schools, staffed the hospitals, and operated the charities which for many people represent the Church at its best. It was and still is women more than men in the pews, standing in line to receive Communion, performing the music, providing the flowers and seasonal decorations, maintaining the spirit and maybe the essence of a church whose hierarchy will not give them full recognition. And who, by focusing an abstract, idealized attention on one woman, Mary, turn away from flesh-and-blood women and the earthly reality they represent.

"Something is terribly wrong with the institution," according to seminary professor and psychologist John R. Lynch. "It's Mark versus Mike, individual vitality versus a run for a bishopric. It's saying that one is unafraid to love but afraid of being engaged. The system fosters fear of engagement. It still fosters the illusion that being in the inner circle is something to strive for."

In 1990, a group of African, Southeast Asian, and Canadian bishops at a Synod on the Priesthood asked the Vatican, for the sake of the Church, to do away with mandatory celibacy. "They went hat in hand, respectfully," says Lynch, "and were told in advance that the topic could not even be discussed."

In the Diocese of Santa Rosa, where public disclosure was viewed as a worse offense than repeated thefts or charges of chronic sexual misbehavior, and a bishop who had submitted his

Agony in the Garden

resignation was performing Confirmation and insisting on the soundness of his own judgment and the correctness of his decisions, the system of secrecy remained in effect. As did the related practice of ignoring or not listening to women.

"It's a male chauvinistic denial hierarchy," says Sister Kelly. "They feel they are above the law." Though she was now receiving expressions of support from laypeople throughout the diocese and beyond, including a pledge of physical protection, if needed, from a group of San Francisco firefighters, as well as saying a daily rosary in behalf of Bishop Ziemann in the hope that he would come around on this, Sister Jane Kelly was to receive, then or later, not a single expression of gratitude or solidarity from a priest.

On June 22, 1999, Santa Rosa Police Detectives Ruben Sanchez and Martha Supernor, responding to a complaint of sexual battery and oral copulation, reported to the law offices of Irma Cordova, the attorney representing Jorge Hume Salas. Following a briefing by Cordova about the history of the case, the detectives interviewed Salas, in the presence of two attorneys. The interview was taped.

Salas presented his version of the relationship: the surprise call from the bishop when Salas was about to leave for treatment in St. Louis summoning Salas to his residence; the caressing leading to a sexual encounter; Salas's reluctance; Ziemann's insistence. He detailed Ziemann's visit to St. Michael's Center in St. Louis, the bishop's continuing demands for sex there and back in California, rigging Hume Salas with a pager, calling him to his residence for required sex. The detectives listened to the Salas–Ziemann tape. The following morning, Detective Sanchez returned to Cordova's office, where he was given a plastic bag containing tissue and a towel supposedly containing the bishop's semen, copies of Hume Salas's daily planner noting times and dates of his meetings with Ziemann, and a copy of the tape.

Agony in the Garden

"Based on my investigation of this case," Detective Sanchez concluded, "I noted that there are abusive characteristics found in this case similar to domestic violence cases. There was a pattern of assaultive and coercive behavior by Bishop Ziemann onto Jorge Hume Salas. This included sexual and psychological abuse, as well as economic coercion." Sanchez felt there was clear evidence, based on the audiotape provided by Salas, corroborating that the abusive behavior existed. Sanchez's report was forwarded to the District Attorney's office for possible prosecution for sexual battery and oral copulation.

The police investigation was now extended through Detective Mariano Guzman in Ukiah to the Latino men who claimed to have been sexually approached by Father Jorge. One of the men interviewed had been at the meeting where the tape of the Latino boys describing being accosted and groped by Hume Salas was played for Bishop Ziemann. Ziemann had assured those present that he was going to take care of it. "Famous last words," the Latino man now said.

Warrants were obtained for Bishop Ziemann's phone records. Detectives Sanchez and Supernor flew to St. Louis, where they obtained hotel records, interviewed the director of St. Michael's Community, and requested access to Hume Salas's psychological evaluation. They interviewed his therapists, Gloria Equidanos and Jay Judin. Hume Salas and his lawyer, no longer negotiating, were playing hardball by releasing personal and probably sexual information to the police.

Ziemann had secretly submitted his resignation to the Vatican in April. Whatever happened, Ziemann was aware that the Church looked after its own. A place would be found for him, arrangements made, just as he had made them for the accused priests of his diocese. The harsh judgment of the secular world would be softened.

Perhaps a transfer could be arranged to another diocese, though there was not the desperate shortage of candidates for bishoprics that there was for priests. A good speaker, bilingual, effective at networking, Ziemann might be assigned to the National Conference of Catholic Bishops, where his experience in establishing outreach programs to Latinos, the homeless, those with AIDS, could be useful to the prelates of other dioceses. He might even be called to Rome to serve as a kind of liaison with the American Church, especially its young people.

There was also the question of Jorge Hume Salas's credibility. With the possible exception of the cartoonist Charles Schulz, Bishop Ziemann was the most prominent person in this part of the country. Hume Salas was an obscure, if not discredited, individual. Surely Hume Salas was no more eager than was Ziemann to have the details of their sexual relationship made public. Any legal action initiated by Hume would seem, to people not involved in the legal negotiations or the investigation, like a nuisance suit, the vengefulness of a discharged priest who was also a known thief. There was a reasonable chance that Hume Salas and his lawyer might at the last moment back off and withdraw the criminal complaint.

On July 16, a lawsuit was filed in Sonoma County Superior Court on behalf of Jorge Hume Salas, alleging a series of sexual abuses by the bishop over a two-year period from 1996 to August of 1998. In his suit, which would now proceed along with the criminal investigation, Hume Salas charged that Ziemann used the threat of going to the police regarding Hume's thefts and alleged sexual abuse to coerce him into sexual favors. The civil suit once again demanded damages of eight million dollars.

Five days later, Ziemann, speaking through his attorneys, announced his resignation "for the good of the diocese." The bomb was dropped, through the media, the following day.

"BISHOP ZIEMANN QUITS" the *Press Democrat* announced in a war-declaration-sized headline. The front page featured a large color photograph of a pensive Bishop Ziemann and a smaller black-and-white of a smiling Jorge Hume Salas. Mike Gienella's story mentioned the police inquiry and Salas's lawsuit, detailing accusations which Ziemann, speaking through his personal attorney, vehemently denied. "The bishop has refused to buy his reputation and peace of mind from this man at the price of millions from the people of this diocese." An accompanying article summarized Ziemann's episcopate as "efforts to do good that were overshadowed by sexual scandals and financial controversies."

The abrupt nature of the announcement of Ziemann's resignation was portrayed by his attorneys, claiming the high moral ground, as an act of principle.

"The threat of this lawsuit has been going on for quite a few months," a diocesan attorney said. "Being aware of it and working all the while to try to resolve the thing, [the bishop] has always anticipated it could end up a lawsuit against him. On that basis, he felt it wise to tender his resignation. He knew it would be a scandal and he didn't want the diocese to be involved in a scandal that is personally directed at him."

A third attorney insisted that "the diocese and Bishop Ziemann have repeatedly stated that the diocese has not and will not make payments in response to claims to purchase silence."

For the present, diocesan affairs would be in the hands of the nearest archbishop, William Levada of the Archdiocese of San Francisco.

In keeping with Ziemann's secretive, micromanaging style, the announcement had blindsided the diocesan staff, clergy, and religious. Keys, contacted on a cell phone, expressed ignorance and shock. "I couldn't even begin to answer these questions that are hitting me at this time."

Sister Kelly said that she was grateful that the bishop had stepped down. "At least the wrongdoing done by some priests within our diocese who were protected by the bishop has finally come to an end."

Aside from the intense coverage the announcement of Ziemann's resignation had received, church officials and their lawyers
had to have been relieved at the way the story had been contained
so far.

Most Catholics of the diocese, clergy and laity, initially dis-
counted Hume Salas's sexual allegations as compromised by his
own history of theft and dismissal, and probably motivated by
opportunism or revenge. If Ziemann believed that the announcement of his resignation would somehow allay either the police
inquiry or Hume's lawsuit however, he was quickly disabused of
that notion. On July 22, the same morning as the front-page news
of his resignation was being read throughout the diocese, six Santa
Rosa Police detectives and a uniformed police officer arrived at the
bishop's residence with a search warrant. Getting no response from
the doorbell, the detectives entered through an unlocked rear door.
The detectives took photographs of the residence and the cottage
behind it, paying particular attention to the description given by
Hume Salas. They also opened filing cabinets but did not remove
any files. When, during this search, a lawyer representing Ziemann
arrived, the detectives gave him, in addition to a copy of the search
warrant, an additional warrant for the blood of the suspect in this
case—Bishop Ziemann.

From the months of negotiation, Ziemann and his lawyers were
aware that Hume Salas and his lawyer had semen samples.
Through DNA testing, a court-ordered blood sample would con-
nect the bishop with the semen samples in a way that would be
impossible to deny.

The following morning Ziemann responded to the second warrant, notifying Detective Sanchez, through his attorney, that the
bishop would appear at the lawyer's office that morning for the taking
of a blood sample. At 10:00 A.M., Sanchez and an investigator from the
D.A.'s office, accompanied by a paramedic, arrived at the lawyer's
office where they were met by Ziemann's attorney and Chris

Agony in the Garden

Reynolds, a private investigator. The men went into a private room, the others observing as the paramedic drew blood from Ziemann's left arm. Detective Sanchez asked Ziemann's lawyer if his client would like to make a statement and the lawyer replied, "Not at this time."

"No questions were asked of Ziemann," Detective Sanchez reported. "I observed the draw of the blood and obtained two vials, which were then booked into evidence."

That same morning, Ziemann's personal lawyer released a statement admitting Ziemann's sexual relationship with Hume Salas. "The bishop did regretfully have a personal consensual relationship with Father Hume that was inappropriate for both of them as priests. It is unfortunate that Father Hume and his attorneys are now using this consensual relationship as a weapon against Ziemann and the diocese."

The attorney characterized Hume's lawsuit as "blackmail and extortion," and insisted that Ziemann had resigned out of concern for the people of the diocese and so that he could confront the allegations.

"Bishop Ziemann is a very holy man," the lawyer concluded, "but he is not without human frailty like the rest of us."

Ziemann's attorneys contended that the issues raised by Hume Salas should properly have been addressed under canon law, the church's system for settling disputes between priests. "Hume should start preparing for a trial right now," a diocesan lawyer challenged, "We're going to find a jury and do it."

Following the *Press Democrat* story, a copy of the tape of Ziemann apologizing for coercing Hume for sex, in Spanish with an English voice-over translation, was played on an evening newscast on San Francisco's television Channel 4, accompanied by still photographs of Hume and Ziemann. Ziemann's lawyers protested, insisting that this was outrageous, setting someone up, taping him. The station replied that the tape had been sent to them anonymously.

Michael Meadows, a lawyer who had secured some five million dollars from the diocese for victims of sexual molestation, expressed sympathy for Ziemann. "He reminds me of Bill Clinton—good policies, bad personal conduct."

The public admission of a priest and a bishop having had a sexual relationship produced an initial reaction among Catholics of shock turning rapidly to confusion, denial, and media blame, and eventually finding its expression among all but people of blind faith in lingering anger and mistrust. Here was yet another sexually based scandal whose existence had to be pried out of the Church through a resort to the media, the courts, and police. It represented yet another rent in the now tattered garment of the Catholic Church's moral authority.

Catholic clergy generally, while urging their congregations not to lose their faith, asked them to remember Ziemann's good works and suggested that his resignation amounted to an act of sacrifice by detaching the diocese from liability because of his personal failure.

These were words that the diocesan clergy would soon have ample reason to regret.

The scandal was further evidence of a serious disconnect between the view of the Church from within and that from outside. The repeated priestly sexual offenses in the Church as a whole, most of which result in financial settlements, are treated by the church as individual occurrences and not accepted by the hierarchy as symptoms of serious institutional wrong. Among the public at large, Catholic and non-Catholic, there is with each revealed incident a growing frustration and anger at individuals in positions of supposed moral and ethical leadership either being dragged reluctantly before civil courts or buying their way out of them with what amounted to payoffs. This changed outlook extends to both prosecutors and police.

Agony in the Garden

In a 1985 report prepared for the National Conference of Catholic Bishops concerning priest sexual abuse, Rev. Michael Peterson, a psychologist and president of the St. Luke Institute, warned the bishops that "Our dependence in the past on Roman Catholic judges and attorneys protecting the Diocese and clerics is GONE [caps his]."

Peterson's report was rejected by the bishops.

Despite the hierarchy's refusal to recognize this hemorrhaging loss of moral authority, the practice of allowing the Catholic Church to handle questions of priest sexual abuse privately is now regarded among police, prosecutors, and judges as political suicide.

"When people call me now with complaints about priests," says Fred Keplinger. "I tell them to go right to the civil authorities."

The cover-ups, in the eyes of most Catholics, are worse than the crimes. They make the Church a conspirator in deceitful behavior, they guarantee that the offenses will reoccur, if perhaps in a different form and in another place, and they demean the entire Catholic tradition of true contrition as a necessary requirement for the forgiveness of sin.

In a statement read, two days after Ziemann's admission of the sexual relationship, at every Sunday Mass in all the diocese's 45 parish churches, Archbishop Levada said that Ziemann had asked him to convey to his former followers "how deeply sorry he is for betraying the trust that was placed in him, out of human frailty. He asks humbly for forgiveness and for our prayers."

The statement smacked of damage control and personal unconsciousness. It was a predictable, off-the-shelf response that concealed more than it revealed, and served only to recall previous crises in this diocese in which church officials and their lawyers had been quick, in the name of forgiveness, to offer the Church itself a blanket amnesty.

Any thinking Catholic remembering his or her first communion, the conditions for the sacrament of penance, recognizes the disin-genuousness of such a statement. Saying "I'm sorry" and asking for forgiveness doesn't cut it. Confession, Catholics are taught, requires us to enumerate our sins, own up to what we did point by point, do our best to make restitution to any and all persons who may have been injured by our acts, and to amend our lives by changing our attitude or the circumstances under which the offenses occurred. Anything less is a false confession, undeserving of forgiveness. The absolution given by the priest in such circum-stances doesn't count, and the false confession is itself a serious sin. Every Catholic who has received his or her first communion has been taught this, which was why statements like the essentially self-serving one Ziemann was making now satisfied nobody other than perhaps the Church hierarchy, its lawyers, and its public-rela-tions people. For many Catholics, it was yet another instance of the institutional church being unwilling to ask of itself what it regu-larly asked of the people—clergy, religious, and laity—of its parishes.

In a study authorized by the National Conference of Catholic Bishops and published in 1972, detailed historical, sociological, and psychological investigations concluded that approximately one-third of Catholic priests in the United States were underdevel-oped emotionally, another one-third were developing, and one-third were considered developed. "These studies," says Richard Sipe, "validated my observation of the emotional health and devel-opment of the priests and religious I had observed and treated at Menninger and Seton and in my therapeutic work and studies."

A subsequent study, in 1977, by Eugene Kennedy, found that fifty-seven percent of Catholic priests were underdeveloped, twenty-nine percent were developing, eight percent were malde-veloped, and only six percent were developed emotionally.

Surely, the Church's continuing denial of the reality of human sexuality, its insistence on proclaiming theories such as on birth control in which the overwhelming majority of both laypeople and clergy do not believe, its behavior in practice that offenses, particularly sexual ones, will be tolerated as long as they remain secret, its hierarchical insistence in the license to make rules for others from which they exempt themselves, contribute to this lingering emotional immaturity. The acceptance of responsibility—legal, financial, moral—which is the essence of manhood or womanhood, is postponed, sometimes for a lifetime. Is it any wonder that given this environment the attitude of priests toward women, toward other men, and occasionally toward children is so often stuck in adolescence?

"At a crucial stage of his personal development," writes Dr. James E. Biechler, an emeritus professor of religion and a licentiate in canon law, "the young seminarian is formed in a culture of denial. He must deny the importance of his natural family, he must relegate marriage and the procreation of children to an inferior level of life and so he must even see children in a diminished light. When the worth of children is diminished, and sexuality is immature, the distance to pedophilia is short."

I n keeping with Church practice in matters of sexual scandal, Bishop Ziemann was dispatched to a treatment center in Pennsylvania, where he remained unavailable to the public and the media. Jorge Hume Salas was said by his lawyer to be with his family in Costa Rica. While the principals, Hume and Ziemann, withdrew from the front lines, their lawyers began exchanging sniper fire.

Hume Salas's lawyer, Irma Cordova, annoyed at the characterization of her client's eight-million-dollar settlement demand as "blackmail and extortion," revealed that negotiations had been in progress since September, that the diocese had offered a monetary settlement, and that Hume had rejected the money when the church insisted he agree not to perform Mass and administer the sacraments.

"She is telling you things that happened in mediation," one of Ziemann's lawyers protested, "and is violating a confidentiality agreement."

Cordova said that full disclosure of the scandal could have been avoided. "Had we known that Ziemann had tendered his resignation in April, there would have been a very different outcome. That would have been eighty percent of our battle right there."

She characterized Hume Salas's criminal complaint and lawsuit as a struggle for human rights. "These are not nice people," she said of the diocesan leadership and attorneys.

This tactical bickering, combined with the continuing police investigation, fed increasing public concern about practices within the diocese and throughout the Church as an institution. What other damaging information had been concealed during Ziemann's term as bishop?

In Crescent City, on the California–Oregon border, it was recalled that a local pastor, who had been living openly with a woman and her child, his son, had been accused of depositing church funds to his personal account, financing retailer credit cards for his relatives, and taking a personal computer purchased with church money for himself. Financial abuses by this pastor, according to an accounting firm which prepared a confidential audit for Ziemann in 1998, were "so rampant we have a hard time understanding how [this priest] can live with his conscience about his treatment of parish finances." The pastor had since been reassigned as a prison chaplain, and the investigation had petered out.

In Eureka, in an echo of Jorge Hume Salas's questionable - pre-ordination resume, the principal of St. Bernard's elementary and high school had resigned amid controversy over his lack of claimed credentials. Ziemann, it was recalled, had expressed public support for the principal. Among the previous principals of St. Bernard's had been the since-imprisoned child molester, Monsignor Gary Timmons.

Archbishop Levada, the man who had inherited this mess, issued a statement saying that he did not plan to review all cases from the past "unless there are reasons to indicate the benefit of contrary action."

There were continuing pleas from diocesan spokesmen, from

priests in parish pulpits, and even from lay members of the diocese, urging Catholics to put this behind them, to stop dwelling on negative issues and move on. There was also a widespread feeling that there was more bad news to come, that there were important issues still to be addressed, and that what was happening in the Santa Rosa Diocese was emblematic of serious institutional wrongs within the Church.

"Bishop Ziemann," the *Press Democrat* pointed out, "is the eighth of his rank or higher in the church worldwide to leave office in this decade after being accused of sexual misconduct. Others include the Cardinal of Vienna, the archbishops of Santa Fe and Atlanta, and bishops in Canada and Ireland."

Accusations of priestly sexual misconduct had by now been reported in all 188 of the Catholic Church's dioceses in the United States.

Father Thomas Doyle, a military chaplain and former canon lawyer who had prepared a detailed report for the National Conference of Catholic Bishops on priestly sexual abuse and how the church should deal with it, which the bishops rejected, was quoted as saying, "Priests take all these oaths to maintain secrecy. It is all about how to protect the system, how to control the situation entirely." Catholic bishops, according to Doyle, even have the power to swear priests to silence.

"Many priests," Richard Sipe points out, "make a complete psychic split between their sexual behavior and their professional clerical life; this is also true of those who involve themselves in heterosexual behavior. The maturity, judgement and values lived and expressed in their professional life are entirely abandoned in their 'play' world, where they operate almost wholly apart from those values."

The public revelation of the sexual relationship between Bishop Ziemann and Father Hume Salas also intensified the existing concern among laypeople, if not priests or diocesan spokesmen, about the prospect of an increasingly gay Catholic clergy. In his 2000 book, *Papal Sins*, Garry Wills points out that of the tens of thousands of priests and seminarians who have left the priesthood in the years following *Humanae Vitae*, the overwhelming majority left to marry. This almost certainly increased the proportion of homosexually oriented men among the remaining clergy. The mandatorially celibate church is, after all, a homosocial society which someone who prefers all-male company might find congenial. What happens if a homosexually oriented priesthood becomes dominant?

"There surely have been gay priests, gay bishops, gay Popes and gay saints," says the Rev. Andrew Greeley, the sociologist and popular novelist, "but one would not want the whole priesthood to be gay because it would mark it off strikingly from the rest of humankind .... [if] the priesthood gets marked as a gay profession in people's minds, it will lose its attraction for heterosexual young men."

The Catholic Church's teachings on homosexuality are self-contradictory. We are told in *Christ Among Us* that "There is nothing evil or wrong in being homosexual." The Church also teaches that all homosexual acts are, in themselves, sinful. Yet responsible homosexual spokesmen as well as common sense and experience in the world tell us that homosexually oriented people are essentially the same as heterosexually oriented people with the exception that they prefer having sex with individuals of the same gender. By insisting on condemning homosexual acts while professing to welcome homosexuals, the Church is forbidding Catholic homosexuals any sexuality at all. There is an eerie counterpart in this to the practice of condemning, among heterosexuals, all sex acts not performed within marriage and with the possibility of conception. Both deny human sexuality generally; both contain a certain sour-grapes aspect of telling people since we can't enjoy sex, we're not going to let you enjoy it either.

A clearer guide to the institutional Church's true attitude to homosexuality is to look not so much at what the church says as what it does.

In July of 1999, Sister Jeannine Gramick and Father Robert Nugent, American Catholics who had conducted a 20-year pastoral work among gay and lesbian Catholics, were permanently barred from their ministry by the Vatican. "An analysis of the documents," says *The National Catholic Reporter*, "reveals that the investigation's goal gradually shifted from determining the orthodoxy of their teaching regarding homosexual acts, to the demand that Nugent and Gramick declare their consciences to be in full agreement with official church doctrine."

In addition to having their teaching declared "erroneous and dangerous," Gramick and Nugent were specifically asked to affirm that homosexuality is an "objectively disordered" condition and that homosexual acts are "intrinsically evil."

This action, by the Pope through the Congregation for the Doctrine of the Faith, raises the question for homosexually oriented priests of ability and conscience of whether it is possible to remain in an organization which is theologically hostile. The alternative is to deny one's sexuality altogether or live a lie, as with birth control, professing allegiance to a teaching which one knows from his or her own experience of life to be false. The question for the Church seems to be not what the relative number of homosexual to heterosexual priests is, but what kind and quality of priests—whatever their sexual orientation—will there be?

The month after the Hume Salas–Ziemann scandal broke, there was an opportunity for at least one portion of the Catholic laity to declare itself on the issues involved. St. Mary of the Angels parish in Ukiah, where the loose threads that led to the general unraveling of Ziemann's episcopate had first appeared, was scheduled to dedicate its new church. A good part of the congregation had gathered in the new structure, a wide, bright natural wood and rock room with an unpainted wood ceiling resembling a natural hardwood floor. Various parish and diocesan dignitaries were introduced along with local civic figures, each of whom received polite applause. Then, the master of ceremonies mentioned the parish's most conspicuous figure, who had deliberately stayed away this day, and whom, it was rumored, many of the clergy had shunned: Sister Jane Kelly received a standing ovation.

In contrast, Archbishop Levada's management was receiving, within the diocese, mixed reviews. While his intentions seemed good enough, his urging of Catholics not to lose their faith and to move beyond this reminded them that Ziemann had used the same spiritual language for purposes of deceit.

In his first address to the people of the diocese, a homily given at St. Eugene's Cathedral in Santa Rosa on August 22, the archbishop expressed sorrow and compassion for Ziemann, "our brother and your former shepherd" who "shared in the mystery of the cross that we are now experiencing.

"The most important thing to me at present is for us as [a] church, in the Diocese of Santa Rosa, not to let the scandal of this tragedy harm the faith and faithful lives of those of us who have Christ as our Good Shepherd."

"Are there those among us," the archbishop said, "who will find in the bishop's fall from grace an opportunity to flee from the demands of faith, to give into the temptations of their own lives? It would be surprising if it were not so."

Levada concluded by, yet again, stressing faith, urging people to pray to the Holy Spirit "to help us . . . to be witness of the firm faith and models of right conduct for our brothers and sister, especially our young people, whose faith and life values are still being formed in the challenging environment of our secular society."

In the Greek in which the New Testament was originally written, the word "faith" actually means "trust." According to the theologian and former Dominican priest Matthew Fox, the Jesus of the

Gospels "time and again assures people that 'your trust has healed you.' He recognizes the salvific power of trust. And he also laments how little trust he finds among people, 'O you of little trust.'"

Trust, says Fox, is a faith issue, in fact it is *the* faith issue, "because trust is the most basic meaning of faith."

Trust cannot be given, it must be earned; and, once lost, can only be regained slowly by performance over time.

"The point I didn't like," said a parishioner following the archbishop's homily, "is he didn't really address the main issue of misconduct. He kind of glazed over it. People need to hear about it in public. We can't pretend it didn't happen."

"It's tough," observed a church usher. "A lot of people are still apprehensive. We've had two bishops who have said they will take care of the problem, and it just seems to occur over and over."

If he had asked for trust, under the circumstances, the archbishop would have found himself laughed at. But that, in the truest sense, was what he wanted. The people of the diocese had heard this before, most recently from the now-disgraced Ziemann. They would listen, with a certain skepticism, to what he said. But they would draw their conclusions from what Levada did or didn't do.

One unfavorable sign was that Levada had retained as the diocese's vicar general and finance officer Monsignor Thomas Keys, whose efforts he praised in an article in the diocesan newspaper. These moves suggested anything but the thorough investigation and housecleaning that a majority of the diocese's Catholics were now demanding. However, any idea of a quick fix and an early return to business as usual received a rude jolt when the Archbishop examined the diocese's books. As of June 30, the cash balance of the Consolidated Account, in which the parish and diocesan funds were concentrated, stood at zero. The Diocese of Santa Rosa was broke.

On August 25, the Archbishop's office announced Keys' resignation as finance officer. While thanking him for his services, the announcement stated that Keys would remain as Chairman of the Scrip Center and pastor of Star of the Valley Church. Star of the Valley is in one of the diocese's most affluent communities. Appointed to the hot seat vacated by Keys was Monsignor John Brenkle, a seasoned priest with forty-one years' service in the diocese.

"When the Archbishop called, I was in my office," recalled Brenkle, pastor of a parish in the town of St. Helena. "He said, 'I need to see you.' When the Archbishop says he needs to see you, you're in trouble." Brenkle, trained in canon law, was secretary to the second Bishop of Santa Rosa, John Maher. When Maher left to become Bishop of San Diego, the Apostolic Delegate, the Pope's official representative in the United States, contacted the Santa Rosa clergy and requested the names of suitable candidates to lead the diocese. Brenkle's name was the unanimous recommendation. Instead, the Vatican, uncomfortable with the turbulence of democracy, looked to the nearest cardinal, in Los Angeles, for his recommendation. Both the bishop chosen then, and the one who followed him, Ziemann, were former Los Angeles priests.

Brenkle, an intelligent, soft-spoken man who resembles an aging cherub, recalled the Archbishop estimating that the financial crisis would take a day or two a week of his time. "Even he didn't know the extent of this."

An audit had revealed that while parishes, schools, and other organizations showed millions of dollars on deposit at the Chancery, diocesan pooled cash and equities were virtually nonexistent. On Ziemann's—and Keys'—watch, the diocese had been raided.

At Levada's insistence, Brenkle acted to stop the bleeding. In late August, all accounts in the Consolidated Account were frozen. Construction jobs in progress throughout the diocese were halted. At the Chancery office, Brenkle was forced to lay off what eventually amounted to almost fifty employees. Ministries were cut drastically. In some Christian Doctrine (catechism) classes, volunteer teachers had to reach into their own pockets to buy books.

For some Catholics, the financial scandal was worse than the sexual one. Human weakness arising from sexuality was shared, explainable, and could be contained. Financial chicanery affected the whole diocese, cut both wide and deep, and pointed to an ingrained embrace of secrecy as a preferred way of doing business. Spiritual language would no longer suffice. Secrecy was beginning to be perceived as habitual within the Church, a web of bonds within which the hierarchy was so enmeshed that it was going to prove difficult, if not impossible to break.

"Two of our parishioners called me last night to tell me they are joining the Lutherans," a Sonoma County pastor announced to his congregation at this time. "What could I tell them? They've had enough."

Among the diocesan staff and clergy as well, the suspicion was strong that the money had been used to pay off the claims, known and unknown, against the diocese for sexual abuse of children and adults by priests. At St. Rose Church in Santa Rosa, on whose grounds were located the chancery offices, distrust ran so deep that the administration called the police.

"On Wednesday, October 13," a Santa Rosa Police detective reported, "I met with Kathy Ryan, Principal of St. Rose School . . . concerning the raising and management of funds for the construction of a multipurpose building on the grounds." Fund-raising for the project had begun in 1991, with the parish and school charged with raising sixty percent of the capital and the diocese supplying a low-interest loan for the remainder. By the spring of 1999, the school had raised its sixty percent, approximately $900,000.

In April of 1999, the same month Ziemann submitted his resignation as bishop to the Vatican, he gave the go-ahead to the parish to begin construction. Later that same month, St. Rose School received an inquiry from Monsignor Keys, then the Diocese Finance

Agony in the Garden

Officer. Keys directed the school to close its own account and move all of its funds to the Diocese's Consolidated Account. This was done. In June, Ms. Ryan was advised by the diocesan office that the diocese was "suffering a cash flow problem." Then, on September 27, she received a fax from Monsignor Brenkle that all Consolidated Accounts were closed, and that new accounts would be opened with zero balances. In return for $900,000 and nine years of fund-raising, St. Rose Church and School was left with a hole in the ground.

Two days later, a Santa Rosa Police detective and a Sonoma County D.A.'s office investigator met with Thomas Beecher, the principal of Cardinal Newman High School. The investigators told Beecher that they were looking into allegations that monies, some of which belonged to accounts for the high school, were missing from the Diocese Consolidated Account. Beecher replied that the school had two accounts, an operations account which as of September 30 should have had a balance of approximately $900,000, and a development account, whose balance should have been $700,000. "Thomas Beecher reported," the police report stated, "that on Sept. 30, 1999, while attending a diocese meeting in Ukiah, he learned from Monsignor John Brenkle that the balance in both accounts was zero."

Like Kathy Ryan, Principal Beecher had received monthly statements for two numbered accounts. No doubt he assumed that these accounts were in a bank and that, if worse came to worst, they would at least be federally insured for $100,000. Instead the accounts were held and administered by the diocese, and thus carried no insurance at all. The investigators asked Beecher if Monsignor Brenkle provided any explanation for the missing funds. "Beecher told me the financial officer's response was 'Don't ask me. I don't know. I can't tell you anything.'"

Bishop Ziemann and Keys, his vicar, had mismanaged the funds of the parish on whose grounds the chancery office stood.

When the extent of the financial bad news began to be made

public, the reaction was instantaneous. Attendance at masses dropped sharply throughout the diocese, and collections fell off even worse. Because of the hierarchy's commitment to secrecy, parish pastors were left with no plausible explanation to give to their congregations. To the miasmic fog of moral and ethical distrust was added a cloud of financial suspicion.

For anyone with an axe to grind against the Catholic Church, the multiplying scandal provided an endlessly spinning stone wheel. Believe that the priesthood is infiltrated by a homosexual conspiracy? Here, exemplified by Ziemann and Hume Salas, was your clerical homintern. Convinced that the clergy is rampant with men coercing sex from minors? Here against a background of previous diocesan molestations was an accused ephebephile. Certain that priests regularly robbed the collection baskets? Here was a priest who had. The idea of the depthless hypocrisy and cunning of the church seemed at this point to break down when it came to finance. The clumsy incompetence of what the Diocese of Santa Rosa did with other people's money is an embarrassment to the Church of the Vatican's own bank, of Richelieu and Wolsey. The Church that was once estimated, by *Time* magazine, as the second most efficiently run organization (after General Motors—how the mighty hath fallen), in the United States, here behaved in the manner of yokels and rubes. Worse. They were the classic confidence-game gulls—people who were financially naïve and ignorant yet convinced that they were smart.

On October 23, a Saturday morning, a police detective and D.A.'s investigator interviewed the newly elusive Monsignor Thomas Keys at his parish in the community of Oakmont. The investigators told Keys that they were conducting an examination into complaints regarding the possible theft of construction funds from the Consolidated Account. Keys said he was not surprised at the inquiry, since he had recently met with some parents from St. Rose School about the subject.

Keys explained how the Consolidated Account, which he described as his "brainchild," operated. "It worked very well when it's monitored," he told the investigators, "but when it's not monitored, it's a disaster."

Keys granted that he recognized that the single account, combined with the participants' belief that there existed individual accounts, represented a weakness in the system. The account was abused by some participants who were allowed to overdraw from the fund's pool of money when they didn't have the balance to cover their checks. Violators would receive phone calls about their abuse, but according to Keys, Bishop Ziemann would not support his position. When he threw St. Bernard's Church in Eureka, almost two million dollars overdrawn, out of the Consolidated Account, Bishop Ziemann had complained that Keys had been "hard-hearted."

Keys told the investigators that he reported the bishop's misuse of the Consolidated Account funds to the Vatican. In a letter sent after this to the Santa Rosa Diocese clergy, however, Archbishop Levada said he asked Keys directly about informing the Vatican and Keys said he never contacted church leaders in Rome.

In an interview, Monsignor Brenkle explained it this way: "Keys says he protested to Rome, but who did he protest to?"

"Ziemann?"

"That's his contact with Rome."

Keys would have been protesting Ziemann's conduct of his office to Ziemann, with the proposal that the protest be forwarded, an easily ignored request in the hierarchical world of the Church. "I'm sure if he ever questioned any of Ziemann's expenditures," says Brenkle, "the bishop would just say, 'Do it.' "

Mike Gienella agrees. "Keys was the money guy, under three straight bishops. The way it worked is Ziemann would say, I need five hundred thousand dollars, and Keys would get it, find a way. The bishop had power over him."

"What recourse does a priest have under these circumstances?" asks Brenkle. "He can resign, that's about it."

He can also go to the police. Or he can go public, like Sister Jane Kelly did. There is a cover-your-ass aspect to what Keys did, or didn't do. By making a protest that you know won't be forwarded, you are on record as having attempted to do something about the situation while continuing to conduct business as usual. This is one of the ways you remain the finance officer and vicar general under three different bishops.

Keys told the investigators that under the Church's concept of Corporation Sole, nothing could legally be done with regard to how Ziemann managed the Consolidated Account. As bishop, Ziemann controlled all assets of the diocese. This, Keys pointed out, was designed to give the bishop more autonomy. It required an honest man to be in the position, and Ziemann, Keys said, "was very generous with other people's money."

Keys was asked if there was any way Ziemann's overspending could have been stopped. Keys cited the Code of Canon Law and explained that the Priest Consultor and Deanery or Council of Priests had been advised seven months after Ziemann came to the Diocese. "Monsignor Keys," says the police report, "learned that the bishop had met with seven senior priests, and that he [Keys] was personally counseled and told to get along with the bishop. Soon afterwards, Monsignor Keys went into the hospital."

Brenkle remembers it differently. "The early meeting of the Priest Consultor and Deanery were in question of Ziemann's style more than any financial irregularities. He would come into a parish, talk directly to people, hand out his card with his personal phone number, short-circuit the local pastor. People wanted to know what gives."

Brenkle believes the problem was in Ziemann's micromanaging style. "It was not operating by any system that got him into trouble, ignoring the checks and balances, not listening to people who wanted to do many of the same things he did—fund the missions, build churches and schools."

Maybe, but he couldn't have plunged into a financial chasm this deep without Keys. And Keys is the man who, whatever the situation, always seems to have an alibi. "Lots of people should have asked questions and didn't," says Brenkle. "The Diocese's lawyers, me, Keys, the holders of the accounts."

It is important to keep two things in mind here. In all this, one member of the clergy and religious, Sister Jane Kelly, seems to have acted in keeping not with the traditional practices of the church, but with the fidelity to one's conscience that the Church professes to teach. And were it not for her, none of the sexual and financial wrongdoing so devastating to the welfare of the diocese and the Church would have been made known to its people.

What of those who had remained on the scene and got on with the job? The parish priests, preparing homilies and speaking individually with parishioners after Mass, making emergency visits to the sick, performing baptisms and weddings; the nuns, teaching in and administrating the schools, nursing in and running clinics and hospitals; the lay Christian Doctrine teachers and counselors and Catholic Charities workers. They were the ones who were left to deal face-to-face with the consequences of what had happened, put in the position of being asked questions for which they had no answers while having their own faith and the appropriateness of their vocations challenged by things they never would have done themselves.

Ziemann was gone, vanished into the insulated world of Church therapeutic programs, counseling, and retreats. Keys, a consistent official presence in the diocese for nearly three decades, remained in seclusion, unresponsive to the media, appearing rarely at his parish, cloistering himself at his residence inside a gated community.

The people of the pastoral church, like the congregations they served, were left largely in the dark about what had been going on until the news broke to the public. They had to continue their work, reduced to pleading ignorance or issuing reassurances while anticipating the next hit.

"I don't particularly enjoy," John O'Hare told his congregation, "getting bad news about the diocese along with my morning coffee." He had begun to refer to the *Press Democrat* as "the diocesan newspaper."

The Church system of secrecy was concentric: just because you were admitted to one circle didn't mean you couldn't be excluded from other, inner circles. Among priests, religious, and diocesan employees there was a sense of betrayal in some ways more intense than among laypeople: as representatives of the church, they couldn't express their anger by staying away from Mass or withholding money from the collection baskets. Right now, while the Archbishop was still trying to assess the damage, there was little that pastoral priests could offer in the way of answers to questions or responses to complaints.

On September 15, Archbishop Levada traveled to Ukiah for a face-to-face meeting, his first, with ninety priests from throughout the diocese. Gathering at the new St. Mary of the Angels Church, they offered prayers for, among other concerns, the spiritual welfare of both Ziemann and Hume Salas. The priests then met behind closed doors for more than two hours while the archbishop delivered his assessment of the crisis and listened to the priests' concerns. He followed the meeting with a news interview.

The diocese, he informed the priests and later the press, was more than $15 million in debt after tapping into restricted funds and money entrusted to it by parishes, schools, and other church entities. Contrary to what most people suspected, most of the money was not used for cash payments to settle sexual misconduct cases against priests. Under Ziemann's relaxed financial standards, most of the money, some $11 million over the past three years, had been used to cover escalating spending on construction projects, new or expanded ministries, and added personnel. The Santa Rosa Diocese, it would later be revealed, had been supporting more ministries than the Archdiocese of Los Angeles.

Since 1995, the archbishop said, the diocese had paid out 5.37 million dollars in settlements for priest sexual misconduct, two million dollars of which was covered by insurance carriers. A series of overdrafts by parishes and schools amounted to another two million dollars. It was these cash payments, combined with escalating deficits, increased subsidies, accelerating demands for parish construction projects and "poor investment decisions" that led Ziemann, former financial officer Monsignor Thomas Keys, and other church administrators to tap into the fund entrusted to the diocese by parishes and schools.

Levada promised that the $15 million "borrowed" from that fund "must and will be repaid with interest." Working with Monsignor Brenkle, he was bringing spending in line with income. This involved sacrifice: halting construction projects, reducing ministries, letting people go. He hoped, within two weeks, to have in place a council of lay financial advisors, which would help shape the diocese's financial future. To cover current operating expenses, a consortium was being formed of California dioceses to help the Santa Rosa Diocese through its crisis. A $5 million loan had been received from Wells Fargo Bank. Certain diocesan holdings, land and buildings, would be sold.

The diocese, Levada insisted, was not paying for lawyers representing Ziemann in either the pending civil suit or criminal investigation. Ziemann, he said, was undergoing "intensive spiritual and psychological therapy to assist him with the issues he faces."

The meeting, and the coverage that it received, answered some concerns and intensified others. At last the parishes had some assessment of the extent of the damage, an explanation as to how much money was missing and where it had gone, and an assurance that the worst of the problems were being addressed. But with awareness of the extent of the loss came the realization that knowledge of it had been forced from the Church only by scandal and had Bishop Ziemann not had to resign because of the threatened exposure of his sexual conduct, the financial misbehavior might have continued for years. Some people, laity and clergy, questioned the thoroughness of the archbishop's disclosure. Levada had stated that payments for priests' sexual misconduct totaled less than $5.5 million, yet a lawyer in Contra Costa County claimed his firm had collected that much from the diocese for his clients alone. Some people, Sister Kelly among them, believed that funds from the Scrip Center, of which Ziemann had been Chairman and Keys President and CEO, had been used for payments to sexual molestation victims. Others wondered whether the diocese was now paying for Ziemann's upkeep, as well as his "extended spiritual and psychological therapy."

Also, the "borrowed" funds were eventually going to be paid back, with interest. By whom? The diocese, which eventually meant, one way or another, the people.

In early December, a letter was sent to the archbishop, signed by sixty-seven diocesan priests, requesting a meeting at the earliest possible opportunity. The letter quoted a Vatican II document stating that bishops "should be glad to listen to their priests' views . . . about matters that concern the needs of pastoral work and the good of the diocese."

The priests requested that, in the interest of restoring trust, a fully documented statement be issued, "to tell our people the total story about what happened throughout Bishop G. Patrick Ziemann's administration." The statement would "include the role of the bishop, the vicar-general, the diocesan finance committee, the administrative staff and the Scrip Center in creating our present situation."

The letter went on to ask that Monsignor Brenkle be put in charge of the day to day operation of the diocese, that the priests be given an active part in the consultation process for the selection of a new bishop, and that "in the future, official communications be given to us by mail or fax prior to their release in the public press."

While commending the archbishop for establishing a Diocesan Finance Council, the priests requested that a case be made justifying continuing participation in the Consolidated Account. They asked that the archbishop's oral promise to repay parish, school, and other debt with interest be put in writing and included in the diocese's annual report, and that the priests' retirement funds be restored and safeguarded.

They also proposed that the Priests' Personnel Board re-establish permanent criteria to evaluate the personnel of the diocese.

In milder, more respectful form, this is what most laypeople were demanding. For better or worse, the continually unfolding calamity had driven the clergy and laity together, adding to the chorus addressing a hierarchy with a history of ecclesiastical deafness.

"There's no means of upward communications," says Father Andrew Greeley. "The Vatican doesn't ask because it knows all the answers. The bishops don't ask anyone either . . . . That seems to be the abiding failure of Church leaders: they don't listen."

Added to the continuing financial bad news were reports from the investigations into possible criminal charges against Ziemann and others, as well as strategic leaks from both sides in Hume Salas's civil suit. As part of the negotiations that had run from the previous September until April, Ziemann's attorneys had retained a private investigator to shed light into Father Jorge's murky background. The private investigator turned this information over to the Santa Rosa police. It included financial records indicating that Hume Salas had spent more money than he earned, along with information from seminaries that he had attended. A letter from the Bolivian Order stated that, while a seminarian, pornography and contraceptives had been found in Hume Salas's belongings. Another letter said that Hume Salas, as a seminarian, had been found in possession of three passports, one of which claimed he was a priest. A letter from the Bishop of Costa Rica accused Hume Salas of forging a letter of recommendation. There was a transcript from the Universidad Intercontinental in Mexico City which differed significantly from the transcript that Hume Salas had submitted to the diocese.

There was also more recent evidence suggesting that Jorge Hume Salas had little intention of changing his ways. In June of 1999, five months after he had been dismissed from the parish in Napa, and after he had been stripped of his priestly faculties in keeping with canon law, Salas had officiated, as a priest, at a wedding in the chapel at the Radisson Hotel in San Jose, Costa Rica. He was supposed to be visiting his sick brother at the time.

This information was leaked to the press at considerable risk to Ziemann, the diocese, and an increasingly demoralized clergy and laity. Salas, it was revealed, prior to seeking a new start in the Santa Rosa Diocese, had been expelled from seminaries in Honduras, Bolivia, and New Jersey. While successfully undermining Jorge Hume Salas's credibility and tending to attract sympathy for the bishop as the victim of a veteran con artist, the information also revealed an appalling cynicism or naivete in the lack of a background check prior to ordination on the part of Ziemann and his administration. It also devalued the earned ordination of every priest in the diocese.

In response to the release of information from previously sealed investigative records, made public after a legal challenge from the

Press Democrat, Ziemann's lawyers attacked the validity of the tape of Bishop Ziemann apologizing to Hume Salas and admitting making him do things he didn't want to do. "This guy goes over there," said one of Ziemann's lawyers. "He is playing to an audience. He knows he is on tape. He is casting it in a light that is best for him."

Another Ziemann attorney depicted Hume Salas as a sinister foreigner: "We Americans have strong feelings about people who do these kinds of things. Why would you do that unless you were trying to set someone up?"

In defense of Hume Salas, his attorney added an amendment to the priest's civil suit. It accused the Latino men in Ukiah, along with another man in Napa, of conspiring with Ziemann "to defame Hume by making false allegations of sexual misconduct to police in Ukiah and Napa and to the press." Hume's lawyer also suggested that Sister Jane Kelly had been part of the conspiracy, that she had been used by the diocese to discredit Father Jorge by leaking unfavorable comments about him. Sister Kelly scoffed at the charge: "How could I be working for the diocese, when nobody in the chancery office has spoken to me for two and a half years?"

For some Catholics, the whole spectacle was simply too much to witness. They preferred to avert their eyes and blame the messengers.

"If it wasn't for Monsignor Brenkle and these other people," a woman said to me, "none of this would have come out."

"Are you serious?"

"Yes. It's like the federal government. It operates at a deficit, but somehow things always work out."

Blind faith. It was the essential co-dependent of the secret system.

For those who chose not to look away, there was compensation of a different sort: the sense of life being lived at a deeper level. The church, to which people brought their individual crises, was itself in crisis. Beneath the surface of everyday life another life was going on, a life and death drama, resembling and in some ways comparable to the Mass. A passion, articulated in fleeting moments in parts of the gospel or a fragment of a homily, but mostly felt, lived more than observed. Through contemplation it offered glimpses of the essence of existence, a purpose to pain and suffering, relief from the triviality of everyday life, a sense of deeper meaning; then, like the Mass, it brought you back through community. A shared expanded consciousness. A revived sense of the significance and value of life. With it came the hope that, within the institution, the passion would manifest itself, because the need for it was so deep.

Two weeks after his announcement that the Diocese had plunged 15 million dollars into debt, Archbishop Levada broke the news that the former finance officer, Monsignor Keys, had resigned as president and CEO of the National Scrip Center. The announcement was made by fax and neither Keys nor Levada was available for comment. The statement said that Keys would remain on the Scrip Center's board and that he would carry the title "President Emeritus" in recognition of his role in establishing the Center. Archbishop Levada would remain Chairman of the Board.

The Scrip Center and the Diocese had, and still have, what might be termed an accordion relationship: it expands or contracts according to what tune needs to be played. When association with the Church for the purposes of nonprofit status or a clerical endorsement would be useful, the space between Diocese and Scrip Center was squeezed close. When distance was more desirable, as during the present diocesan financial crisis, the space between the two expanded. The Center was begun on a $25,000 loan from the Diocese in 1988, and was incorporated into a separate nonprofit California Corporation in 1994. The bishop—Ziemann and now Levada—had always been its chairman, however, and the membership of the board was largely diocesan

Catholic laymen. When, in 1998, the Scrip Center bought out its largest competitor, the diocese had guaranteed the $5.1 million purchase price with a promissory note.

"There has been an intermingling of funds," Monsignor Brenkle admitted, "and there still is, but it has worked both ways, to the benefit of Scrip and now kind of to our benefit."

According to a diocesan audit, the Scrip Center was the largest depositor in the Diocese's Consolidated Account, the pooled fund that was exhausted under Ziemann and Keys. At the time the Consolidated Account was frozen, the Scrip Center had $2.1 million on deposit, and the Diocese now owed that amount to the Center. As President and CEO of the Scrip Center, Chief Finance Officer of the Diocese, and the originator and administrator of the Consolidated Account, Keys would appear to have been in a three-way collision of interest.

"The Scrip Center," explains James Dillon, a retired banker and chairman of Levada's new Diocesan Finance Committee, "is a not-for-profit corporation that is basically owned by nobody. It is run by directors appointed by the archbishop. In the event of liquidation, the Center's assets come to the Diocese of Santa Rosa.

"The potential is quite high. They are about to launch a Scrip Card [a buy-by-scrip MasterCard], and make a lot of money. They pay tax on income, and what they earn beyond that goes to 'a charitable institution.'

"The Scrip Center is on the verge of becoming a cash cow."

Uh-oh.

In all this faxed, leaked, or press-released information, none of the big questions were ever satisfactorily answered. Was Scrip Center money used to pay off sexual misconduct complainants? Through the Consolidated Account, it would have been easy. Was Keys, its founder, president and CEO, now president emeritus and board member, still calling the shots? Was Ziemann or his family going to offer to make at least some token restitution? Was the Vatican, which had chosen and appointed him as bishop, going to make good on the damage done by his mismanagement? Information was given for the most part grudgingly, as was cooperation with the District Attorney and the police. The feeling prevailed that the Church, as an institution, did not believe it should be subject to public scrutiny or civil law. The Church clung to secrecy, the black curtain, as the people, in frustration, tore at it. With each revelation, the Church was seen to have been incompetent in areas of sexuality and finance that laypeople understood better. Anyone who sustained a loving relationship, held a regular job, raised children, paid taxes, balanced a checkbook, knew that, the Commandments aside, lying, cheating, stealing, and an obsession with secrecy just doesn't work as a long-term way of life. You get caught. People don't want to do business with you. Your kids go wrong. Your marriage breaks up. Eventually, other people don't want to be around you. People who live and work in the world know this, and it was apparent to them, at a visceral level, that the Church hierarchy didn't. It preferred to remain deaf to the underlying message that people were pleading to be heard:

"For Christ's sake, *own up!*"

In the Diocese of Santa Rosa as well as in the rest of the United States, sexual misconduct by priests is often accompanied by financial misconduct such as extortion, embezzlement, theft. Secrecy in the one breeds secrecy in the other. But there is another aspect to this, and it is also related to obligatory celibacy. The Catholic Church does not pay its priests decent salaries.

Traditionally, in the European system, parish priests were supported by benefices—earnings from lands, crops, and money to which the pastor held title. The benefice system, which began its decline with the end of feudalism and the political changes that started with the Reformation, was not officially scuttled until

Vatican II, when the church recognized the need for a new way to support its priests. For the Church to be an effective preacher of justice, the Synod of Bishops stated in 1971, it must appear just in the eyes of the world. "Such justice is to be evident in the way the church compensates its workers, including priests and religious."

By the 1960s, most American dioceses had moved away from benefices and established modest salaries for priests. To this were added car allowances, stipends, and "stole fees"—monies priests are paid for occasions when they don the ceremonial priestly stole: mostly baptisms and weddings. The bulk of priests' remuneration still came "in kind" as lodging, utilities, domestic service, food, and food preparation. Money retained from collections (by means other than Jorge Hume Salas's), a holdover from the benefice system, was still used as a source of priest payment in some dioceses.

According to a 1999 survey of Priests' Compensation of Roman Catholic Dioceses in the United States, conducted by the National Federation of Priests' Councils, the average monthly salary for a priest in the Diocese of Santa Rosa is $1,212. This is less than the standard monthly Social Security payment at age 65. Compared to any full-time adult job in the outside world, this is paltry compensation.

There are, of course, the fringe benefits: food, shelter, utilities, some degree of domestic service. Here, a fairer comparison might be made with the military. According to the monthly basic pay table of the Department of Defense, as of January, 2000, the monthly salary of an enlisted person, rank E-3, which would be an Army private first class, with two years' service, is $1,235.70. This is almost $25 a month more than a Santa Rosa diocesan priest. Someone with a master's degree or equivalent, serving people at the most spiritually crucial moments of their lives who, in a profession desperately short of trained personnel, can commonly work a 60-to-80-hour week, and sometimes serve two or more communities. And the Pfc. gets medical and dental care as well as PX privileges.

This is not just compensation. It is contrary to the church's own teaching, particularly the encyclical on labor of Pope Leo XIII, which states that "The laborer is worthy of his hire," and that everyone who works is entitled to enough money for food, clothing, and shelter, plus something extra for himself. In practice, it leaves priests who do not have an independent income with nothing apart from month to month maintenance. They have no savings, no nest egg to tide them over if they decide to quit and seek a new career, no travel or vacation money, no investment or retirement funds other than a skimpy (and in the Santa Rosa Diocese, threatened) pension. It is any wonder, under these circumstances, that there are under-the-table payments, favors, and occasionally thefts? Or that priests, with the public's trust in the priesthood already shaken, would be tempted to steal?

It also adds a financial reason for the Vatican's refusal even to allow discussion of the possibility of expanding the priesthood to include married men. Priests who are husbands and fathers mean wives and children to support. And a celibate all-male clergy is one of the ways the Catholic Church has been able to support missionaries at an estimated one-fifteenth of the cost for married Protestant ministers. Low-paid celibate priests are dependent on the system, with no financial independence and little opportunity to choose where they will be assigned and how their lives will develop.

"When an individual is not sufficiently rewarded, whether in the present or in the anticipated future," concludes a study of men who withdrew from the priesthood in the years following Vatican II, "and when he has little hope of finding self-rewarding activity, he is, in fact, estranged from himself."

The police and district attorney's investigations into possible criminal charges were getting tepid cooperation from the church. Requests to interview Ziemann were declined by his attorneys. Diocesan officials insisted on having a church attorney present in all meetings with investigators. "The presence of a lawyer," observed Mike Mullins, the D.A., "always chills certain dialogue." The only statements from Ziemann regarding the investigation were news media accounts of Ziemann's lawyers' representations and the tape recording surreptitiously obtained by Salas. The bishop remained in exile, the subject of extended counseling and therapy, his protracted absence further undermining his already shaky credibility. Through his attorneys, Ziemann had initially denied, in the news media, any sexual relationship with Salas. The following day, he had admitted it. He had impeded the investigation of the thefts from the Church in Ukiah by Salas through inappropriate measures that could amount to obstruction of justice. And he remained out of state, like a fugitive seeking sanctuary, refusing any opportunity to give direct testimony to the police.

Agony in the Garden

In a meeting at the Chancery office with Monsignor Brenkle, the current chief financial officer for the diocese, plus the diocese general counsel, comptroller and business manager, the detectives were told that the Diocese knew where all of its funds had gone, and that the financial problems that the diocese faced amounted to gross mismanagement related to power and abuses rather than criminal acts. "The diocese officials," said a joint memorandum issued by the police department and the D.A.'s office, "said they are examining the financial situation and would rather handle the matter as an internal problem." What the people and the management of the parishes whose funds had disappeared thought about pursuing the matter was not included. They had not been consulted.

In both the sexual and financial investigations, the attitude was implicit that the Church did not really consider itself accountable to either civil law or its own laity. And that Church affairs remained ideally conducted in secret and managed from the top down.

A survey conducted among Catholics attending Mass at one of the diocesan parishes confirmed the deep disconnect between the people in the pews and the prelates in the chanceries. Parishioners at St. Leo's in Sonoma County were handed questionnaires as they entered church, which they were asked to fill out and return later. Sunday Mass, formerly a neutral corner away from the sexual and financial conflicts of the world, was now part of the battleground.

Eighty-eight percent of the parishioners who responded were "concerned or very concerned" about the sexual misconduct of priests in the diocese.

Ninety percent were "concerned or very concerned" about the diocese's financial difficulties.

Ninety percent believed that the laity should play a "strong or very strong role" in dealing with the diocese's current problems.

Ninety-seven percent said that the parish should investigate the possibility of joint lay meetings with other parishes concerning the present diocesan problems.

Eighty-three of the people responding volunteered the comment that priests should be able to marry and that the vow of celibacy should be reconsidered.

"The overriding response," said *The National Catholic Reporter* in an analysis of this survey, "reveals a mature Catholic population that understands its rights and roles within the Catholic community."

The question was, would a church hierarchy, increasingly defensive about its shrinking moral authority, be willing to hear such news and to take the necessary corrective action, at the expense of its own power?

"This is a crisis," concluded one of the respondents, "but not a crisis of faith. Rather, the veil of secrecy has been at last ripped away, revealing the hidden cancer of power-seeking. Forsaking the gospel of love for the gospel of power, clericalism and self-will run riot. It's our role as the Church to call the hierarchy to repentance."

On November 10, 1999, the Chief of Police of Santa Rosa and the District Attorney of Sonoma County held a joint news conference at the Finley Center, a meeting and recreation complex that is the crown jewel of the city's Parks and Recreation Department: acres of lawn, oak trees, an Olympic-size swimming pool. In a session that filled two meeting rooms with media representatives, police and county prosecutorial personnel, and various interested parties, the Chief and the D.A. announced that no criminal charges would be filed against Bishop Ziemann. The elaborate setting and the joint nature of the announcement of a nonprosecution were a deliberate attempt to make a statement. Though the police chief, Michael Dunbaugh, and the district attorney, Mike Mullins, were not convinced that Ziemann could be successfully criminally prosecuted, they clearly did not believe that he and the other diocesan financial authorities were innocent of wrongdoing.

Mullins, a practicing Catholic, under pressure of being accused of going easy on the Church, said that a six-month investigation by police and district attorney's investigators had produced evidence showing probable cause that Ziemann had coerced Jorge Hume Salas into a sexual relationship. The problem was that whatever had happened between the bishop and the priest had occurred without third-party witnesses. It was essentially Hume Salas's word against Ziemann's. But Hume's credibility was so damaged by a history of alleged criminal conduct and personal misrepresentations that the D.A. concluded he could not prove sexual coercion beyond reasonable doubt.

In response to a question, Mullins said he thought the secret tape of Ziemann apologizing to Hume Salas would have been admitted as evidence. "It would have been a hotly contested issue, but I believe we would have prevailed."

Despite the tape, Hume's history of alleged thefts and extortions in Napa and Ukiah and evidence that he was thrown out of four seminaries and had masqueraded as a priest before he was ordained to obtain money would have tainted his value as a witness or as a source of evidence.

Ziemann, said Mullins, had his own credibility problems. He had suppressed evidence of Hume's wrongdoing both in Ukiah and in Napa. He had apparently done the same thing earlier in Ventura County, where a priest had been accused of theft. The coverup in Ukiah might amount to obstruction of justice, "in and of itself a criminal act."

In the end, neither the accuser nor the accused could be believed. "I'm convinced that neither party is credible," Mullins said.

Nevertheless, Ziemann still faced a civil suit for sexual harassment and in this the police chief, Dunbaugh, believed that Hume Salas had an effective case. "Let me state that at a minimum, Father

Salas was a victim of sexual harassment in the workplace, being victimized at the hands of Bishop Ziemann. To this, Father Salas has a legal remedy he can pursue in the civil courts."

This was hardly a red-letter day for the Church. And the financial misconduct was yet to come.

After examining the financial issue, in response to complaints from parishioners, Chief Dunbaugh said investigators had so far found no evidence of criminal conduct, but instead gross mismanagement to the point of being "reprehensible."

Church authorities had been less than fully cooperative in both the sexual and financial investigations. "There were individuals in the hierarchy," said Dunbaugh, "who were helpful and would talk to us and there were individuals who were not.

"It is incumbent on the representatives of the Catholic Church to come forward with any future evidence that might support existence of criminal conduct and to do so with a new-found willingness to cooperate in the prosecution of any responsible parties."

Mullins placed responsibility for the financial mismanagement of the diocese's finances on the crowned head of Ziemann. "He was warned that his practices would result in the depletion of the consolidated account. He ignored those warnings and allowed the funds to be depleted."

Lawyers for Hume Salas and Ziemann tried to put their own spin on the proceedings. A member of the bishop's defense team said that Ziemann "was grateful investigators took the time to look at all of Hume's credibility problems. He has admitted his own wrongdoing and is accepting the consequences and is trying to move on with his life." Hume Salas's lawyer, Irma Cordova, "welcomed Dunbaugh's comments, saying police investigators have told her they felt they had a strong case against Ziemann." In a press release issued after the news conference, however, she criticized Mullins, "a Catholic, whom she suggested that in deciding not to file a criminal complaint buckled under to political, religious, and financial pressure and news reports adverse to her client." Mullins vehemently denied any such influence.

For the public, Catholic and non-Catholic, the news conference revealed the continuation of a process of covering up priests' wrongdoing that had existed in this diocese for more than thirty years. For any thinking Catholic who chose neither to turn away completely from the church or to blindly embrace it, the news added to a lingering cloud of skepticism that all the wind about forgiveness and moving beyond this could not blow away. The fact was that two priests, one of them a bishop, as well as a significant portion of the Roman Catholic hierarchy had been demonstrated as unworthy of trust. Or, in the original meaning, faith. And the church's continuing reluctance to cooperate with any sort of outside examination or investigation made any thinking person wonder how willing the organization was to go about the long, hard, humbling work of earning that trust.

The police report of the investigation concluded: "Unless the Church is in a position to assume an active role as a victim in this case, the Police Department has been left without a criminal complaint to investigate."

This is impressive organizational loyalty. And lousy citizenship.

There has existed, on the part of the hierarchy of the Roman Catholic Church, a certain historical antipathy toward the United States based on the sense that the country represented, at its essence, an Enlightenment idea, the ascendancy of reason over faith, a challenge to traditional authority, dogmatism, and censorship. A rival appeal, in the Declaration of Independence and the Bill of Rights, to individual conscience and idealism. The belief in government as the proper and rational instrument of progress. At what other organization could these claimed universal valid principles governing humanity, nature, and society be aimed? The

more combative, more direct threats in France and in Russia came
and went. In the long history of the Church, they were but ill-
nesses, sieges of the flu. The United States remained, an opposition
denied, at times partly embraced, its danger instinctive, perhaps
mostly unconscious, its success a threat to the political power of
the Church and, in its manifest allure of a secular, materialistic
world, a threat to spirituality itself.

The great paradox of the development of the Catholic Church in
America is that the era of its greatest expansion, from the middle
of the nineteenth century up through the middle of the twentieth,
coincided with one of the most theologically reactionary periods
in the Church's history.

In 1850, Pope Pius IX, who had been ousted from Rome and
stripped of the Papal States as a consequence of the European liberal revolutions of 1848, returned to Rome accompanied by a
French expeditionary force. Pio Nono, who had suffered from
epileptic fits as a young man and was especially receptive to
accounts of spiritual manifestations such as stigmata and appearances of the Blessed Virgin, had seemed sympathetic toward the
liberal–nationalist point of view upon his elevation to the papacy
in 1846. He had declared an amnesty for political prisoners and
endorsed the unification of Italy. Now, however, he returned to the
Vatican a confirmed reactionary. He looked on the absorption of
the former Papal territories into the Kingdom of Italy unhappily,
and referred to himself, confined to a temporal state of a few acres
in the city of Rome, as "The Prisoner of the Vatican."

In compensation for this loss of temporal power, the pope
began an expansion of papal authority in spiritual matters that put
the Church hierarchy firmly at odds with most of the sweeping
political and social changes that had been occurring in Europe, as
well as with the Enlightenment ideas that were at the heart of the
philosophical foundation of the United States.

In a series of doctrinal announcements the Pope, as if in

keeping with the yearning of traditional European political authority to reassert itself, took several questions which had been the subject of theoretical discussion and debate within the Church and froze them into inarguable dogma.

The first of these, in 1854, was the papal bull *Ineffabilis Deus*, which declared the dogma of the Immaculate Conception: that Mary, the mother of Jesus was, from the moment of her own conception, "immaculate and free from all taint of Original Sin." This had nothing to do with the Virgin Birth, though many Catholics still assume that it does, and was announced by the Pope without the participation or consultation of the Church's bishops.

The next reassertion of authoritarian Catholicism was the *Syllabus of Errors*, published in 1864, in which eighty "erroneous propositions" were specifically rejected by the Church, with the understood recommendation that all good Catholics were expected to do the same. Among the errors to be rejected were the notion that mankind can find the path to eternal salvation in every religion and that the Church is to be separated from the state and the state from the Church.

The climax of this withdrawal from "progress, liberalism and modern civilization" was the affirmation, in 1870 by the First Vatican Council, of the doctrine of papal infallibility, that the Roman Pontiff, when speaking ex cathedra, acting in his capacity as head of the church, on matters of faith or morals, "partakes of the infallibility with which our Redeemer intended his Church to be endowed."

The implication of these statements, their lack of tolerance toward other religions and other points of view, their discouragement of free and open inquiry and their rejection of the need for separation between church and state, made an awkward fit at best with the nation of Jefferson and Adams, of the spirit of the Declaration of Independence, and the letter of the Bill of Rights.

"The Church is not a democracy," the defenders of the hierarchy insist. Yet it is founded on the egalitarian teachings of Jesus, and at its most autocratic and corrupt still historically sustained in its monasteries and convents the idea of election of rulers by vote as well as the installation of women in positions of responsibility and leadership. At the same time, it preserved the bricks and mortar of democracy, the literature of ancient Greece. Most important, as the leading vehicle of Christianity, the Church imbued the individual with a conscience and told him to follow it, thus creating an enemy to all tyrannies—even those which arise within the Church itself.

The financial bad news kept piling up like a multicar collision on Highway 101. In December, it was revealed that Ziemann, using the bishop's discretionary account, which supposedly had a $25,000 ceiling, had over the past five years spent some $561,000 on payments to victims of sexual abuse by priests. The total amount that had gone through the account was estimated at two million dollars. The half-million-plus dollars was in direct payment to victims or their therapists and was independent of money paid to victims as the result of lawsuits. One of Ziemann's lawyers characterized the payments as a kind of insurance: had Ziemann not offered therapy and financial assistance to these people, the diocese could have faced even more expensive lawsuits. The fact that this in effect made priest sexual molestation a continuing operating business expense was not mentioned.

In his police interview, Monsignor Keys had told the investigating officers that he, Keys, had been in the hospital when Ziemann had opened his own sub-account and begun writing checks on it. "The Monsignor reported that he was advised by the Diocesan CPAs to get Ziemann out of the account." Keys had not done this because, he told the police, he did not see Ziemann personally benefiting from his discretionary account "as he was not driving a new car or wearing fancy clothes."

"A finance council," said a spokesman for Archbishop Levada,

Agony in the Garden

"would have seen a budget and would have said, 'What in heaven's name are we doing with a six-figure discretionary account?' " In the Diocese of Santa Rosa, however, there was no such council. And, as it turned out, no budget.

To help bail itself out of debt, the diocese was considering selling some of its real estate, including a 14-acre parcel adjoining St. Eugene's Cathedral in Santa Rosa. In Ukiah, parishioners of St. Mary of the Angels, already a million dollars in debt for the construction of their new church, learned that another million dollars in church and school savings, entrusted to the diocese, was gone.

Some time after this it was revealed that, apparently as a desperation measure, Keys had invested five million dollars of diocesan funds in an investment scheme based in Luxembourg that was under investigation by U.S. federal authorities. The diocese had been promised a 400 percent annual return on its money, which was apparently used to finance the purchase, in Europe, of homes, boats, and automobiles. The diocese had issued a cease-and-desist order, hoping to cut the investment "off at the ankles."

"Other dioceses have had financial disasters," John Brenkle reflected, "Fresno, Tucson, where they bought TV stations. But this one did the deepest damage. Although the amount wasn't as much as other dioceses, they didn't hit the retirement fund, the health-insurance funds for clergy and lay employees like this one.

"The truth is, we ourselves don't know where a lot of the money went. I'm getting bills for massage therapy for a victim of sexual abuse. Massage therapy? *Come on.*"

In the courtyard outside the Chancery Office of the Diocese of Santa Rosa, a group of some thirty people, mostly women, moved in a silent file along the walkways. Some of the women carried hand-lettered signs, OPENNESS NOT SECRECY, IT'S ABOUT MORE THAN MONEY, SEX, LIES AND SECRECY, but there was no singing, no chanting, no yells. It was a cold night, with a threat of rain, and the women wore down jackets, parkas, coats, and gloves. They were unlikely protesters: mothers of grown men and women who as children had been molested by priests; women who had raised funds for their individual parishes, demanding to know where the money had gone; former diocesan employees angry at job cuts; women who had questions about the scandal and were dissatisfied with the official answers. Sister Jane Kelly was there, along with women who had husbands at home and families left to fend for themselves at dinner. Reduced to silence by the Church, the women were demonstrating that silence can be eloquent.

Inside the Chancery building, a converted parish school, the archbishop was holding his first working meeting with the members of the newly appointed finance council, trying to come to terms with Ziemann's devastating legacy. Most of the women outside had attended Catholic schools like this one, with the tall paned windows that open out at the bottom and the little gable with the cross on the roof above the door. It was a stock reproduction of the place where they had been taught obedience to authority as well as the values they were now using to question it.

"We patterned this group on the Madres of Argentina," explained Mary Shea, a college teacher unaccustomed to being on this side of protest. "We're here to bear silent witness, as the mothers of the missing did outside the presidential palace in Buenos Aires."

In an open letter, she had asked the archbishop "How can we say one thing publicly as a church and then ignore other private behavior? Merely paying off lawsuits and claims will not make the problem disappear. If it is inappropriate for us to raise this difficult question in such a public manner, we ask: where and how should we get these concerns addressed? Unless this question can be answered satisfactorily, we, the faithful, have no recourse but the public stage."

Agony in the Garden

In the Diocese of Santa Rosa, the secret/celibate system had met its instinctive opposition: Catholic women.

It was a woman, Sister Jane, who had begun the chain reaction of diocesan exposure. The church had tried to reduce her to silence by ignoring her. It was women, mostly, in the pews at Mass. A woman attorney in the town of Windsor had prepared a petition protesting the financial mismanagement of the diocese and demanding that the Vatican, which had appointed Ziemann, make the diocese financially whole. She had collected hundreds of signatures and personally delivered the petition to Rome. She counted, among her clients a number of older people, on fixed incomes, who sacrificed to make regular donations to the Church, which had squandered them. It was women running and staffing the hospitals and schools, operating Catholic Charities, and providing hospice services. And it was women, throughout the Church, coming forward in the hundreds to tell their stories of how they had been used to help priests quell their sexual anxieties and comfort them while they climbed the ecclesiastical ladder and assist them to grow beyond emotional adolescence. The priests remained in the system, exempted by the rule of celibacy from any obligation to marry. The women were left behind.

In the process of exalting an abstract woman, the Virgin Mother Mary, the Catholic Church demeaned, exploited, and ignored actual women. And depended, to a degree uncomfortable to admit, upon their silence. "Nuns don't like priests," Father Andrew Greeley says, "because we've treated them like cheap help in the Church for ages—they kept the schools and hospitals going on minimal salaries. And there aren't many doing it anymore. It's hopelessly unfair." When women spoke, the Church was threatened to the point of being terrified.

Representing varying degrees of anger, the women outside the Chancery were united in insisting that things within the church must change. There needed to be an end to the Church's stubborn

silence regarding priestly sexual misconduct. Public acknowledgement must be made of the acceptance of responsibility to repay
money that had been misappropriated. Vendors and employees
needed to be paid, crucial ministries needed to be salvaged. The
death-embrace of secrecy had to end.

"At Cardinal Newman High School," one of the women
explained, "we got a lousy twenty-five thousand dollars a year from
the diocese. We had to do the rest of the fundraising ourselves. Now
that's gone, and we wonder how we're going to keep our lay
teachers."

"We've turned over Peter's rock," said Sister Jane Kelly. "And
look what we've found."

"It's always the same people," another woman objected, "on the
finance committee, on the board of the Scrip Center, there's no real
parish-level inclusion."

"I don't see," said the father of a molestation victim, "how a
woman can even *be* a Catholic."

A priest came out of the building, leaving the meeting early, heading
for his car in his black suit, hurrying through the courtyard of
protesting women as though caught in a driving rain. Some of the
women greeted him: "Good evening, Father." The priest, a tall, stooped
man, hurried through the line, saying nothing, appearing terrified.

"Equality of women," writes Richard Sipe, "is the single most threatening factor to the homeostasis of the system as it now exists. . . .
The place of the priest's mother is often enhanced by devotion to the
Blessed Virgin Mother Mary. This spiritual emulation tends to fixate
the priest in the role of a son who is affiliated with a male-centered
idolatry."

A celibacy that is dependent on immature sexual identity will be
threatened by women, says Sipe, and will be frightened of them.

The attitude of priests, as experienced by women, is: "I don't see
you, therefore you don't exist."

Agony in the Garden

There was the feeling this night that a split already existed here between Catholics of the old school, meeting inside, and Catholics outside doing what the faithful traditionally never did: protest against the Church. It was the idea of protest that shocked, the fact of women—the ignored and neglected backbone of the church—objecting, complaining, calling priests to account.

There had been, earlier on, a confrontation. While the protesters were walking with their signs outside the chancery office, other women began arriving in cars, the mothers of children being brought to the same school building for CCD—catechism class. There was a certain amount of glaring, then one woman, a short, russet-haired person shepherding her daughter, burst out: "I'm ashamed to be a Catholic for the first time in my life!" Aghast at the spectacle, the idea of protest, the presence of signs, she stood in place, seething. One of the woman protesters walked over to talk to her. "Now you know how I felt when my son was molested at the same age as your child." The scene was primal, passion-laden, suggestive of the pain of childbirth. And the death of innocence. The woman with her daughter was unappeased. Children should not see this. The people demonstrating insisted that the opposite was true. Children benefited from being made aware of the potential danger of molestation. The intensity of feeling resembled a Vietnam War protest: righteous indignation on both sides, accusations of disloyalty versus people's right to know, a desperation that those in power will not listen, a conviction that a wrongful course must be stopped.

"It is cold and dark here outside your meeting," Mary Shea concluded her letter to the archbishop. "We are silent but not complacent. Christ himself went out among the thieves and whores, but we are alone. We deserve better."

On a crisp, dark February evening, Catholics of every temper converged mothlike upon the glowing parish hall/gymnasium of St. Eugene's Cathedral in Santa Rosa, California. Priests and nuns in mufti, too embarrassed by events to be seen in public in clerical garb; social conservatives alarmed at the disappearance of at least $16 million in diocesan funds; liberals bent on reform by all means short of Martin Luther; molestation victims and their therapists; parents concerned for the fate of their children's Catholic schools; the curious and the furious, the devout, the depressed, and the deranged, all headed toward a gathering that promised to be anything from massive group therapy to a lynch mob.

In three earlier meetings that week, in other towns and cities of the Diocese of Santa Rosa, spokesmen of the Finance Committee had appeared before the public in town meetings, attempting to explain what had gone wrong and what was going to be set right in the Catholic Church in the northernmost corner of California. The spirit of convocation and confrontation had been growing, night to night. On Monday night in Ukiah a nun, Sister Jane Kelly, had admonished the archbishop, scolding him publicly for ignoring his people in a scene that looked as if it might be climaxed by the archbishop getting whacked with a ruler. Molestation victims bared their souls in public; businessmen and women accused the Church hierarchy of financial malfeasance bordering on insanity. Night by night it had built, fueled by newspaper reports of additional losses to a total of thirty million. The lid was off, the pot was being stirred, people hungry for information were determined to be served.

On the apron outside the entrance of the Monsignor Becker Center, a local car dealer had parked a VW Bug, with balloons attached, taking advantage of the occasion to do a little marketing. It was a scene out of *Butch Cassidy and the Sundance Kid*, where a pitchman uses a crowd gathered for the formation of a posse to introduce "the future" in the form of a bicycle.

Inside, where maybe 500 folding chairs had been set up on the basketball court floor, the seats were half-filled a half hour before the meeting's scheduled start. This was going to be standing room only, the hottest event in town. The audience, mostly middle-aged and beyond, half men, half women, was animated, talkative, adrenaline-laced, like the crowd gathering at a prize fight: they knew that this was news, and they were part of it. "Aren't there any introverted Catholics?" my wife asked.

Off to one end of the court, a semicircle of people, mostly women, stood beneath a folded backboard, saying the rosary. A microphone was set up in the center aisle. Another mike stood in the side aisle, and a third to the front of the crowd, on a raised dais, backed by chairs.

People continued crowding into the gym. "They should have charged admission," a white-haired man remarked. "Help pay off the debt."

"They might pass the basket yet," suggested the woman sitting next to him.

The air of anticipation was almost palpable. Would Bishop Ziemann leap naked from a cake, private parts concealed by stacks of missing money?

At seven o'clock, the announced starting time, the seats were filled and rows of standees lined the walls of the gymnasium. Monsignor James Gaffey, pastor of St. Eugene's, opened with The Prayer of St. Francis:

> Lord, make me an instrument of your peace.
> Where there is hatred, let me sow love.
> Where there is injury, pardon.
> Where there is doubt, faith.
> Where there is despair, hope.
> Where there is darkness, light.
> Where there is sadness, joy.

The three people on the dais were introduced: Monsignor John Brenkle, the Diocese Financial Officer, James Dillon, a retired banker, and Dierdre Fronczak a diocesan spokesperson. She was the designated moderator, the referee, and she began by reading a message from Archbishop William Levada. The archbishop urged faith, solidarity, reason, reconciliation, rebuilding. He attacked critics who ignored the positive aspect of these meetings. There were groans from the audience. "Where's he tonight?" someone shouted. There was a smattering of applause at the conclusion of the message. Keep the lid on, was the tone the archbishop was trying to establish; but this was no Catechism class.

The moderator asked the audience to maintain civility, compassion. And, when the question period began, to please limit the length of their remarks.

Monsignor John Brenkle spoke first. In his late sixties, gentle, avuncular, and smart, Brenkle was probably the most respected priest in the diocese. In 1992, when the previous bishop left an already troubled ministry, forty-three priests of this diocese sent a

Agony in the Garden

letter to the Vatican requesting that Brenkle be appointed their new bishop. Pope John Paul II, uncomfortable with the turbulence of democracy, looked instead to the nearest ranking hierarch for his recommendation, Cardinal Roger Mahony of Los Angeles, who sent one of his auxiliary bishops, George Patrick Ziemann, off to the boonies. Former L.A. clergy now occupy the dioceses of Fresno, Stockton, Monterey, San Francisco, Orange County, Boise, and Salt Lake City, and several of these bishops were also Mahony's former classmates. Brenkle, the man whose appointment would have prevented this mess, had now been handed a mop and told to clean it up.

Brenkle began by an appeal to faith; but the appeal was personal rather than institutional, informed by events, not blind. "I have been asked, again and again, during this crisis, 'Does faith help?' My answer is that it means absolutely everything. We must believe that God is getting us to wherever we need to be. In my office, I have a sign on the wall behind my desk: 'The sign of God may be that you may be led down paths that you choose not to follow.'"

He spoke in the fatigued, philosophical tone of a man who had been left holding the bag and was intelligent enough to realize it. A decent man rocked by repeated unpleasant surprises. And the hits kept coming. Two nights ago, an hour before one of these town meetings, it was revealed that the previous administration, desperate to recoup losses, invested five million dollars with a firm based in Luxembourg that was already under investigation for fraud by the U.S. Government. The Diocese's then Financial Officer, Monsignor Thomas Keys, had been promised an annual return on his money of 400 percent—a proposition that makes drug dealing, by comparison, seem like a calm, reasoned investment.

We are going to discuss numbers, Brenkle continued, but this is a lot deeper than numbers. "It is about what happens in our faith life, what kind of Church we are going to be in the future.

"When this news broke, in July of last year, I was devastated. I didn't believe the accusations against the bishop. I thought it was another Cardinal Bernardin thing, a man being falsely accused. Then the bishop came out, admitted his sexual misconduct, and we priests were just shocked. Priests had prepared homilies for Sunday Mass, which they had to rewrite. I know I had to rewrite mine many times.

"As things began to unfold, I found myself angry. I keep shaking my head as these financial implications keep coming. I felt duped, lied to and manipulated. Anger was followed by guilt, what could I have done to prevent this, there were red flags, I could have pursued it. I was on the Priests Council, one of the consultors. We would go to a meeting where we would be introduced to these new people, very able most of them, brought in to take care of the various ministries. We were told, 'We have the money.' "

Brenkle recalled that one priest, Father David Shaw, demurred, "It isn't our money. It's the people's money." Widespread applause at this.

The monsignor recalled being contacted by someone from the Campaign for Human Development about some $90,000 that had been reported collected not having been passed on. "Why did I not pursue that? Well, I had other things to do in my life. My own parish to administer. I trusted the bishop. 'We have the money. We'll take care of it.' "

Brenkle described being contacted by the archbishop. How the archbishop himself was unaware of the extent of this. "What has happened here has sent shock waves through the dioceses of the nation. We could prove to be a model for other dioceses."

There was rueful laughter at this.

Brenkle tried to offer some good news. St. Bernard's parish in Eureka, which had chronically hemorrhaged money and was cut off by the diocese early on, had found an angel. The parish had been given an $800,000 endowment to assure the future of its con-

Agony in the Garden

solidated grammar and high school. The donation, made anonymously, had been given along with additional matching funds on condition that none of the money was to be deposited in diocesan accounts. Brenkle, years ago, had been principal of St. Bernard's. So had Gary Timmons.

"I had to apologize to the Native American Mission," Brenkle continued, "because we couldn't send them the ten thousand dollars we had collected for them. It was gone. They notified us the other day, they are sending us twenty thousand dollars."

There is hope and there is charity; Brenkle suggested there should also be faith. "I've been through some wonderful times with this diocese, and I'm not going to bail out now that we're going through some difficult times. That's life. You go through good times and bad times, and you grow through both of them."

For 1,500 years, the Catholic Church's most lucrative piece of real estate was Purgatory, the place somewhere between heaven and hell where just about all Catholics, except saints and martyrs, went after death to do time, suffering until their souls were cleansed enough to enter heaven. In grammar school, *The Baltimore Catechism* awarded indulgences, so many days off suffering in Purgatory for certain prayers; the souls in Purgatory were mentioned at every Mass; there were times when indulgences were for sale—Luther denounced the practice, and was excommunicated for his courage and candor; Purgatory made the Church the broker of everyone's eternal happiness or suffering. Now it is gone, along with Limbo and the fish days. I have not heard Purgatory mentioned in a Catholic Church in years. "You're all going to heaven, don't worry about it," the pastor of my church declared just last Sunday.

Monsignor John Brenkle, anguished, called to account publicly before angry Catholics for a mess not of his making, was in Purgatory.

✝ ✝ ✝

Jim Dillon, a lean, crisp, silver-haired retired bank executive, was Chairman of the Diocese Financial Council. He had moved to Northern California three years ago from Connecticut and was charged tonight with explaining the numbers.

"I knew Bishop Ziemann," Dillon began, a polished finance officer, making a boardroom presentation. Would there be slides, charts, an overhead projector? "I was impressed with his charisma. I had a tough time accepting what had happened."

His tone and posture changed from cool appraising banker to impassioned Catholic layman. "There is no 'we' and 'they' anymore. The people who created this are no longer in control of the finances of this diocese. The laity's voice will be heard."

This was the official line as put out by the diocese; but the people who created the mess *were* in control of its most crucial commodity, information. In an interview, Monsignor Brenkle told me that "the reason we haven't been more forthcoming with information is that we don't know ourselves where some of the money went." Only Ziemann and Keys knew this, and a five-million-dollar bomb of bad news was dropped by Keys only that week. There was an overall feeling that more bad news could come at any time. That may not be control, but it is definitely power. By remaining unavailable, still possessing useful information, Ziemann and Keys made people come to them, protect them, counsel them, harbor them. It was passive aggression made manifest.

Dillon, still in theological mode, quoted Luke, 8:17: " 'For there is nothing hidden that will not become visible, and nothing hidden that will not come to light.'

"The black curtain is gone. If you see people fleeing now, it is not because there is a black curtain."

Dillon became again the cool, appraising banker studying a spreadsheet. "The numbers. Generally, there were too many ministries, too many employees, no concern for financial responsibility. For eight years, there was no budget. The chancery office was running an annual deficit in excess of two and a half million dollars. Monsignor Brenkle has cut the budget in half. He had to fire thirty-seven people, some of whom have since been re-hired. The money all went to operating expenses. There were no vacation homes, no Cadillacs, no expensive gifts to people. It all went to ministries. Another three and a half million dollars went to pedophilia victims and counseling. Two million dollars was covered by insurance, five and a half million dollars in all."

Five and a half million dollars in sexual misconduct settlements for a diocese of 140,000 people.

"The Bishop had a discretionary account, linked to the Consolidated Account. He wrote checks on it. Last year alone, he wrote checks in excess of nine hundred seventy thousand dollars." There was a gasp from the audience at this. "A total of two million dollars went through the Bishop's discretionary account." Been molested? Need therapy? Need books, a roof over your head? Someone to pay your hospital bill? Your insurance premium? The sexual partner you picked up? We have the money.

The roll call continued, like the sad courtroom biography of a bankrupt or a congregational confession of sins. In the early church, long before the introduction of the private confessional booth in the sixteenth century, Christians used to lay out their sins before their brothers and sisters, then ask for forgiveness. Perhaps something like that is coming back into the church again—but where is the expression of contrition?

"Five million dollars went into a high-risk overseas investment. We have filed a class-action lawsuit, and most of the overseas investment will be recouped. Five hundred seventy-seven thousand dollars is gone, supposedly to benefit something called 'The Diocese of Santa Rosa, Luxembourg.' "

It was easy to imagine the salesmen pitching this investment. "High risk? Why the Catholic Church has invested in it."

Promising prudence while shearing the sheep, dangling the lure of tax-exempt status.

"The auditors wrote down two and a half million dollars in loans to seminarians, money for the training of priests. We assume that we get some of this back in new priests."

"We had three million dollars in new construction. We can [ac]count for a total of about twelve and a half million dollars. Another twenty million dollars went to improvident spending."

How aware was Bishop Ziemann of what he was doing? A friend of mine, a lawyer who has represented embezzlers, says that people who embezzle money always insist it was borrowing, a temporary use of funds they fully intended to pay back. What did the bishop tell himself, how did he justify to his own conscience what was happening? "I don't know what it was," Brenkle had told me, "a need to be loved maybe." Or perhaps his family heritage, speaking through him: for the important things, education, the Church, good works, money will be found. Or a pastoral need to bend the rules of an unyielding church: perfect celibacy, no birth control or abortion, no Eucharist for Catholics who have divorced and remarried, impossible rules, at odds not only with human reality but with any teachings we have of the historical person Jesus. Ziemann worked out of an office that was a converted garage, drove himself around in an Olds Cutlass, was undemanding of ecclesiastical ring-kissing or ass-kissing. And drove his diocese into financial ruin. My kingdom is not of this world. Render unto Caesar the things that are Caesar's. Money is not a problem when you have contempt for it. Easy to give away when it's not yours. We have the money.

The litany continued. "We closed the Consolidated Account. It was a good idea, but nobody was monitoring it. That account disappeared, deposits and reserves, nearly eleven and a half to twelve million dollars, resulting in a nine-hundred-thousand-dollar overdraft." The priests' retirement fund, two and a half million dollars—gone, $790,000 in cemetery funds borrowed and not paid back—even the souls in long-abandoned Purgatory have been ripped off.

Eventually the mind glazed over at these figures, leaving a dull, numbed rage. This is not right, this is not okay, people who insist on trust (or faith) using it to lie, cheat, and steal. The lyncher's bile rises: grab the rope, get the tar and feathers. But the culprit was gone, hidden behind a screen of lawyers, therapists, cover-your-ass hierarchs who counseled faith, forgiveness. We were left to choke on our own rage.

Dillon tried to strike a positive note. The Archbishop had appointed the Finance Council. "We have refunded two million dollars to the Priests Retirement Account. We have cut the budget. We are paying down our bills."

New construction must be closed. Settlements with people who were victims of priests' impropriety were being reviewed.

"Under the Discretionary Funds," said Dillon, "Two million dollars is unaccounted for. We don't even know who some of these people are. We have diocesan property up for sale. We have performed a full audit. We are encouraging fundraising.

"THE BISHOP'S ANNUAL APPEAL—that name has had a sharpened stake driven through its heart."

Monies collected will be used for ministries, but not to repay chancery costs. There are safeguards and firewalls. The Financial Council is going "to be around biting at the ankles of any bishop who comes in and thinks he is going to run roughshod over the people of this diocese."

In the past, he admitted, money to the tune of two million dollars was taken up in special collections in this diocese that never went to the missions for which they were given. This is robbing the poor box, not with a mask, but with a bishop's crozier.

What loomed ahead was a diocesan capital appeal to repay the loans made from other dioceses, on which this diocese was now running. "The minimum goal is fifteen million dollars. Even if we sell substantial financial assets, we will still need thirteen and a half million dollars. We will need the efforts of everybody. We are the 'we.' We are the body of Christ."

Later, in a statement from the floor, a man from the audience put it more concretely:

"I understand. We are going to be allowed to pay ourselves our money back."

While Banker Dillon had been reciting this litany of the financial sins of what seemed the world's largest dysfunctional family, its sons and daughters had been lining up behind the microphones, waiting for a chance to speak. Some had waited years for this: the Church that would not listen to them had promised that they would at last be heard, in public. The line stretched behind each mike all the way up both aisles to the standees lining the walls.

To accommodate all those wanting to be heard, Deirdre Fronczac announced that the speakers would alternate, a speaker at one mike followed by a speaker at the other; she also again requested that, in the interest of time, the questions or statements be brief.

The first speaker was a woman, probably in her early thirties, heavy-set, round-shouldered as if under a burden of indignation and grief. In a voice thick with anger, moist with emotion, she asked to know "why this diocese acts with threats, oppression and condescending replies in response to a person who has been abused by a priest." She was an abuse survivor. "The reality is that the priest-perpetrators are not blamed, the victims are."

There was dead silence in the audience at the public enunciation of a painful truth. According to Richard Sipe, whose *Sipe Report* is the most thorough study on the subject, Church policy over decades regarding molestation has been the avoidance of scandal, the removal of the priest, and the arrangement of therapy for the priest. Consideration for the victims came only after a chain of successful civil lawsuits. In the last two decades, the Catholic

Agony in the Garden

Church and its insurers in North America have paid out over a billion dollars in settlements to victims of clergy abuse, and some of the clerical responses have been appalling. Children have been characterized as seducers, their sufferings dismissed as harmless maturing experiences, their parents blamed for not keeping closer track of their kids. In what has become a stock response to each new incident, Church spokesmen profess shock, urge forgiveness for the all-too-human sinfulness of the accused priest, and urge Catholics not to lose their faith. The accusers are dealt with, often humiliatingly, by lawyers. There is never, on the part of the Church, an admission of wrongdoing or an apology. There are sound legal reasons for this. It is also a moral outrage.

"Church leaders," the woman testified, "are ruled by fear. A priest said to me, 'Ignorance is bliss.' I say, knowledge is power."

There was thunderous applause at this. Acknowledgement of suffering, relief at a spoken truth, endorsement of indignation, sympathy for a broken life. All of these, and more.

At the other microphone, a man in his thirties wanted to know why the tax I.D. number of the overall account was still that of the diocese. Why couldn't there be an independent bank account for each parish? Dillon explained the advantages of consolidation at a single bank: interest on checking, greater leverage on loans. Monsignor Brenkle, he pointed out, had taken his name off the diocesan account—he didn't even have access to it.

A stocky man in his fifties announced that he was a descendant of the Carillo family. "My great-great-great grandparents built the first European house in Santa Rosa, the Carillo adobe. Now the walnut orchard around it owned by the diocese is about to be sold. Will there be any effort to preserve this home?"

A Latino man, indignant, stood at the mike and demanded, "These people have to come back and answer for their deeds! You didn't find them out!"

His anger lit a fuse, and a woman in the audience went off,

shouting from her seat, shaking a finger at the trio on the dais, "Keys is not accountable? Why is he not here? Why is he still a pastor?"

Brenkle tried to calm her: "The Archbishop is working on it."

"NOT FAST ENOUGH!" the woman shouted.

Responding to another indignant question of why the Vatican wouldn't help financially since Ziemann was the Pope's appointee, the beleaguered monsignor said he could not fathom that Rome would come to the financial rescue of a diocese in wealthy Northern California. "They have much more desperate situations on their hands."

It worked, calmed the crowd, as people realized that their diocese had no monopoly on human anguish.

A balding man, in sweater and slacks, announced himself in a brogue as Father Dennis O'Sullivan, pastor of St. Rose parish, less than two miles away. "You've said you're going to sell the chancery building. You can't do that. It's our building. The chancery offices are tenants of St. Rose, and have been for two years. It's not an option for us at St. Rose to sell that building. I certainly, as a pastor, don't want to be part of it."

There was applause at this, and an embarrassed sense from the dais of tales being told out of school, of Father Dennis going public, not playing by the rules. Distrust of the diocese was clearly not confined to the laity.

A matronly woman thanked the committee and the Council for taking on such responsibilities, then lit into them for having only two women on a nineteen-person council. "Once again, women are grossly under-represented in the management of the Church. Catholic Charities, Memorial Hospital, St. Eugene's School, all are running admirably, managed by women. There must be a greater role in the church for women."

The woman in the audience sounded off again, a one-person Greek Chorus: "WHEN WILL THIS HAPPEN?"

A man professed his loyalty to the idea of the Church, and to his parish. "But, personally, I don't trust anyone above the rank of Monsignor."

Asked when and how a new Bishop would be chosen, Monsignor Brenkle said, "I don't know who would want to come here. There is an old joke, about the bishop who was sent to hell. He was there three days before he realized where he was." Would the choice be based once again on the recommendation of Cardinal Mahony of Los Angeles? He sent Ziemann who didn't understand the people here or the surroundings. "The next bishop," assured Brenkle, "definitely won't be chosen by the Cardinal in Los Angeles."

"I'm a former teacher and a school board member," said a woman in a suit, "and I can't understand the lack of oversight in this matter. Where was Rome? Where was the Archbishop?"

The archbishop, Brenkle explained, is the metropolitan. When the other bishops meet, he presides. That's it. "The only person a bishop has to report to," added Dillon, "is the Pope, and he only has to do it every five years."

"Incredible," said the woman.

The deeper you got into this, the more you realized why monarchy went out of fashion as an effective form of government. The organization of the Church is a legacy of the old Roman Empire, when the man in charge as the representative of the emperor had life-and-death authority over the people, and lived in terror of his superiors. Republican forms of government are tedious and sometimes confrontational; you spend a lot of time listening to pointless gripes, but at least people are heard, elections get held, change isn't entirely dependent on the ruler's death. Everything doesn't come down to bullying, toadying, threats, and force.

A man from the town of Cotati lamented his town's and parish's loss: "We had a chapel, it was the oldest building in Cotati. The property was sold to Lucky Stores for one and a quarter million dollars. Now the chapel is gone and the money from that sale is gone." It was lumped, Dillon explained, with the $12 million now owed to the diocese. Translation: good luck.

A man who said his name is Le Beque, "which means bishop," said, "We are pilgrims, but we've had poor leadership. I say, no money for a year."

Okay, Brenkle suggested. "Then I'll play golf three days a week instead of one. But you aren't going to like it when your services are cut: Catholic Charities, St. Vincent de Paul, Christian Doctrine classes, instruction, CYO."

"WHAT ARE YOU GOING TO *DO?*" the Greek-chorus woman yelled.

Another woman in her thirties, chunky and depressed, stood at the mike. "No one, no priest, has ever said, 'We are sorry, we are *responsible* for the way you can't walk into a church anymore.' All I want is my damn therapy being paid for. It's done some good, or else I'd never be able to come here and say this. You guys keep hurting me, again and again. Fill out forms and you're re-traumatized. You know all about what happened to us, *and you use it against us.*

"Maybe, someday, I'll be able to go to church again."

Brenkle, shaken, was even more soft-spoken than before. "It's trite to say this, but I *am* sorry. I truly am, for what you've suffered. And for the others who have suffered too.

"The first week I was in this job, a man called me from Eureka. His two kids had been confirmed, last year, in Eureka by Bishop Ziemann. They'd had their picture taken with the bishop, and the family kept the picture in a frame. After this came out, the kids brought out the picture, stood in front of their parents, and tore it up. I am sorry for them, as I am sorry for you.

"The first seminary had the greatest teacher of all. There were twelve seminarians. Two of them failed their teacher. One of them,

Agony in the Garden

Peter, came back. The other, Judas, hanged himself. One in six. We all have terrible choices to make."

The town meeting, scheduled for an hour and a half, had lasted three. The crowded gym was stifling on a cold night. The speakers whose number, of necessity, had been cut off, had been heard; now the audience stood and drifted off into the night, into clear winter air, high from the bracing experience of a nonhierarchical church: scruffy, teeming, messy, democratic. A church that is changing, whether it wants to or not.

The parish where all this began, St. Mary of the Angels in Ukiah, now had a lay, woman pastor. The priest in charge, burned out by the scandal and its aftermath, had resigned. What appeals to conscience, scripture, reason, and logic could not change, necessity is turning into a *fait accompli*. The Church of pay, pray, and obey is gone from this part of the country, and all the thundering edicts of aging patriarchs is not going to bring it back. It's now the people, not the Church, who do not listen.

The Catholic Church is being revolutionized, one person at a time.

Ziemann remained, at this time, a kind of fugitive, given sanctuary within the institutional Church, refusing interviews with the news media or the police. When, in March, he appeared at the offices of a San Francisco law firm to give a deposition in the sexual coercion lawsuit, he refused to answer reporters' questions and the session was suspended by his attorney. His refusal was based, said Ziemann's lawyer, "upon his concern that there may be criminal charges as a result of his civil testimony."

Until there had been some admission of wrongdoing, an acceptance of responsibility for what had happened, ideally an expression of true contrition as a prerequisite for the forgiveness of sins, the healing that church officials kept advocating could not take place. The reasons given for this reticence, legal liability or the loss of insurance coverage, had become a self-justifying defense, where the diocese wouldn't go after priests for legal and insurance reasons and the priests wouldn't apologize because it might leave the diocese without the necessary coverage. This put the Church's management of this matter purely on a business basis and eroded yet more of its spiritual and moral authority.

Agony in the Garden

Especially embarrassing was the fact that, in another Northern California diocese, a similar situation was being handled according to the principles that all Catholics are taught.

The chancery office of the Diocese of Oakland is less than sixty miles from the chancery of Santa Rosa; but the difference between the two when it comes to priestly misconduct and official response resembles the difference between the Enlightenment and the Dark Ages.

In March of 2000, while the people of the Santa Rosa Diocese were still being addressed mostly through the statements of lawyers and public relations officers, the Diocese of Oakland held a public apology service, the first of its kind in California. The service had been in preparation for nearly a year and was in part a response to the call of Pope John Paul II for the Church to reach out during the Jubilee Year 2000 and ask forgiveness of those it has harmed.

"We weren't interested in apologizing for anti-Semitism or slavery," says Sister Barbara Flannery, the diocesan chancellor. "We wanted to address the things that need correcting now."

In a departure from traditional hierarchical top-down dictates, the Oakland Diocese chose to work with the priests' council, the body representing the parish priests of the diocese. They also decided to work with survivors of priestly abuse. The committee planning the service included Sister Flannery, a parish pastor, and seven members of the West Coast Survivors Network of those Abused by Priests (SNAP). The diocesan bishop, John Cummins, also attended some meetings.

In respect of the pain and anger of the abuse survivors, the committee agreed to hold the service away from any church. Instead, on March 25, some 130 people, including abuse survivors and their families, gathered at Leona Lodge, in a wooded Oakland park, to hear the Catholic Church publicly apologize to its living, not just its historical, victims.

There was little religious ritual. Instead, Bishop Cummins

addressed the men and women who were sexually abused by priests when they were children, teenagers, or adults. "For our lack of facing the truth regarding abuse by clergy and others, for our tendency to retreat into denial and self-protection in the face of such abuse, for our response of fear and avoidance rather than of care for the survivors of clergy sexual abuse, we ask pardon and forgiveness."

For any Catholic, practicing or nonpracticing, this was immediately identifiable as a true confession: an enumeration of sins based on an examination of conscience.

Bishop Cummins and other diocesan leaders acknowledged the failure of the Church to confront clergy sexual abuses head-on, to inform themselves of the deeper issues involved in such abuse, and to remove priest abusers and other offending employees from the active ministry. "This," admitted Bishop Cummins, "has been one of the most distressing aspects of the Church's recent history.

"Many dioceses in the United States took no decisive action, but rather counseled priests and placed them in new assignments elsewhere in the diocese or religious community, where acting-out may have continued unabated.

"In times past, the ignorance about the subject of sexual abuse— an ignorance that was culpable on the part of many people living in denial—was almost total in society as a whole, even among healing professionals. Unfortunately, the Church was part of that ignorance."

Survivors were invited to speak. Person after person rose to tell how the abuse had ripped their psyches and challenged or destroyed their faith. "Some individuals," reported *The Catholic Voice*, the diocesan newspaper, "chose not to come to the front of the room to tell their stories because the row of clergy in their black suits brought up too many painful memories."

Part of the service was a responsorial reading with survivors describing the horror of their abuse and Church leaders admitting the institution's transgressions.

Agony in the Garden

"We came back to the Church seeking healing and we were hurt again. We were told that we were liars. We were told that we were whores. We were told that we were hysterical. We were treated as if we were the ones who had brought shame and embarrassment on the Church.

"What we are doing here today will be, at best, the beginning of a process of healing and reconciliation and not its culmination."

Part of every traditional Catholic confession, along with a promise to do penance, is a pledge to amend one's life. It is a condition of any forgiveness of sin. "We protected our colleagues," the diocesan spokesmen replied, "who had stolen people's innocence and murdered their souls while maintaining an illusion of faithfulness and productivity. We pray for God's mercy and forgiveness and ask for the courage to amend our lives."

This was no blanket amnesty, but an acceptance of responsibility and accountability. How had the lawyers, the insurance actuaries, the public relations counsels let them do it?

"We didn't worry about attorneys," says Sister Flannery. "What attorneys say didn't count. We came to the position we did in association with the survivors of clergy abuse. Until you've done that, no real healing can begin."

Five of the abuse survivors at the meeting had come from the Santa Rosa diocese. When asked if the Diocese intended to hold a similar ceremony, a diocesan spokesman replied that Santa Rosa was considering adopting the Oakland policy on clergy sex abuse, which had been in effect since 1987.

The difference was while the Santa Rosa Diocese had consulted its lawyers, the Oakland Diocese had listened to its conscience.

On April 9, 2000, Bishop Ziemann made his first public statement in nine months to the people of the diocese whose most prominent figure—whose Corporation Sole—he had been.

In a letter read in each of the diocese's forty-five parishes at

Sunday Mass, Ziemann linked his message with the Pope's invitation to the whole church to ask pardon for its sins and with the penitential season of Lent nearing the conclusion of Easter.

He was taking this occasion, Ziemann wrote, "to express my most profound sorrow for the pain I have caused this diocese, both because of my failure to abide by my sacred vows and also because of my failure regarding the management of diocesan funds . . . I acknowledge with deep regret my responsibility for the current state of affairs about which you are justly angry."

The letter went on to ask for forgiveness, particularly from the youth of the diocese, and to reiterate Ziemann's faith in his vows even though he had failed to uphold them. "I know that you all are living daily with the consequences of my actions, and I cannot express to you enough the deep remorse and repentance I feel for letting you down.

"I urge you not to lose faith in God or in your Church because of me. . . . I pray that God will heal the wounds I have caused in the Church of Santa Rosa."

The letter concluded by requesting and promising mutual prayers.

Though unquestionably sincere, the apology fell considerably short of the full confession that the situation demanded. For one thing, it was mailed in. Unlike the bishop in Oakland, or Monsignor Brenkle and the Finance Committee Chairman in Santa Rosa, Ziemann had not appeared in person either before the people of the diocese, or the news media, or the police, to answer questions. The letter dealt in generalities instead of enumerating specific offenses, offering useful information, and suggesting a deep examination of conscience. What had he done with the money and why? What was his role in raiding the diocese, and what was Keys'?

Would Ziemann or his family offer restitution of any of the squandered funds?

Agony in the Garden

Also, the top-down tone of the letter was discouraging. It was mostly about Ziemann; his pain, his sorrow, his deep feelings for the former members of his flock and for their continuing faith in the Church. It reflected a larger self-absorption and refusal to listen that characterized the Church hierarchy in general. There was a definite Wizard of Oz quality to this, of a lonely man still thundering from behind a tattered churchly curtain to people who no longer put much trust in either.

At a time when directness was called for, the message was phrased in the spiritual language that had been previously used, by Ziemann, for deceitful purposes. It smacked of button-pushing, evasion and manipulation, of a failure of empathy and imagination, and a clinging to the wish for a quick return to business as usual. Even people who couldn't articulate what was missing sensed that something essential was not there.

"I just feel that there has to be more than an apology," said a Catholic woman in Eureka. "There has to be some financial way to get the money back."

"It was a heartfelt letter, and maybe a first step," conceded a woman in Sonoma Valley. "I don't feel animosity toward him. I do feel animosity toward a system that allowed this to happen, that allowed this activity to go on unchecked."

The church hierarchy, she concluded, "is a top-down system, which is way out of tune with the democratic principles in this country and in the world. . . . There has to be accountability and responsibility. The best way to do that is have things open and a lot more people participating in the process."

The release of Ziemann's letter was timed to coincide with the naming of his successor. On the following Monday, April 12, it was announced that the Pope had appointed Las Vegas Bishop Daniel F. Walsh to take over the Santa Rosa Diocese. Walsh, prelate of a diocese that had doubled in size during the previous decade, had a reputation as an effective administrator and money manager, a thoughtful, steady man whose lack of personal charisma promised relief after the rollercoaster regime of Ziemann. His appointment was not the outside job it might at first appear: Walsh, who was 62, had been born and raised in San Francisco, was ordained and had risen through the ranks of the San Francisco Archdiocese. His return to Northern California, rumored to be undertaken with a good deal of personal reluctance in the spirit of a good soldier, was in many respects a homecoming. While Walsh expressed skepticism toward the suggested creation of a lay congress to help guide the diocese, he had a history of establishing a working collegiality among laity, clergy, and hierarchy. The Diocese of Santa Rosa was no longer going to be run as a one- (or two-) man show.

One thing was certain: under the circumstances, nobody was going to write Walsh off as an opportunist.

The installation of the new bishop was scheduled for May 22. In the meantime, priority had to be given to establishing as clean as possible an administrative slate, starting with the lawsuit by the priest against the previous bishop.

For all their lawyers' macho talk about drubbing the other side, neither Jorge Hume Salas or G. Patrick Ziemann looked forward to having his sex life publicly examined in civil court. Negotiations had resumed after Ziemann's resignation and continued throughout the months of revelation of financial scandal and the seclusion and silence of both men. While their lawyers bickered privately, both men remained adrift, each withdrawn from the society at large and suspended from his priestly functions. Different as they were in affluence, nationality, and education, they shared the loss of what mattered to them most, their priestly identity. There was a fundamental need on the part of both men to have the issue settled.

For the Diocese, the need for closure was even stronger. How could the new shepherd be expected to function with the sins of the old hanging over him, maybe even detailed every day in the media? In order for the diocese to move forward, the matter had to be put to rest; that was the priority. A settlement was in the best interests of all of those most concerned, and what the laity or even the clergy of the diocese thought of the terms of the settlement had to be secondary to that.

On April 25, the diocese announced that a settlement had been reached in the sexual coercion suit brought against Ziemann by Jorge Hume Salas. Under the terms of the agreement, "solely for the purposes of settlement," Hume Salas was to be paid $535,000, money which the diocese's lawyers insisted would be paid by an insurance carrier. The money, they insisted, would not come from the depleted coffers of a diocese left 16 million in debt by fiscal mismanagement and payment of six million dollars worth of claims related to sexual misconduct by priests.

The settlement, Ziemann's lawyers said, was justified because "each side recognizes the legal complexities involved, the pain already imposed on the Catholic community by the issues in this case, and the need to bring the matter to a close and move on."

In what was to prove the most provocative part of the settlement, the announcement stated that while Hume Salas was to resign his ministry in the Santa Rosa Diocese, he would remain a priest.

The deal, described by a diocesan spokesman as allowing "newly-appointed Bishop Daniel Walsh [the opportunity] to give his undivided attention to his important pastoral and administrative responsibilities" struck many Catholics, clergy and laity, as another hierarchical cover-up, and maybe the most offensive yet.

"This is outrageous," said Sister Jane Kelly. "The Church is doing what it's always done: paying to settle claims involving priest misconduct and then letting the wrongdoers move on."

"For the first time in my life, I am ashamed to be a Catholic," wrote Mary Shea, who had helped organize a series of silent protests outside the chancery office. "It seems our values have been sold for 535,000 pieces of silver and a priesthood has been purchased. Our local Catholic Church has displayed moral cowardice of the worst kind, and this settlement was cavalierly designed to 'bring closure' and to 'allow us to move on.' I can't believe the lawyers and the insurance companies control so much of our spiritual health."

Michael Meadows, the lawyer who had represented victims of clergy sexual abuse and had collected at least five and a half million dollars in settlements from the diocese, said that none of his clients had received as much as Hume Salas had, and that he believed no other victims had either.

In a statement issued on behalf of the diocese, its public relations representative insisted that the decision to allow Hume Salas to remain a priest was not part of the deal. "It is independent of the settlement," he said.

Yet the issue of Father Jorge's remaining a priest was exactly the one that the diocese had balked at in the previous negotiations, the ones that had been broken off when Hume Salas's thefts became public knowledge. What was unacceptable then had become, after Ziemann's exposure and resignation, negotiable.

There were adequate safeguards to prevent future misconduct on Hume Salas's part, the diocesan spokesman maintained, because he remained legally tied to the Santa Rosa Diocese through the church process of incardination. If Father Jorge petitioned any other diocese in the world to resume active ministry, that process called for a background check to be made with the Santa Rosa diocese. This was the same process, however, that the bishop and the diocese had ignored in ordaining Hume Salas in the first place. The obligation to investigate a priest's background rested with the bishop of the new, hiring diocese. In the present climate of a church drastically short of priests, knowing Hume Salas's skills at dissimulation, what was to prevent a strapped bishop in the United States, Central America, or South America from taking a chance on a bilingual priest with American ordination credentials without undertaking a detailed personal investigation?

"The bottom line," commented Monsignor Thomas Green, a canon law expert at Catholic University, "is that, amazing at it may seem, there is virtually little that can be done to attack the validity of a priest's ordination, even if there was fraud involved.

"A bishop has wide latitude in regards to accepting any priest into his diocese. If he believes it's worth ignoring a troubled past, he can do so."

The financial settlement also provoked more questions than it answered. If the diocese was broke, and Hume Salas was to be paid by an insurance carrier, who was the carrier? What firm would be willing to insure an organization that already had six million dollars in sexual misconduct settlements charged against it? In later statements, diocesan spokesmen explained that the Santa Rosa Diocese was now being carried by a self-insurance plan offered by The Ordinary Mutual Insurance Company, which is incorporated in Vermont.

The Ordinary Mutual Insurance Company is part of a Risk Retention Group, incorporated in 1987. The company provides coverage for members in Arizona, California, and Idaho. Its standard policy provides coverage for sexual misconduct liability along with other standard automobile and general liability coverage. The members are Catholic dioceses or archdioceses only. According to the 1996 Report on Examination submitted to the State of Vermont, the board of directors of The Ordinary Mutual consisted entirely of Roman Catholic monsignors and bishops. Its president, in the 1996 Report and in the annual statement for 1998 lists, as the President of The Ordinary Mutual, the Reverend Monsignor Thomas J. Keys.

I nside the church, a contemporary stone, wood, and glass structure with a glass wall framing towering, twisted pin oaks behind a stylized, nonsuffering crucified Jesus, a special Mass was being held before a packed house in the middle of Sunday afternoon. The congregation was mostly female, uniformly old, white, and expensively dressed. Most of the people in the pews were holding rosary beads. On easels before the altar were large framed portraits—one of St. Faustina, a Polish nun recently canonized by Pope John Paul II, and one of Jesus, with the exposed Sacred Heart, both decorated with evergreen fronds. From the number of parishioners present and the elaborate nature of the setting, including the portraits, there was a sense of eventfulness, like that surrounding a wedding or a funeral, of the Mass taking on an extra planned and anticipated air for the purpose of making a statement not just about this parish but about the Catholic Church at large.

Not the least contributing element to the special-event nature of this Mercy Mass was the fact that it was being celebrated by the parish's recently elusive pastor, Monsignor Thomas Keys. In the months since Ziemann's resignation, the gregarious Keys, described by the *Santa Rosa Press Democrat* as moving "in and out of diocesan events and programs with such regularity that there were few places that Keys was not seen," had become a near recluse. "In recent months," complained the *Press Democrat*, "Keys has been unavailable for comment. Attempts to reach him by phone were unsuccessful . . . both lines are no longer in service." Reporters' knocks on the door of his private residence inside the nearby gated community where Keys lived elicited no response, and inquiries to the parish office as to when Monsignor would be saying Mass produced the blanket reply, "We never know in advance which priest will be celebrating a particular Mass." But the Mercy Mass had been announced in the parish bulletin, with Keys officiating, and intentionally or not it had taken on some of the air of a comeback performance. The clouds of controversy, the occasion seemed to say, on this sunsplashed spring afternoon, had blown over, and it was time for Monsignor Keys' reputation to bud and bloom anew like spring flowers.

The Mercy Mass itself, once it began, proved to be a throwback to old-time bead-rattling, incense-swaying, Host-adoring, Latinsinging Catholicism, and nobody who hasn't experienced it in its heyday, as most of the people present had, can fully understand its eloquence and power. Incense, flowers, rosaries, music, Latin: the full Catholic voodoo, with Keys, a priest from Central Casting, pink-faced, with a thick shock of white hair, wearing rimless glasses and singing prayers with a light brogue, definitely the man to deliver it. While not the powerful preacher Ziemann was, there was about Keys a birdlike alertness to the congregation, a certain watchfulness that suggested the calculation with which this particular event was orchestrated. There were droning repetitions of prayers by the congregation, counted by the decade on maybe 200 rosaries, a concluding doxology, followed by a benediction, including adoration of the Blessed Sacrament displayed in a gold sunburst monstrance. For people of a certain age, this can be very potent stuff, and it was clear that for members of this congregation, located in an affluent retirement community, it hit home.

Behind a glass rear wall which all the congregation faced as they exited was a room with rows of folding chairs, a table with a metal cash box, and, above it, on the wall, a large sign:

BE A GOOD NEIGHBOR.
BUY SCRIP.
DON'T LEAVE HOME WITHOUT IT.

There were also admonitions in the parish bulletin about the practicality and importance of parishioners' doing as much of their shopping as possible in scrip, issued by Monsignor Keys' enterprise, the National Scrip Center, and which could be conveniently purchased on the way out of church. The pitch for scrip, unlike the portraits, flowers, incense, and music, seemed permanent as opposed to linked to that particular day, suggesting a long-term if not permanent union. It also suggested a condition where the money-changers were not just in the courtyard of the temple, but enjoying, in effect, dual occupancy. The divided nature of the entire scene—of traditional, even reverse-gear Catholicism combined with modern consumer marketing—was also suggestive of a similar split in the nature and character of the pastor.

"I first met Tom Keys in 1991," recalled Bob Coyle, Sr., a Fresno, California, businessman. "I was in the insurance business. My son Bob was CFO of a wholesale food distributor. We had done sales for years. We had introduced a plastic card, a local store card, run it through a terminal, similar to the concept used now, but more universal. Keys told me about his scrip program, which was just a local operation at the time. We felt the scrip thing had potential. Keys didn't have a clue. We felt it could really take off. I called him up, said I had a couple of ideas. Went up to Santa Rosa and talked to him. We said we could automate it—he was doing a by-hand operation then out of St. Vincent's parish in Petaluma. We showed him how to do debiting and crediting. We did a handshake, agreed to a joint venture. Market outside his local area. Blow it up.

"'You guys are saviors,' he told us. 'I've been trying to do this for years.'"

"We were going to do a joint venture, sixty-five percent for us, thirty-five percent for him. That was supposed to be the deal."

"We're Catholics," added Bob Coyle, Jr., "we'd got a handshake from a priest, we thought that was that. We were running around, doing all the sales, set up Keys' Automated Clearing House, which allowed him to go to other areas of the country."

Keys was supposed to bring everything concerned with the business to the Coyles in August of 1992. When they hadn't heard from him by September, they traveled to Santa Rosa to see him.

"We had to wait an hour and a half," said Bob Coyle, Jr. "then he handed me a letter saying that the Diocesan Finance Council had made the recommendation that the relationship should be ended. This was the same Finance Council that Keys was using as a rubber stamp. He said they couldn't continue to expand the business into our Fresno operation. It could be considered a business, and jeopardize the diocese's tax-exempt status. No diocesan funds could be given outside the diocesan program. It would involve too much diocesan bookkeeping.

"My brother John and I decided the hell with them, we'd just do what we had been doing, and compete with them."

The Coyles started their own firm, Scrip Plus, operating in Fresno, with inventory and start-up funds provided by the diocese, while Keys' National Scrip Center continued its business in Santa Rosa.

Keys recalled the relationship very differently. According to the monsignor, the Coyles were not partners, but employees hired to assist him in developing a new medium for scrip, a charge-type card; the monsignor says he soon realized the Fresno businessmen were out of their depth.

"I payrolled them for a few months, but I wasn't working with them long before I realized that it was much more complicated than walking to the local bank and asking for a credit card. They came to the end of the research, and I had to cut them."

"We found out later," said Bob Jr., "that before we ever got to the chancery office in Santa Rosa, Keys had hired five guys and opened an office in Washington D.C. He'd sent out a letter to ten thousand schools. He'd already hired these guys. Now that we'd showed him how to do it, he said, I don't need these guys."

Where was Bishop Ziemann, officially the Chairman of the Board of the National Scrip Center, when this was going on? "Ziemann didn't orchestrate anything," said Bob Coyle, Jr., "even though this was about the time he took over the diocese. It was all Keys."

The Coyles are not the only would-be partners who later found themselves dismissed as hirelings by Monsignor Keys.

Bob Curry is a former Catholic priest of the Santa Rosa Diocese who now works for the Tobacco Prevention Program run by the State of California. According to Curry, "Tom Keys had a little group of people set up who didn't know one another. After he got what he wanted, that was the end of them.

"Keys was working with my brother, who was putting on presentations concerning safety. He got into a deal with Keys concerning the Scrip Center. My brother was being paid by Tom to do business. One of the things was a Scrip Card.

"I was leaving the priesthood. I sat down with Tom; the diocese was between bishops and Keys was in charge. I offered to work on the Scrip Program with my brother. It would be a kind of transition thing, very little money, and get more down the road. That was what we agreed to at the time. I didn't have it in writing.

Agony in the Garden

"We went down and met with the Coyles, to see if they were compatible. The way Keys worked, he was continually stalling. You had to clear everything with him, but he wasn't available. He didn't return calls. Tom had four or five different groups of people working on different parts of the puzzle.

"In 1992, as the whole idea was taking shape, he brought in Wendy Perryman, as one of the managers of the Scrip Center. I said, 'I know there are other people working on this.' I said everybody should meet and discuss the whole problem. Tom said, 'I have another meeting, I have to leave.' Later, he told me privately, 'I really don't want to discuss in front of the ladies what is going on. It's just not the time.' "

According to Curry there were all kinds of meetings, with John Klein, the lawyer for the Scrip Center and the Diocese, at the bishop's residence in Santa Rosa. "We were looking to put together a nonprofit that would solely benefit the diocese. We would be involved in management. We wrote up a business plan and sent it off to the state. Klein was set to make final signatures. Form a corporation. He sat on it, because Keys told him to. Keys said the Diocesan Finance Board, which was nonexistent, didn't want to put diocese money into it." The purely diocesan enterprise, which Curry and his brother believed they had a stake in, appeared to be evaporating.

"We said, wait a minute. We weren't consultants, we were *in* it.

"The matter eventually went to arbitration. I got nothing, because I had nothing in writing. My brother had stuff in writing, so he got something. In the arbitration, Keys basically lied."

The Coyles had a similar arbitration experience with Keys.

They had found an outside partner to invest in their Scrip Plus operation, The Signature Group, a subsidiary of Montgomery Ward, which bought a 10-year stock option in April 1996. In December 1997, after Montgomery Ward filed for bankruptcy, Signature exercised its stock option and fired the Coyles. Security guards were sent to escort them from the premises. The next month, Signature closed the company. Within a week, Monsignor Keys began confidential negotiations to acquire Scrip Plus from Signature. With the Diocese of Santa Rosa serving as guarantor, National Scrip in February 1998 bought Scrip Plus's inventory and assets for $5.1 million.

"When they bought the assets of Scrip Plus," said Bob Coyle, Jr., "Ziemann signed a promissory note pledging seven million dollars of Diocesan assets. They even had to change the National Scrip Center corporate charter. They just did it. As Corporation Sole, Ziemann had full say."

As part of the deal, the Scrip Center acquired a covenant that Bob Coyle Jr. and John Coyle had made with Signature, pledging not to open a rival business to Scrip Plus during the length of the option. The Coyles, well-versed now in the scrip business, wanted to begin again with new investors. Bob Sr. started up again as Scrip Advantage, but National Scrip obtained a court order enforcing the noncompete covenant against the two Coyle sons, preventing them even from working with their father. National Scrip rejected a $100,000 offer from the Coyles to buy back the covenant.

According to Keys, the right to keep the Coyle family out of the business was part of what he bought from Signature, "and we paid dearly for it."

"Keys testified when we were in arbitration, trying to settle with the Signature Group," Bob Coyle, Jr. recalled, "He walks into the building like an eighty-year-old priest, 'Oh, you've got a beautiful building here.' He goes into his Irish thing, 'Heavens to Betsy,' 'Jesus, Mary and Joseph.' He claimed in the arbitration that we stole his idea. He said we were employed by him. We never were. There's no record of any such thing. Keys lied his ass off. They threw what he said out.

"Nobody takes the collar off and puts it back on better than he does."

Agony in the Garden

+ + +

The house, on a quiet cul-de-sac in an upscale Santa Rosa neighborhood, is an enlarged, elaborate version of a California ranch house, a single story extending the length of the lot, faced with wood and brick, with a gate leading back to a garden, garage, and private office. It is an expensive house into which the diocese, according to an individual once intimately associated with the diocese's finances, says has "stuck a lot of money. It's a beautiful place." This is where Jorge Hume Salas was regularly summoned to sexually service Bishop Ziemann. In addition to being Ziemann's home, it had been the residence of the diocese's two previous bishops, Mark Hurley and John Steinbock, as well as that of the Diocesan Vicar General and Chief Financial Officer, Tom Keys.

Ziemann, arriving in 1992 to take over a diocese that had once gone bankrupt, found things apparently in good shape financially. He was coming into a situation that had been in place for ten or 15 years. There had been a turnaround and things now seemed to be in excellent condition, thanks largely to the financial acumen—perhaps genius—of Monsignor Keys. Freed from pressing financial concerns, Ziemann could concentrate on the aspects of his episcopacy that appealed to him most: expanding ministries, and approving new construction. "We have the money."

The problem was that Ziemann's area of expertise, or even interest, did not include finance. "If Ziemann looked at the books once a year, I'd be surprised," says a corporate officer who dealt with the diocesan management at the highest levels. "Where financial questions were concerned," said Ray Decker, a retired priest of the San Francisco Archdiocese, who has given considerable study to conditions in Santa Rosa, "his relationship with Keys was deferential."

"Ziemann relied on Keys to do all his fiscal stuff," said Bob

Coyle, Jr. "At board meetings of the Scrip Center, he never opposed Keys. Whenever there was an issue that might find the Chairman and the CEO on opposing sides, they never both appeared."

"Ziemann told me," recalled Bob Curry, "I don't know anything about finance. I rely on Tom for that."

"Normally," said Bob Coyle, Jr., of the Scrip Center meetings, "Ziemann just sat there in a stupor whenever Keys talked."

"Ziemann was an immature man," in Ray Decker's view. "He spent no time in the office. Instead, he drove around, popping up here and there, talking on his car phone, playing at being bishop. He paid no attention to the administration of the diocese."

Also, as Ziemann's housemate for more than three years, Keys would almost certainly have been aware of Ziemann's sexual orientation. "Keys would have known everything about Ziemann's sexual practices," said Bob Coyle, Jr. "He makes it his business to know your business." This could have developed into a quid pro quo: you do your thing sexually, I do my thing financially, and there'll be no questions asked on either side.

Through this complex interweaving of business, spiritual, sexual, and personal interests, Keys, who had been, as acting bishop, in charge of the diocese for the nine to ten months following the departure of the previous bishop, Steinbock, remained in charge in most respects after the arrival of the new bishop, Ziemann. If anything, Ziemann's love of the ceremonial aspects of his episcopacy, his preaching skills, his tireless capacity for showing up at events throughout the diocese, his glad-hand ability to communicate with people on an individual basis, his interest in expansion, freed Keys to concentrate on the financial and administrative tasks which were his forte. Under Ziemann, he had more room to maneuver than he had ever enjoyed before, without the burdens of politicking or covering ceremonial occasions. He had achieved a private, unacknowledged combined financial and clerical clout that was about to be exponentially magnified by the power of electronic banking.

Carey Daly is President, CEO, and Chief Technical Officer of The Pathways Group, Inc., a Santa Rosa–based developer of smart-card technology, which provides clients (banks, retailers, school systems, transit systems), with secure, tailored solutions for capturing and processing data and electronic transactions. A senior systems engineer with degrees in law and accounting, Daly first met Monsignor Keys in 1987.

"I first met Tom Keys at a computer conference. He was putting together Project Hope, a sacrificial giving program for fundraising."

Keys' business computer system, his DFM, was not working, and he asked Daly to rewrite it, and while he was at it, the software for Project Hope. "A lady from his office and I started working together on it," Daly recalled, "and we wound up getting married. That's how close he and I were.

"When I first knew Tom Keys, it was like he was an ex-priest who was still wearing the uniform. He told off-color stories, swore like a drunken sailor, wanted to be one of the guys. Then I saw him say Mass, and it was like two different people."

The DFM system became complex. Keys' demands were proving

to be 180 degrees away from what he had outlined. "We were not getting paid," said Daly. "I was helping various churches put together systems. My partner and I were afraid that if we didn't continue working on Keys' project, he'd pull the plug and we'd lose our paying church business." Daly finally got the system working and added things to it.

This system, with the software written by Daly, became the basis of the Diocese's Consolidated Account. "If it would have been used only to run the chancery, run the schools, Catholic Charities, I would have been happy," Daly reflected. "Instead, as it turned out, I gave him a tool to do some things that I'm not so happy about."

At a subsequent computer conference, Daly, like Bob Curry and the Coyles, got a harsh first-hand look at Keys' proprietary attitude toward other people's work and ideas.

"At this conference, Keys was the speaker. He got up and explained to the audience how he had written this software and that it belonged to the diocese. I talked to him afterward. I told him that he talked as if he was a senior systems engineer. Keys said, 'But I did design it.' "

Keys filed a copyright on the software saying that he was the designer. Daly also filed a copyright on the same software.

Shortly after this there was an unrelated meeting at the Becker Center adjoining St. Eugene's Cathedral. Daly was giving a software presentation to diocesan fiscal managers. Following the meeting, Daly encountered Keys in the parking lot outside the Center. "Here's Tom Keys with this over-the-hill attorney blocking my way. Keys challenged my copyright. I told him, 'We did the design and engineering, and we haven't been paid for it.' Keys said, 'You said you were going to donate this to the diocese.'

"I lost it. I got into a shouting match with Keys. The lawyer tried to step into it: 'Don't you talk to a monsignor that way!' There was a circle of people around us. It was ugly. I walked away. I was boiling.

"That night, Keys called me. He was very conciliatory." Keys, said Daly, had the ability "to convince people of things that would leave them with their heads spinning. Even when you caught him in a lie, he'd come up with a series of answers. He would be in the office phoning to correct things, before you could check."

Daly agreed to meet with Keys the next morning over breakfast. Keys, recalled Daly, "said he was in a bad place, he said, 'I can't have you talking to me like that in public.' About an hour into our breakfast, the lawyer turned up. Oh, look who's here, why don't we ask him to join us. Keys had timed it for the lawyer to be there at a certain point in our conversation."

Daly had also been giving thought to the marketability of the software product. With the dispute over the copyright, it would be tainted. "I told them look, I'm not going to sell the DFM product. I'm going to write a letter and donate it to the diocese. That way, at least we'd get a tax write-off."

Keys, essentially, got what he wanted. And Daly continued to work on the product.

"There were one hundred thirty-five [eventually 215] accounts. School accounts, altar society, women's clubs, Boy Scouts, all of these accounts got interest on interest-bearing balances. It was an accounting nightmare, keeping track of daily balances.

"As part of my background, I had worked for a company that made bank stationery. I knew how bank clearing worked, how documents were processed. If, on the standard individual bank account form, line E13B was encrypted with special code, then we could handle each of these accounts, write checks on it. The special code let the bank split interest and the account's bank balance out. The churches, local parishes, all got new checkbooks, all specially encrypted. The bank had no problem with it if it was okay with the diocese. And Keys was the diocese, financially.

"In the Consolidated Account," Daly explained, "overdrafts were virtually nonexistent. Here's how it works. Say you have three bank accounts, two traditional accounts, which you never overdraft.

Agony in the Garden

You keep a hundred-dollar minimum in each account. You always rely on these. The third account has five dollars. When you combine them, you have two hundred and five dollars to play with. Now you can continually overdraft the third account, but you never get caught by the bank because you maintain a minimum in the other accounts."

And play with the diocese's money is what Keys did.

"We were at a diocesan conference in Konocti, on Clear Lake," Daly recalled. "Keys said to me, 'Tell me how I can use the overnight balances to leverage into the money market.' I said, 'Give me a direct connection to Wells Fargo.' The bank won't let you do this. Instead we devised a concept of dialing in."

Keys had grasped the idea of the overnight money market, which banks use with their own depositors' funds. At night and on weekends, money from depositors' accounts is invested in instruments of the International Monetary Fund, which pay substantially higher interest than normal bank rates, at little risk. Interest from these investments is swept into a bank account, some of which is distributed, at normal bank rates, among individual depositors' accounts, at a tidy profit to the bank.

"Keys," according to Daly, "calculated the interest he paid to the one hundred thirty-five [eventually 215] accounts in the Consolidated Account on a monthly rate published in *The Wall Street Journal*." The parish managers were happy, they were getting regular monthly statements, and they were earning interest on accounts they'd never enjoyed before. The money they were earning, unfortunately, was, said Daly, "drastically lower than what Keys was earning. He put the excess money in the money market and in the stock market."

In essence, then, Keys was functioning as an unlicensed, unregulated, and untaxed bank.

"Not just as a bank, but as an investment bank. He was investing at times in private companies, including mine. I let Keys buy stock in my company. Ten thousand shares in his name. The stock went from two dollars to twenty dollars a share. He sold his shares. Who knows where those profits went? To the Priests' Retirement Fund? I don't think so.

"It's like I am taking profits on money you've entrusted to me, to buy things that I am selling back to you, at a profit."

According to a petition, filed by the Coyle family with the Tribune Rota of the Catholic Church in Rome, Monsignor Keys, by this method, was able the first month to "gather in interest $23,000, a sum which progressively increased."

This figure has been confirmed by its source.

"It was," said Carey Daly, "on Monday morning, let the fun begin. You download Monday night, know what bills have to be paid, the chancery, the schools, and the excess money and fees can be used for whatever."

"Take the Priests' Retirement Account. You have money coming in, from annuities and such, and very little coming out. The overnight money market is practically risk-free. If you have a substantial amount in there, that much money running through, you're going to get substantial earnings. You can direct profits to go into a separate account within the Consolidated Account. It becomes a slush fund—self-propagating. A spider web."

Keys also grasped the concept of the "short month." "You make your investment after the start of the month, then sell before the end of the month. It doesn't appear on the monthly bank statement. There's no accounting. The money-laundering people use this." So, apparently, did the Diocese of Santa Rosa.

"The banking world doesn't know what it missed when Tom Keys took his vows. He had seen the power of compounding, consolidation. It was like he was the first banker to discover it."

What did Keys do with his exponentially expanding cash flow? Well, for one thing he founded and funded two corporations, making himself CEO of both and also making himself, from the Consolidated Account, when needed, zero-interest loans.

"Keys was bragging about the huge buy he had made of scrip from the J.C. Penney Company," Carey Daly remembered. "Where did he get the money? He said, 'I got a free loan, got it from the Consolidated Account.' A week later, we had our set-to in front of St. Eugene's. I thought, when he comes down, he's going to come down hard."

Keys' second corporation, The Ordinary Mutual (acronym T-O-M) is a insurance company incorporated in Vermont, where corporate regulation is lenient. "Keys hatched it," says Daly. "He was active in it."

The Ordinary Mutual, according to Don Hoard, a longtime insurance executive, provides coverage for members in Arizona, California, and Idaho. Their policies provide coverage for sexual misconduct liability along with standard automobile and general liability coverage. The members are Catholic dioceses or archdioceses only.

In practice, The Ordinary Mutual seems to function as a flag of convenience under which Church dioceses are able to pay off sexual misconduct claims, almost always in exchange for confidentiality agreements, without the money appearing to come from diocesan funds. When the Diocese of Santa Rosa made its half-million-dollar settlement with Jorge Hume Salas, and Catholics complained that they did not want their parish donations used to reward an admitted thief, liar, and fraudulently ordained cleric, diocesan officials assured the laity that the money would be coming from an independent source, an insurance carrier, The Ordinary Mutual.

This is less than the truth.

The Ordinary Mutual is a self-insurance operation, a form of insurance used by entities—like municipalities—who know that they are going to be sued. "It's not insurance the way people normally think of insurance," explained Don Hoard. "Self-insurance means you pay it back. It's based on not *if* something is going to happen, but *when*. The insurance covers risks and immediate administrative costs. What you will do, you will pay back any indemnification amount in higher premiums over time. It's like a loan. For municipal entities, whose vehicles are inevitably going to be involved in lawsuits and judgments, the payments are carried, over time, by the taxpayers. For a diocese, faced with the continuing prospect of sexual misconduct judgments against priests, the money will come from parishioners."

Though as CEO of the Scrip Center, Keys took no salary, he hardly needed to. He also had given himself a CEO's heavyweight expense account. As the success of the Scrip Center grew, Keys expanded his good fortune to include that of his family, relatives, and friends from Ireland.

Tony Culley-Foster was a boyhood friend of Keys' in Northern Ireland. He is, says Daly, "on a retainer of twelve thousand dollars a month from the Diocese, plus expenses." Culley-Foster lives in Virginia and supposedly functions as some sort of lobbyist.

"Keys was bringing folks over from Ireland," says Bob Curry, "and paying them under the table. He'd bring them to a parish, or buy scrip, then pay people, so it looked like they were being paid from the parish. They're legal now, but they weren't then."

"The family lives an extravagant lifestyle," said Carey Daly, "relatives always coming over, enormous amounts of money. No taxes."

"I had hired one of Keys' nephews," Daly recalled. "He had no papers. Keys offered to pay his salary. I said, 'No. If he works for me, I pay him.' The kid worked for me for about eight months. It didn't work out. Then he had to go back to Ireland: in the interim, Keys hadn't got the kid's papers."

Agony in the Garden

+ + +

Monsignor Keys' transatlantic success story reached its climax in August of 1996, when he celebrated his Jubilee, the 25th anniversary of his ordination, with a gigantic party in his hometown of Derry, Northern Ireland.

"It was a five-day party," Carey Daly recalled. "A hotel had a bash at its restaurant. There were parties at people's homes, parties at parish halls."

"A Derry-born priest," reported the *Derry Journal*, "who has been described as one of the most dynamic and famous members of the American clergy was in his native city last weekend for celebrations to mark the twenty-fifth anniversary of his ordination."

The centerpiece was a special Mass celebrated at Long Tower Church, followed by a reception at the Everglades Hotel in Derry. There were speeches by the present and previous bishops of Derry, by former Santa Rosa bishop Mark Hurley, and a joint appearance by the Colmcille Ladies Choir and Saint Columb's Male Voice Choir, "each of which have visited the Diocese of Santa Rosa."

There had previously been a local version of Keys' Jubilee in Santa Rosa. "Tony Culley-Foster went around asking political figures for letters, pumping people up," said Carey Daly. "He got assemblymen and stuff writing glowing tributes to Keys, people who never knew him."

In Ireland, where the sending of such courtesy letters, usually written and sometimes signed by political staffers, was largely unknown, these letters were accepted as personal endorsements.

Bishop Hurley, the *Derry Journal* said, "gave an overview of Monsignor Keys's remarkable ministry in the United States, and the accolades he had earned from his fellow priests, parishioners, the Church hierarchy, educators, and President Clinton. He said everyone in Derry could be proud of Monsignor Keys's service in the priesthood and that he was justifiably regarded as one of the most dynamic and famous members of the American clergy."

Daly, who stayed with Keys' brother in Ireland, said that among people in Derry and Donegal, "Keys is a sort of Rodney Dangerfield figure. Some people in his family think he's a genius. Others just shake their heads: 'Well, the Keys boys have convinced the world they know what they're doing.' "

Who paid for this fulsome extravaganza in Ireland for a monsignor from California? "It was always a question of creative accounting," said Daly, "who paid for the Jubilee. In Donegal, I was introduced to people from a major Irish bank. The connection there was more than friendship. Keys had a 'special relationship' with the bank."

At this time, Daly had a contract with the National Scrip Center, signed by Keys, to develop a Smart Card together. Daly's company, The Pathways Group, Inc., had leased office space on Dutton Avenue in Santa Rosa, across the street from the offices of the Scrip Center. "We had an office geared to do card processing and fulfillment. We had fifty thousand smart cards printed."

At this crucial point in his own company's history, Daly was having serious doubts about the advisability of continuing to work with Keys. The Scrip Center, which had been spun off, supposedly as an independent entity by Keys in 1994, was being included in the Consolidated Account.

"The breaking point was when the National Scrip Center came in," Daly recalled. "I was involved with it. I knew it was not nonprofit. The Scrip Center insists that it has nonprofit status from the State of California, but only Federal matters." The National Scrip Center has been rejected four times for Federal nonprofit status.

Daly felt Keys was going to get in trouble by commingling, in the Consolidated Account, nonprofit and for-profit funds. "There was also the question of The Pioneer Flag Company, a nonchurch entity in Sonoma, using funds from the Consolidated Account." Daly believed that Keys owned a piece of it under another's name; that this was more creative accounting, applied to the Consolidated Account.

"I decided I didn't want to be part of it," Daly said. "I told Keys I didn't want to be part of something that violated tax laws."

Keys, on the verge of rolling out the Smart Card, changed his mind. He decided he didn't want to issue the card after all.

"We sent him a demand for payment," said Daly. "I reminded him that we had a contract. Keys denied the signature on the contract was his. I said, 'I was there, I saw you sign it.' Keys, backed by Culley-Foster, said he was sick at the time, that he apparently didn't realize what he was signing. We had a quarter of a million dollars in raw costs at the time, plus a hundred-fifty-thousand-dollar lease on an office building. I didn't want to sue the Church. I have to live here, do business here. So I walked away from it. Our Board of Directors was unhappy. Our stock dropped."

The National Scrip Center eventually concluded an arrangement with MasterCard. As of this writing, it still does not have federal nonprofit status.

According to tax-operational statements filed with the State of California, Monsignor Keys was working 50 hours a week at the National Scrip Center. The bishop, Ziemann, not particularly interested in management routine, was, most of the time, in his car or on his cell phone. What was the atmosphere like at the administrative center of the diocese, the chancery office?

"I've worked for the government," recalled Carey Daly, "and I never saw any place as totally locked down as the diocese chancery office. Every door in the office was kept locked whenever people weren't in it. The building was totally locked down at 5:00 P.M. Sister Patricia, the diocese fiscal manager and assistant vicar general, was in charge. Whenever I'd meet with Keys there, and he didn't want to keep me waiting in the conference room, he'd have Sister Patricia usher me into his office. She'd sweep every paper off

Keys' desk, rather than let me be alone in there with that paper. The atmosphere was totally paranoid."

The diocese's outlays for approved new construction, combined with Ziemann's penchant for new ministries (the Santa Rosa diocese was now supporting more ministries than the Archdiocese of Los Angeles), combined with the increasing costs of settlements involving sexual misbehavior by priests and Ziemann's unrestricted use of the bishop's discretionary account, was beginning to tax even Monsignor Keys' ingenuity for generating additional cash flow.

"My opinion," concluded Daly, "is that Keys knew he was in trouble for quite a while, and that he took chances he wouldn't have otherwise. Opening an offshore account in the diocese's name was typical of him. Put it in the diocese's name, so if he got caught, he wouldn't be associated with it."

In June of 1999, the month before Ziemann's resignation, there was an annual priests' gathering in the city of Napa. At this conclave, the priests played golf and had meetings. Keys, as the Chief Finance Officer of the Diocese, addressed the gathered priests. "He told the priests that the financial condition of the diocese was all okay," said Bob Curry, "when at the time he knew it was a disaster. He stood up and lied to them all."

"Right up to the last moment," said Monsignor John Brenkle, the man brought in to deal with the diocese's financial mess, "they were hoping for a bailout from this overseas investment. The people who had talked them [Keys and, presumably, Ziemann] into it, promised them they'd have first consideration in any sharing of returns."

Then, with the civil suit against Ziemann for sexual harassment, the revelation of DNA evidence, Ziemann's admission of a sexual relationship and his resignation, the roof fell in. The diocese's financial crisis was revealed. Promises were made of a thorough financial investigation. They were not kept.

Agony in the Garden

"Authorities in the Church did not do that," says Ray Decker. "They did not investigate thoroughly. They did not want more scandal. There was a suspicion that Keys was manipulating everything.

"Keys made people indebted to him. That's why there is not a lot of criticism of him on the part of the clergy. He entered into agreements over local things. He was in a powerful situation, and he could make side agreements. That's how he operated. It's hard to find people in the church who would speak out against him." The accountants hired to do a diocesan audit were the same accountants Keys had used. Keys' lawyer was still the diocese's lawyer. "If you incriminate Keys, you're incriminating yourself."

The Church hierarchy, says Bob Curry, convinced themselves that it was better not to go public. "They keep saying it's not that big a deal. We have to go on, move forward, get beyond this. But they are dealing here with people's lives and livelihoods. It is important to them. It is tremendously important to them."

Among the people unhappy with the Church authorities' decision not to pursue financial wrongdoing was Santa Rosa Police Chief Michael Dunbaugh. When, in January of 2000, during the series of diocesan town meetings, Monsignor Brenkle was quoted as saying that police had "made the judgment there was not enough activity there to press charges," Dunbaugh responded that "The simple fact is that the diocese failed to cooperate fully."

"The criminal investigation," Dunbaugh said, "was stymied from the beginning by the lack of cooperation from key church leaders, leaving police and district attorney investigators unable to evaluate the circumstances thoroughly enough to reach any conclusion."

Once again, when push came to shove, the Catholic Church, in the interest of avoiding scandal and risking the loss of people's faith, had—to maintain silence and secrecy—collaborated with people who had committed criminal acts.

"The decision not to prosecute," says Ray Decker, who at one time was assigned to be Jorge Hume Salas's defense counsel for a trial under canon law, "was an amnesty for Keys, but not for Ziemann. What Ziemann did was out of human weakness. What Keys did was calculating and premeditated."

"I had no particular fondness for Ziemann," said Carey Daly. "I didn't particularly like the man, but when he got caught and resigned and everybody pointed fingers at him for all the financial stuff, and nobody came forward, I thought he got a raw deal.

"Basically, they threw Ziemann under the bus."

18

A t noon on a sunny May Monday in Santa Rosa, the priests of the diocese, each in a ceremonial white robe, flocked like doves around the exterior of St. Eugene's Cathedral. Because of the diocese's financial difficulties, this was to be a somewhat scaled-down version of the traditional installation Mass for the new bishop, Daniel Walsh. Nevertheless, the presence of priests from throughout the diocese, some 100 in all, combined with past and present bishops from Santa Rosa and San Francisco, the scarlet-clad cardinal from Los Angeles, and the pope's apostolic nuncio from Washington, gave the occasion, despite the bright sunshine and the California traffic flowing by, a certain dark, medieval majesty.

Among the priests standing on the lawn and walkway between the Cathedral and the rectory, one white-robed, white-haired figure moved with a certain animation among the clusters of diocesan clerics. Monsignor Tom Keys, bouncing back from seclusion, was working the crowd: talking to priests who responded to him with varying degrees of body-language reticence or enthusiasm, shaking hands, smiling.

Agony in the Garden

"A number of priests," said Bob Curry, "are just disgusted with Keys. I'm sure he has convinced himself that he didn't do anything wrong. He's started showing up everywhere."

"I believe that a deal was cut," said Carey Daly. "Keys got away with his scalp in return for his silence. I also think he's lonely. He's done in so many people, he doesn't have many friends."

There were people, mainly women, who continued to think highly of Keys. They remembered his coming to the aid of an alcoholic parish priest who was told, by the diocesan bishop at the time, that the priest or his family would have to pay the costs of his treatment program, some $30,000. Keys, privately, said, "I'll take care of it." And did. Unfortunately, two men who told him he had molested them as boys eventually confronted the same priest. The priest admitted it, and there had been a financial settlement.

"I would like your readers to know," a woman wrote to *The Santa Rosa Press Democrat* in March of 2000, "that Monsignor Keys was immensely helpful in the process of revealing the crimes of Gary Timmons." In 1994, the paper had printed the story of how this woman's son had been molested by Timmons, at that time a respected North Coast monsignor. The statute of limitations prevented criminal prosecution. The only way to nail Timmons was to expose him through the media. "Your reporter . . . was not prepared to go ahead with his story without further corroboration. He contacted Monsignor Keys who acknowledged that the story was true. The article was printed and Monsignor Keys was quickly and cruelly vilified by many of his fellow clergymen and lay people alike. . . . Whatever else has happened, Tom Keys showed great strength of character at a time that was very traumatic for our family."

Keys' knowledge of Timmons's molestations, and the anger and frustration of his victims and their families was, says Bob Curry, part of the problem. "Keys acted as bishop for ten months prior to Ziemann's arrival. He knew of everything. The whole Gary

Timmons mess. He had the power, under canon law, to stop it. As bishop, he controlled all of us. He could have stopped it. And he didn't."

From inside St. Eugene's Cathedral, a trumpet fanfare echoed. The priests and bishops outside, formed a file, by rank, parish priests first, followed by monsignors, then some thirty bishops, then the cardinal and the papal nuncio and headed in a slow procession up the steps and through the cathedral entrance, the living incarnation of the male, hierarchical Catholic Church.

In his homily that day, Daniel Walsh, who had been seated in the thronelike bishop's chair, where he was given his crozier, the shepherd's staff symbolizing his pastoral office, spoke to the concerns of clergy and laity throughout, and beyond, the diocese.

"These tragedies," said Walsh, "have undermined the credibility of the role of bishop and the diocese and the life of the Church. Our parishes have suffered; individuals have suffered. Our good priests have suffered."

As bishop, Walsh said, he would see that a system of checks and balances was installed for the good of all church members. He said that there must be accountability in all aspects of religious life, and that there would be no place for secrecy in his diocese. "There can be no code of silence or cloak of secrecy that protects those who harm and destroy the faith of others."

It was an impressive statement of purpose which, unfortunately was not applied to the past offenses which continued to haunt the diocese and the Church. In March of 2000, the National Scrip Center had amended its charter so that the Diocese, which originally funded the operation, was no longer entitled to fifty-one percent of the proceeds if the Scrip Center was sold. Instead the money would go to a "public benefit corporation." The people whose money had actually funded the Scrip Center, the laity of the diocese, were not consulted. The true confession that all Catholics knew at faith level was required, the owning up to the details of what was done and how before absolution could be given, was not forthcoming.

"This stuff, unexamined, happens again and again," said Ray Decker. "It happened in the Vatican, with the bank scandal. Guys get in there, get corrupted by power."

"Let us speak of this, you who are wisest, even if it is bad," wrote Richard Sipe, concerning the Church, quoting Nietzsche.

"*Silence is worse; all truths that are kept silent become poisonous.*"

A month after his installation as bishop, Daniel Walsh made his first official visit to the parish where this whole story began. St. Mary of the Angels' new church in Ukiah was spacious, radiant with light, a clean, modern structure of wood and glass and stone, one of the few positive manifestations of the expansionist spirit of Ziemann's episcopate. The evening meeting had brought a near capacity turnout in the pews, and among the people seated there was Sister Jane Kelly, looking fit and feisty in a flowered skirt and blouse, toting a bottle of water as she moved about the church from pew to pew, visiting with parishioners. During the past week, there had been a private meeting between Bishop Walsh and Sister Jane which carried with it something of the air of a reconciliation. Sister Jane, the diocese's most effective and respected internal critic, appeared to have come on board in support of the new regime.

After some initial prayers Walsh, wearing a regular priest's black suit, spoke to the gathered parishioners and other interested parties in a straightforward, unpretentious manner.

There had been some question whether this meeting should be held in a church, the bishop began. "I insisted, because we are church people of prayerful dialogue and discipleship. We must have prayerful dialogue, in the presence of God, inspired by scripture.

"I am no miracle worker," he told the gathering. "I am here to serve you, the people of God . . . In the name of my Church and in my own name, I apologize. I assure you that together we will strive to see that . . . the sexual misconduct and financial mismanagement that have undermined the credibility of the diocese cannot and will not happen again.

"I am here to walk with you. All of us must work for the good of the whole Church. This diocese has been tested and is stronger for the experience."

"We want to be like the Church described in the Acts of the Apostles. Like the first Church of Jerusalem, listening to the words of Jesus, when he assured them, and us, 'I am with you always, even unto the end of the world.' "

Then, to the longest ovation of the night—sustained, standing applause—Bishop Walsh introduced Sister Jane Kelly, in her glasses and flowered skirt, holding her water bottle, at that moment the individual of most respect in the diocese. Clearly the bishop was hoping that the nun would add some heavy artillery to the legitimacy of his administration without proving to be a loose cannon causing more internal damage.

"It is with great pleasure that I am here to introduce Bishop Dan Walsh," Sister Jane, in an experienced, take-charge classroom manner, began. "I have known him since he was in the sixth grade at St. Anne's School in San Francisco. I was deeply affected when Dan called on Tuesday and asked to see me.

"I have a real sense of hope," Sister Jane continued. "I believe that we have a challenge, each of us, and that is to respond to what Dan Walsh calls 'a prayerful dialogue.' We must be honest, we must say who we are. I am going to take up this challenge tonight."

At these words there was, in the manner of the clerics present in the church, particularly Bishop Walsh and Monsignor John Brenkle, a certain visible stiffening, as if the room temperature had been lowered 20 degrees. Bracing and shocking at the same time. Here, you could feel them saying to themselves, it comes.

"I cannot believe," resumed Sister Jane, "that any reconciliation can occur as long as Monsignor Tom Keys is pastor of one of the wealthiest parishes in this diocese."

There was applause at this, some cheering, and downcast faces by the bishop and the monsignor. Sister Jane was still clearly not shrinking from telling people what they didn't want to hear.

"He's the one," she continued, "who paid men and women for their therapy and their silence. Keys and Ziemann made a vow of obedience, and kept silent. This man must be made accountable."

From the bishop and the monsignor there was no response. Not even a nod. They were good soldiers. And the orders, in this matter, had been given.

Sister Jane was not finished. "Why can't Ziemann be back here, apologizing and giving accountability?

"I, Jane Kelly, cannot be fully healed or reconciled, until I see Tom Keys made accountable for sexual offenses and financial mismanagement.

"I hope that the other priests who have molested, who have sexually abused and who have stolen, will be brought to justice. That is my hope, and I believe that Dan Walsh will do this."

As a parting shot, Sister Jane turned to the now stunned-looking bishop.

"Be honest," she told him.

In a desperate attempt to change the subject, Monsignor Brenkle began a rundown of the diocese's financial condition. Among the pews, there rippled aftershocks of Sister Jane's rhetorical earthquake. Enough's enough, a woman muttered, got up, and walked out. Another woman was arguing with a suddenly defensive priest. What was to have been a comfortable recline upon the familiar divan of Church doctrine had turned out to be another urgent need to compress broken springs popping up all over.

Eventually, after Sister Jane had left, the evening settled down into a question-and-answer session with most people speaking from their own individual positions. Toward the end of the evening, one of the parishioners popped the question. What was going to be done about Ziemann and Keys?

"At this point, I have no plan," Bishop Walsh admitted. "Perhaps it will wash out in time. We are still trying to figure it out."

"How can you ask us to give more money," the same parishioner, a woman, asked, "when you won't tell us where the money we gave went?"

"Some of the money," explained Brenkle, "from discretionary funds, went to people who have been molested. We can't reveal that without identifying a number of young people.

"To stop the bleeding has taken all of our time."

By the third anniversary of Ziemann's resignation, the bleeding had been stanched, but the blood-soaked rags and wounds, the aftermath of financial violence, were everywhere. $12.6 million dollars in emergency cash spent to pay bills, restore pension funds, cut staff, halt construction projects, and pay claims arising from priests' sexual misconduct. $21 million in other obligations including payback of the $16 million lost in the Consolidated Account, repaying external organizations, and setting aside reserves. The total recovery obligation stood at $33.6 million. Through loans from other California dioceses, gifts from foundations established by wealthy Catholic families, the sale of diocesan real estate and recouping certain high-risk investment, San Francisco Archbishop William Levada and his advisors were able to raise $22.8 million to help offset the fiscal carnage—some $10.8 million short of diocesan obligations. The diocese was also obligated to repay some $10.9 million to Wells Fargo Bank and other dioceses, while diocesan parishes and schools owed the diocese some $10.8 million borrowed in years past in the form of long-term loans.

By focusing on the future and ignoring the past, the diocese of

Agony in the Garden

Santa Rosa had achieved a certain stability. But it had come at the expense of justice.

"If the Consolidated Account had been operated honestly," said Carey Daly, "Santa Rosa would now be lending other dioceses money instead of borrowing it."

Once again it was the people in the pews, the parents of children in diocesan schools who were left with reduced ministries, repeated appeals for funds, the threat of closure, of the withdrawal of the means for meeting their spiritual needs. The wounds had cut deep, the scars would last long, and the people responsible for inflicting them remained frustratingly beyond reach.

George Patrick Ziemann, still a bishop, was, as of July 2000, at a monastery in rural Arizona, using his bilingual skills to administer to the needy in a predominantly Latino and Native American area.

The Reverend Jorge Hume Salas, who would have realized some $350,000 after legal fees from his financial settlement with the diocese, was in his native Costa Rica, where he was reportedly seeking restoration of his priestly faculties with a new diocese.

On July 1, 2001, the diocese of Santa Rosa ceased all involvement with the National Scrip Center. As part of the separation, the Center agreed to forgive an undisclosed amount of the $2.1 million loan it had made to the Diocese. It also adopted new by-laws, and Santa Rosa Bishop Daniel Walsh had resigned from its board. The Center, the nation's largest seller of discounted gift certificates, had yet to show a profit.

Monsignor Thomas Keys remains pastor of a church in one of Northern California's more affluent communities. He claims he has no ambitions to return to administrative work, but the simple pastoral duties he professes to prefer do not seem to command much of his time. He lives in a gated community, drives a Lexus, and makes regular trips to Ireland and to his favorite American destination, Disneyland.

John van der Zee

✝ ✝ ✝

The principals in this story, as types, in the worldliness of their values, are certainly not unique to the Santa Rosa Diocese, and nothing new in the history of the Catholic Church. Indeed, the Church may owe its institutional survival to a certain element, in its ranks, of ambition, greed, status, or reputation. They are all there, embodied in types, in the fourteenth-century England of Chaucer's *Canterbury Tales*, the Pardoner with his sleazy collection of relics, the haughty Prioress, the corrupt, indulgent Friar, and, in the one who in his simple nobility, is a living rebuke to them all, the Parson,

> Who truly knew Christ's gospel and would preach it
> Devoutly to parishioners and teach it.
> Benign and wonderfully diligent,
> And patient when adversity was sent.
>
> Nay rather he preferred beyond a doubt
> Giving to poor parishioners round about
> Both from church offerings and his property:
> He could in little find sufficiency.
>
> His business was to show a fair behavior
> And draw men thus to Heaven and their Saviour,
> Unless a man were obstinate;
> And such, whether of low or high estate,
>
> He put to sharp rebuke, to say the least.
> I think there never was a better priest.

211

I n the ballroom of the Commons at the Student Union of San Jose State University, maybe 500 men and women had gathered to hear a talk on the graces and griefs of being Catholic. There were priests present, and nuns, ex-priests and former nuns, straight Catholics and gay and lesbian Catholics, pro-choice and pro-life, Catholics who had divorced and remarried, some of whom had lost their jobs with Catholic organizations because of their remarriage. There were Catholic academics and therapists, social activists and altar society members, daily communicants and Christmas-and-Easter Catholics, the people from the classrooms and the hospitals, the parishes and the pews. It was the Church minus the hierarchy, come here to an academic but nonreligious setting, a neutral corner, from throughout the Western United States, to try and help renew the Church in the spirit of Vatican II.

The West Coast Conference of Call To Action was a regional expression of an independent national organization of more than 18,000 people and forty local organizations. Founded in 1976 by Catholic laity, religious, and priests, CTA is committed to the belief that "the Spirit of God is at work in the whole church, not just in its appointed leaders."

"We are convinced," the organization describes itself, "[that] the Church must be open and just in its own structures and practices. We believe the entire Catholic Church has the obligation of responding to the needs of the world and taking initiative in programs of peace and justice."

The conference seemed to represent the pastoral rather than the institutional Church, attempting to reconcile the spirit of the Gospels and the sacraments with that of the nation of the Declaration of Independence, the Bill of Rights, and the Gettysburg Address.

The keynote speaker, Anthony Padovano, a wry, rumpled figure resembling the young Walter Matthau, was a former priest who had studied at the Jesuit College in Rome, holds doctorates and professorships in theology and literature, has written some 26 books, and is the founder of Ramapo College in New Jersey. He was, on this California summer conference weekend, the only person wearing a suit.

Padovano, married for twenty-five years, is one of the men the Church hierarchy characterizes as having "left the Church to marry," as though having been overwhelmed by lust rather than experiencing a crisis of conscience in the narrowing direction of the Church in the years following Vatican II. As though these priests—by now numbering in the tens of thousands—had all failed the Church, instead of the hierarchy failing them.

In this year of the 2,000th anniversary of Jesus' birth, addressing a mostly gray-haired and female crowd, hoping to return the Church to the simple power of its roots, Padovano began where the Church began, in the first century.

It was, Padovano explained, a Christ-centered system of belief. The Church, as an institution, was not yet powerful. For the first twenty-five years after Jesus' death, his followers were observant Jews: they went to temple, observed the dietary laws, had their sons circumcised.

The Gospels, Padovano continued, say nothing about Church, ministry, marriage, sexual norms, doctrine, almost nothing about Mary. "The issues that are our major concerns are almost nonexistent in the gospels." With Paul, Jesus' death and resurrection became the center of Christian worship. *The Acts of the Apostles* was based on the preaching of Jesus. Christ was still at the center. Christianity was strongest in preaching and the sacraments of baptism and the Eucharist. Confirmation was part of baptism; marriage and holy orders didn't exist. There was a profound sense of inclusion.

"There was no Christian marriage for a millennium. Marriage was performed by pagans. If you were a baptized Christian, it was a Christian marriage."

This was the Christianity, strong in its combination of preaching with the sacraments of Baptism and the Eucharist, weakest in its definition in law, to which Martin Luther urged a return.

"The Church definition in law," continued Padovano, "is medieval. Most Catholics today define themselves by it. Law is more important than sacraments. There is no divorce, but it is relatively easy to get annulments. The emphasis is on legalisms. The Church legislates rules, and chooses law over sacraments. Laws are useful, but when they become central, things go wrong."

In the Christianity of the first century, no one had the authority to impose anything apart from the community. The Church was seen as the People of God. "Most Catholics today believe the Church is the Pope. Unfortunately," Padovano looked suddenly mischievous, "the Pope also believes that."

"We don't really know," he maintained, "what The People of God means. We have private teaching and private ordination in which people are not present. Annulments are decided in secret.

Agony in the Garden

The Swiss theologian Hans Kung, ordered to Rome for trial, asked: could he be represented by a lawyer? No. Confront his accusers? No. Have the right of appeal? No. There is no open process. We don't have one. Why would you expect justice from our church?"

"We have gotten so far from the idea of Church as people."

There are other organizations or movements within the Church, Opus Dei or RCF—Roman Catholic Faithful—combining laity and clergy who maintain exactly the reverse: that they are following the legitimate dictates of Vatican II in urging a return to a more strict obedience to authority. From their point of view, the abuses within the Church—priest sexual abuse, misuse of funds, declining vocations and attendance—are all traceable to a moral laxness that has crept into the Church due to misinterpretation of what was actually decided at the Church's last Council. But do these movements, some of which are influential at the Vatican, have the deeper resonance with the people in the pews, the nuns in the hospitals and the schools, and the priests in the parishes that Call To Action represents? Do they listen? Or are they simply a reinforcement of the top-down hierarchical system, with its dependence on silence and secrecy that has caused so much damage by keeping closed that which needed to be addressed openly? A system which, as it turns out, is of relatively recent origin and questionable historical legitimacy.

In the first century, Padovano continued, believing Christians thought that Jesus was coming back soon. "They got it wrong." So they devised the idea of the Paraclete—the Holy Spirit—to serve as a substitute for Jesus. "This meant that anything could happen in the Church. It was what made Christ more real." The Bible should be written. Slaves should be free. The Church can create structures—orders whose members elect their leaders, who serve at the pleasure of the men and women who elect them.

"The spirit was in people, not in tradition or the Bible."

In the first millennium, laity were considered Church members, and voted. There were seven Councils called in the first 1,000 years, all of them by laity. The Pope was not invited. At the Council of Constance, in 1415, a time when there were three Popes, each of whom had excommunicated the others, the Council fired all three. People's voices were heard. They carried weight. One council was called by a woman, the Empress Irene.

In the first century, the community held itself together through stories. Parables, rather than dogma. For dogma, people are not necessary. The law is laid down. But the hallmark of parables is compassion. "Parables are for everyone. Everyone knows what it's like to lose a child—the Prodigal Son. The Good Samaritan. The Woman in Adultery. You only need to be human to understand a parable."

Dogma is always intimidating, parables are inclusive. "Do most Catholics see the Church as intimidating, or inviting?

"If I come out, get divorced, resign my ministry, they will hurt me.

"There were a lot of downsides in the first century, but the priorities were right. We at least knew where we should be."

Did anything good happen after first-century Christianity under the Catholic Church? Quite a bit, maintained Padovano; significant values were developed by the Church, without Christ, following the lead of the Paraclete.

The first of these was the papacy, "an enormous asset. A brilliant, creative, unifying structure. The Catholic Church is the largest, oldest institution the world has ever known." The Orthodox and Protestant churches tried to operate without a pope, and lost unity. The problems that people have with individual popes should be like problems people have with the President. You may not agree with the man, yet you still respect the office.

The sacramental system represents another asset, an enormous and continuing release of creativity. "When Catholics are good at this, they are very good." Ritual and symbol create loyalty and commitment more than anything else. They give expression to feelings we are unable to articulate fully and unite people of differing, sometimes opposed political beliefs in the community best expressed in James Joyce's characterization of the Catholic Church: "Here comes everybody."

"To exclude someone from a family ritual, Thanksgiving or Christmas, is devastating. The sacramental system binds us together."

The development of church law. Canon law protected people from arbitrary and capricious leaders within the church, even at times and in places when there was no equivalent protection in civil law.

The Ecumenical Councils, the first of which, the Council of Nicea, was held in 325 A.D., "are the oldest democratic gatherings you can think of." The councils, with the exception of Pius IX's Vatican I "which was a charade," allow freedom of speech and democratic elections, "which is why popes don't like them. People say, 'The Church is not a democracy.' Of course it is, in its ecumenical councils."

Monastic and religious life. This was based on the idea that it was possible to create a community, apart from marriage, using the family as a model. "All these communities were built on democratic principles. You elected your abbot or abbess. Everyone served for a while. Terms were limited, the leaders were elected at the pleasure of the group, and women served in positions of responsibility. Hildegard of Bingen, the mystic, artist, and musician, was an abbess.

The New Testament. They got the story of Jesus down, in all its strangeness and power, the words that continue to speak to us through our own lives and the changing world around us, from four different sources, the message of *how to be*. "The existence of the Church," insisted Padovano, "could be justified for this alone."

Longevity. "The Church has locked within it a bed of unconscious

theology that brings it back, even when you think it's finished."
There are buried riches, like the work of mystics, again like Hildegard of Bingen, rediscovered in the light of modern psychology, a
legacy bequeathed to all by ignored or forgotten theological ances-
tors, gifts waiting to be opened.

The Church's global condition. "The Church seems to avoid,
when the chips are down, both the challenge of utopian communities and the chaos of anarchy." The Church has never tried to perfect the world, or the people in it, nor does it claim to possess any
such recipe; rather, it presents to the existing political and economic order the need for and possibility of another system based
on the needs of the individual human soul. "There is a quality of
accepting the world as it is, and people as they are, and working to
make the best of both." Is there another church whose clergy still
suffer and die, as priests and nuns do in Latin America and Africa,
for the poor?

Marian theology—"until it got extreme with Pius IX." C.G. Jung
claimed that the declaration of the dogma of the Assumption of
the Blessed Mother—a papal declaration that many Catholics still
have difficulty swallowing—was the most significant event in
Christianity since the Crucifixion. In Jung's view, it elevated the
feminine principle to the godhead and completed the quartite
nature of the Trinity. "Catholic Marian theology," said Jung, "has
always tried to find the feminine face of God."

It has been trivialized and used for political purposes, Padovano
pointed out. "In all her apparitions, Mary always seems to show up
at those times when she is needed for political purposes. Lourdes,
when Piux IX was pushing the idea of The Immaculate Conception. Fatima, at a time of fear of Communism. At these appearances, did Mary ever say anything that was worth the trip?"

Yet Marian theology, as an expression of feminine consciousness within the Church, continues to act against the formal
institution.

Agony in the Garden

The university system was created by Catholics on the basis of free inquiry and open research. The university was an attempt to apply the ideals of the monastery to the secular world. Without the universities, and before them, the monasteries, there would have been no Western intellectual tradition.

The emphasis on social justice. "Catholics," according to Padovano, "are brilliant at this." Pastoral letters issued by the American bishops. Encyclicals like *Rerum Novarum*, on the social order and the rights of labor, *Mit brennender Sorge*, against the Nazi regime in Germany, and John XXIII's *Mater et Magistra*, which made current the Church's teaching on social matters. The Church, when it wants to be, is in touch: the machinery for saying what needs to be said is in place.

The development of spiritual theology. The Catholic Church is the source of the most brilliant spiritual theology Christianity has seen. Augustine, Aquinas, Cardinal Newman, including women: Hildegard, Catherine of Siena, Claire. "It is," concluded Padovano, "a brilliant theological system, and options.

"At its best moments, the creativity of the Church was absolutely breathtaking. The question is, *what went wrong?*"

The development of an imperial papacy, maintained Padovano, is the primary thing that went wrong. "The Pope as emperor" is a system "excluding as it now does, all bishops, priests, nuns and laity. Nobody is anything. All of us are equally insignificant, a Church of a billion nobodies—how did we get from the New Testament to that?"

Everyone is seen as an extension of the papal monarchy. "Cardinal Newman said that nobody should be pope for more than twenty years, because they become cruel. What happens when the pope is, in essence, no longer part of the Church, excluded from all the Church's checks and balances?"

Padovano identified the supremacy of canon law as another

wrong turn. "Law has become the center of pastoral ministry. Has anyone ever heard of a pastor being fired for being lousy with people? You only get fired if you break the law." And law has dislodged the spirit of Christ at the center of the Church. "Canon 333," said Padovano, "says that neither recourse nor appeal is allowed to any Christian on the decision of the Roman Pontiff: There is no appeal to the Church at large." This is how far things have come from first-century Christianity, when the people, in community and later in council, decided everything.

The development of bishops and priests into a hierarchical order was, according to Padovano, another unfortunate change of course. "Bishops and pastors have no accountability to the laity unless they choose to. They don't have to listen to parish councils."

In the Diocese of Santa Rosa, this shirking of accountability to a degree unacceptable in any business inflicted terrible financial wounds and maimed the diocese's parishes and schools for a generation. "The culture dismisses the experience of lay Christians. Sexual ethics are decided by people who are supposedly not engaged in sexual experience." Like the old Groucho Marx gag, "Who are you going to believe, me or your own eyes?" people are expected to accept rules that are in conflict with their own knowledge of life.

"The Church," said Padovano, "says that holiness lies with order, not spirit." But there is still the matter of individual conscience. "If our experience shows us that women are equal to men, then that's it."

"The Church cannot canonize Cardinal Newman, because he was honest. Instead of some of the silly people we have canonized as saints, I would like to see us canonize five honest plumbers, a dozen kind cab drivers, half a dozen women who've raised families. Francis of Assisi was canonized almost immediately after his death. Why are we going to canonize Pius IX, when Bishop Oscar Romero of El Salvador is a saint? He gave his blood at the altar."

Agony in the Garden

Mandatory celibacy is and has been a disaster for the Church. "Celibacy is beautiful, which is why it doesn't have to be mandated. It should be allowed to develop naturally."

If celibacy really is a more effective way of life in terms of altruism, effectiveness in the ministry, and service to humanity, then celibates should rise anyway to positions of leadership in a mixed married and celibate church. The ancient abuses of simony and lay investiture don't seem particularly threatening in the modern world. Though in 1999, the People's Republic of China appointed five Roman Catholic bishops (where did they find them, in jail?), in what seems to have been a political arrangement accepted by the Vatican, other faiths—the Protestant churches, the Orthodox Church, Judaism—do not seem to suffer from religious property being bequeathed within families, or the state interfering in nomination to high religious office. Surely the downside—continuing instances of priest sexual abuse, and with them Church involvement in cover-ups—at least justifies opening the subject of mandatory celibacy to discussion.

"Celibacy," Padovano pointed out, "shouldn't have been linked to order, making people hang on to it as part of clinging to authority, power."

Divorce and remarriage. The Church used to allow it. The idea of restricting it was not to make it too easy. The mistake was in making marriage a contract rather than a relationship. The drastic punishment remains for those who divorce and remarry: no Eucharist, no employment in the Church. "Instead, we give annulments. The Church plays sexual games. Marriage is a commitment of one human being to another, for as far as you can see."

The Church's preoccupation with sexual concerns, Padovano maintained, represents yet another wrong turn. "Birth control. Masturbation a serious sin. In this system, sexuality achieves a gravity which Jesus never gave it." It gets associated with rules, prohibitions, dissociated from dignity, love, feeling. "A healthy sexual life would be there, if we allowed it."

The treatment of women was not just a wrong turn, said Padovano, but a tremendous and missed opportunity. "The Church was brilliantly poised to move in the direction of women. There were women saints and martyrs, women mystics. They lost it when it appeared that women, if granted full rights, might gain authority over men." The all-male hierarchy, feeling itself threatened, chickened out.

There is a continuing problem with the magisterium, the Church's teaching power or function. Because it is top-down, dictatorial, not open to colloquy, it endows official teaching with an authority it doesn't have. Galileo. Birth control. The ordination of women. Married priests. Issues are closed to discussion—this is not the attitude of a confident, truth-seeking, reflective body. Even priests who support change qualify their support for it: "Not under this Pope," "Not for another century." Instead of open inquiry, there is a sense of stalling, of bureaucratic delay in the interest of postponing the inevitable.

Considering this enormous inertia, the ingrained habits of institutional closed-mindedness, and obstinate clinging to power and authority, what are the realistic prospects for the future of the Catholic Church? Could it become a kind of rump-religion, an exercise in nostalgia, with people enjoying Gregorian chants and cathedral architecture at the purely esthetic distance we apply to Shaker furniture?

Padovano thought otherwise. "I think the future is bright. Collegiality and inclusivity is the way of the world at large. Teilhard de Chardin was silenced, and he shut up. Now, no one stops speaking and writing. Hans Kung. Charles Curran. People sense that the right to speak out comes from the teachings of Jesus, not from the Pope.

Agony in the Garden

"The Church cannot function in the world with the rigid system we have. There is a sense in the Church at large that we cannot go on this way any more.

"There is a sense among Catholics that conscience is central.

"The Church is reliable. They never lost the gospel, never lost the sacraments; priests still preach the parables, instructing with examples that touch us all as humans. There is, at base, a profound sense of toleration." The idea that we are all in this together, of the tragic sense of life that rescues us from trivia. "There is a deep hunger for good priests and good preaching. The Church still honors and values good priests.

"There is a growing resistance to flamboyant and autocratic leaders. A silent resentment among Catholics against leaders they do not deserve.

"If the word of God is in you, nothing is lost. Once this Church had the word of God, and nothing else. With the word of God alone, it prevailed. We have the word of God. Why do we keep thinking we need anything else?"

On a dark December evening, the Church of Our Lady of Guadalupe was radiant with light. A stream of people flowed through the front entrance and the vestibule, filled the pews, and spilled over to the standing room along the sides and at the back. Before the altar, a chamber orchestra tinkered, tuning up; behind it, in three robed ranks, stood the men and women of the Sonoma County Bach Choir; to the sides of the orchestra, sat the smaller, in individual size and overall number, members of the Santa Rosa Children's Chorus. In a setting brisk with anticipation, Bach's *Christmas Oratorio* was about to be performed in a setting both similar to and different from that of its original performance.

The music began, jubilant, intricate, soaring, filling this modest church as Bach's music had the church in Leipzig where it was originally performed in 1734. A work of art as an act of faith, singers and players alive in great music as they had been more than two and a half centuries earlier.

Before the changes of Vatican II, Bach's music could not be played inside a Catholic Church: he was a Lutheran. Now, here,

Agony in the Garden

beneath the figure of Jesus splayed on the cross, surrounded by stained-glass windows, flickering devotional candles, an enshrined portrait of Our Lady with her womblike nimbus, Bach's clean, austere notes seemed complemented and fulfilled, head and heart rising together, with nothing held back. The church was bursting with unspoken reconciliation: Bach's Lutheran music joined with Catholic pageantry; the fleeced and lied-to people of the diocese hearing and feeling the power of an earlier, exulting Christianity; the sense of a gathering from the scattered corners of this sprawling diocese, pulled here at last for a positive purpose.

There were people in the pews rubbernecking at the stained-glass windows, the Christmas decorations, the candles, the robes, the gleaming instruments, and the faces of the choir. Others were tapping their feet, cheering the soloists like ballplayers. A few people were following Bach's music from scores or reciting the lyrics *en deutsche*. In its combination of people of differing ideas, tastes, and intellect, for one unifying purpose, the crowd was the Church made manifest. The idea that there is room for everybody, sharing a common hunger for a spiritual experience, combined with the essence of great art, that it is available at different levels.

With the demise of the Soviet Union, there has arisen in this country a triumphal worship of the market, in all its aspects, that means death to the human soul. Believers in money insist that theirs is the only reality, maintaining that adherence to other values represents either naivete or hypocrisy. The language, suggesting that the matter is closed—bottom line, real-world—is a dead giveaway: they are unwilling to be open to question, and at the same time laboring to convince themselves that half of life is all of it. The message is so insistent and pervasive it is intuitively obvious even to ecclesiastical authorities.

On January 1, 1999, Pope John Paul II, in his annual World Peace Day message, delivered, in the midst of the longest sustained economic boom in American history, a denunciation of "materialist consumerism" as an ideology in which the "exaltation of the individual and the selfish satisfaction of personal aspirations become the ultimate goal of life" creating a world view in which "the negative aspects on others are considered completely irrelevant."

Coming as it did from what many people would consider the center of established authority, the pope's message had a combined truth-telling shock and bracing effect like Dwight Eisenhower's parting message to the American people, warning them against the dangers of the military-industrial complex. Only the pope wasn't going anywhere. In a life with more than its share of principled stands, this would be one of the most memorable.

The history of the twentieth century, the Pope stated, had shown the tragic danger that results from forgetting the truth about the human person. "Before our eyes we have the results of ideologies such as Marxism, Nazism and fascism, and also of myths like racial superiority and ethnic exclusivism.

"No less pernicious, though not always as obvious," he emphasized, "are the effects of materialist consumerism."

In an obvious dig at the World Trade Organization, about to hold its protested international meeting in Seattle, Pope John Paul insisted that "nations and people have the right to share in the decisions which often profoundly modify their way of life.

"Who is responsible," he asked, "for guaranteeing the global common good and the exercise of economic and social rights? The free market cannot do this because in fact there are many human needs which have no place in the market."

"The technical details of certain economic problems give rise to the tendency to restrict discussions about them to limited circles, with the consequent danger that political and financial power is concentrated in a small number of governments and special interest groups."

As the Pope spoke these words, a monsignor in the Diocese of

Agony in the Garden

Santa Rosa was trying to make a killing in offshore investments, putting diocesan money at risk in a desperate scramble to recover secret losses. And a bishop was about to break off settlement negotiations with a priest who was his former sexual partner. They were part of the hierarchy of the same Church, which nevertheless held within it the power to restore equilibrium.

"The effects of recent economic and financial crises," the Pope continued, "have had heavy consequences for countless people, reduced to conditions of extreme poverty. Many of them had only just reached a position that allowed them to look forward to the future with optimism."

"Through no faults of their own," he continued, "they have seen these hopes cruelly dashed, with tragic results for themselves and their children. And how can we ignore the effects of fluctuations in the financial markets? We urgently need a new vision of global progress in solidarity, which will include an overall and sustainable development of society."

The simple truth is that, at the big moments—falling in love, being fired, having a lab test come back positive, someone we love dying—the money system fails us. It leaves us bereft. It is then that we need the solace of the combination of meditation, connection with the infinite, and restoration to community that can be found in religious faith. Elements of it are available elsewhere, but formal faith gives us the means to oppose the seductive and ultimately despairing message of the money world at all its levels: reason, myth, symbol, the shared sense of a common journey, of participation in a moral drama beyond the economy.

"All citizens have the right to participate in the life of their community," said the pope. "But this right means nothing when the democratic system breaks down because of corruption and favoritism. All human beings, without exception, are equal in dignity. Consequently no one can legitimately deprive another person, no matter who they may be, of these rights."

Nobody else, in any comparable position, was saying these things. And they have been reiterated and expanded upon over time. Is this not part of the unconscious body of theology, referred to by Anthony Padovano, that brings the Church back, just when you think it's finished?

In a series of surveys of American Catholic laity, funded by *The National Catholic Reporter*, the Louisville Institute, and various private individuals, the Gallup organization was able to identify certain long-term trends in Catholic identity. The surveys, taken in 1987, 1993, and 1999, represent a national sample of the American Catholic population, each survey based on 800 or more interviews, with a margin of error of plus or minus four percent. The studies indicate significant changes in the definition of what it means to be a Catholic.

Laypeople, the data suggests, were less attached to the Church in 1999 than they were in 1987. By 1999, only thirty-seven percent of surveyed Catholics attended Mass on a weekly basis. Seventy-one percent maintained it was possible to be a good Catholic without obeying the church's teaching on birth control. The number saying one can be a good Catholic without obeying the church's teaching regarding divorce and remarriage rose from fifty-one percent in 1987 to sixty-four percent in 1999. Those saying it was possible to be a good Catholic without obeying the Church's teaching on abortion climbed from thirty-nine percent to fifty-three percent. A majority of Catholics said they intended to stay in the Church even though they disagreed with these teachings.

"It's not that they are increasingly angry at the Church," *The National Catholic Reporter* interpreted the survey. "Rather, as more and more Catholics make up their own minds about what it means to be Catholic, they seem increasingly indifferent to the institutional Church."

At the same time, there were what appeared to be opposing

trends toward more personal autonomy regarding rules of sexual conduct and toward a desire for more lay participation in the institutional Church's decision-making processes.

Three-fourths of the Catholics surveyed thought that the laity should be involved in selecting priests for their parishes and in decisions about ordaining women. Seventy-one percent said it would be a good thing if married men were allowed to be ordained as priests; seventy-eight percent agreed it would be good if priests who have married were returned to active ministry.

"Even as lay people are distancing themselves from the institutional Church as the absolute source of moral guidance," concludes *The National Catholic Reporter*, "they appear to embrace the People of God idea that emerged from Vatican II.

"In this reading, the whole Church—not just the hierarchy—are the people of God, and Church teachings should reflect this reality."

If, as the pope says, all citizens have the right to participate in the life of their community, doesn't that community—and that right—include the Church?

The Gallup survey indicates that there is, among American Catholics, no going back to a rigid, authoritarian Church. The change is one of conscience, within individuals. Mandates and coercion won't work. There is for strict, top-down, hierarchical authority, no *sensus fidelium*. Trying to browbeat people into letting what is essentially a group of old Italian men do their moral thinking is only going to produce greater emptiness in the pews and a further shrinking of vocations. Is it not possible that the answers to the church's problems lie, where they did originally, among ordinary people who are familiar with the world and ready to apply their knowledge of life-as-lived to the greater spiritual benefit of all?

The institutional Church and the pastoral Church need one another. Who else can speak, as the pope has done, to the world on the perniciousness of money worship and be taken seriously? Who can better apply moral leverage in behalf of the cause of reform in Latin America? Who else can address world political figures without being accused of having a political agenda of his own?

"I loved being a priest," says a man I have known since first grade, at one time a California diocesan administrator. "I'd return to the priesthood in a minute if the Pope ever came to his senses and allowed priests to marry." Must priests who have married and women who wish to be ordained be viewed as nonpersons, liabilities, even threats to the Church? Are they not buried assets, like the scholars and mystics, people like Meister Eckhart and Juliana of Norwich, waiting to be rediscovered and reapplied by the evolving consciousness of a changing, renewable faith?

This is the moral quandary of the contemporary Catholic Church: that the changes demanded by an overwhelming majority of the laity, and, in increasing numbers, the clergy, are not possible without the death of a Pope whom, in many ways, they admire.

The *Oratorio* has ended; Bach's notes linger in the air. The size of the departing orchestra and chorus almost equals that of the audience: nobody can be making money from this. Yet here it is. Perhaps some of this music will remain in the atmosphere, descending on the parishioners, prompting them on Sunday to sing better. The crowd, riding the occasion, heads up the aisle and into the night, borne by a shared sense of spiritual replenishment. It can't be sustained, the world wears it away, but it can be renewed, here, through the gospel, the Eucharist, the pilgrim sense of a shared spiritual journey, in the resounding echo of two millennia of human hope.

Tod, Teufel, Sund und Holle	Death, devil, sin and hell
Sind ganz und gar geschwacht;	are quite diminished;
Bei Gott hat seine Stelle	the human race has its place
Das menschliche Geschlecht.	At God's side.

Chapter Notes

Introduction

xiii *In a Sunday homily to his congregation . . .*, "Praying for courage to name the pain," *National Catholic Reporter*, April 5, 2002.

Prologue

xv *My old friend Lucky . . .* Not his real name. Or nickname.

xvi *Kevin Dugan . . .* Not his real name.

xvi *Nicholas Topfer . . .* Not *his* real name, either.

Chapter 1

2 *The only problem was that some of this money—along with money from other parish collections—was disappearing . . .* Interview with Chief Fred Keplinger, November 22, 1999.

2 *The thefts went back months and months, and a member of the church staff was suspected . . .* Ibid.

3 *Hume Salas had been ordained without graduating from a seminary, after serving 15 months as a deacon . . .* Sister Jane Kelly, interview, October 27, 1999.

3 *Guzman found that Hume was removing bank bags from the safe, breaking a seal, and removing cash . . .* "Ukiah priest's misconduct

kept under wraps by SR's Ziemann. Accused of theft, sexual abuse." *Santa Rosa Press Democrat*, January 22, 1999 p. 1.

3　*The identified missing money amounted to some $1,200, though the total thefts were later estimated as high as $10,000* . . . Sister Jane Kelly, interview.

4　*Detective Guzman was ready to make an arrest that night. But Bishop Ziemann called Father Hans, the pastor, and asked him to intervene* . . . Chief Fred Keplinger, interview.

4　*In the meeting, the bishop was very demanding. "This is the way it's going to be"* . . . Ibid.

5　*The only time I ever allowed my religion to get in the way of my job* . . . Ibid.

5　*There was no precedent for the training of a nonseminary student* . . . Sister Jane Kelly, interview.

6　*The ministry is job security* . . . *Anything that alters it, threatens it* . . . Ibid.

6　*Sister Jane has been active in social causes in this county for years* . . . Fred Keplinger, interview.

7　*There was a big growth in the Latino population and few Mexican clergy* . . . Monsignor John O'Hare, interview, Sept. 13, 1999.

7　*It was in July of 1992, only days after Ziemann's appointment to the Santa Rosa Diocese, that Jorge Raul Hume Salas wrote his letter of introduction to the new bishop* . . . "Hume's road to ordination: Booted by three seminaries," *Santa Rosa Press Democrat*, September 19, 1999.

8　*I believe he is an unsophisticated person, Ochoa wrote* . . . Ibid.

8　*Shortly before Jorge's ordination, Bishop Ziemann came to the parish in Ukiah* . . . Sister Jane Kelly, interview.

9　*The avoidance of scandal . . . is the primary goal when the sexual activity of a priest comes to the attention of authority* . . . A.W. Richard Sipe, *The Sipe Report*, no. 18, www.thelinkup.com

9　*At St. Mary of the Angels things reached their nadir when a county judge* . . . Sister Jane Kelly, interview.

Chapter 2

12   *Oakland, California, where Jane Kelly was born in 1931 . . .*
"Hellraiser . . . Meet the feisty nun who rocked the Diocese of
Santa Rosa," *Sonoma County Independent*, September 9–15,
1999.

14   *Hume Salas was notified by Bishop Ziemann that he was being sent
to St. Michael's Community in St. Louis . . .* Santa Rosa Police
Dept. *Crime/Case Report #99-10694*, p. 3.

14   *On June 27, 1996, according to Jorge Hume Salas . . .* Ibid., p. 5.

14   *Salas then said that Ziemann embraced him and began to caress his
face . . .* Ibid., pp. 5–6.

15   *Afterward, Salas asked Zieman why he had done what he had done
. . .* Ibid., p. 6.

15   *Bishop . . . I believe that Jorge is a pathological liar . . .* Letter, Sister
Jane Kelly to Bishop Ziemann, August 2, 1996.

16   *Bishop Ziemann made regular calls to the secretary at St. Michael's
. . .* Santa Rosa Police Dept. *Crime/Case Report*, p. 6.

16   *Once they were in Ziemann's room, the bishop asked Salas how
things were going . . .* Ibid., p. 7.

17   *After the meal . . . [Ziemann] took $80 from his wallet and slipped
it into Salas's pants pocket . . .* Ibid., p. 7.

17   *The following day, Bishop Ziemann arrived at St. Michael's early
for the evaluation . . .* Ibid., p. 8.

18   *While he was living in this apartment . . . Hume Salas continued
to be asked by Ziemann for sexual favors . . .* Ibid., p. 9.

18   *Ziemann told him, said Salas, that the bishop was the only friend
Salas had . . .* Ibid., p. 10.

19   *In January of 1997, Hume Salas called Gloria Enguidanos . . .*
Ibid., p. 16.

20   *She was concerned that he might do away with himself . . .* Ibid., p. 17.

20   *If we truly love . . . we do not ever want to treat another person as
a 'thing,' . . .* Wilhelm, Anthony *Christ Among Us*, p. 296.

20   *Dr. Judin also felt that, based on the serious nature of the allegations*

CHAPTER NOTES

. . . Santa Rosa Police Dept. *Crime/Case Report #99-10694*, supplement, p. l of 24.

Chapter 3

21 *Ziemann injected a spirit of dynamism, a possibility of positive change within the existing structure* . . . "Mass Appeal," *Santa Rosa Press Democrat*, October 12, 1997.

22 *Because I've seen it delegated by other bishops and that has not healed* . . . Ibid.

22 *In what had been the North Coast Counties' religious scandal of the decade* . . . "Catholics ponder impact of Timmons," *Santa Rosa Press Democrat*, September 8, 1996.

22 *He was, in many ways, the best of the four bishops we've had here* . . . Monsignor John O'Hare, interview.

22 *I was teaching an English as a Second Language course* . . . Mary Shea, interview, January 6, 2000.

25 *A graduate of Santa Clara University in Northern California, with a law degree from Georgetown* . . . *Judicial Profiles of the Superior Court of Los Angeles County*, Los Angeles Historical Society.

25 *George Patrick Ziemann's maternal grandfather, Joseph Scott, was* . . . "Poor Immigrant became 'Mr. L.A.'" *Los Angeles Times*, November 28, 1999, p. B3.

28 *In 1933, Joseph Breen, public relations man for the Hays Office* . . . *retained Joseph Scott to speak on behalf of the Catholic bishops* . . . Lynn, Kenneth S., *Charlie Chaplin and His Times*, pp. 364–365.

28 *Accusing his audience of being "disloyal" Americans* . . . Ibid., p. 364.

28 *Zukor, the president of Paramount Pictures and the dean of the industry* . . . Ibid., p. 365.

30 *In 1944, Joseph Scott was once again retained to aim his heavy courtroom artillery in the direction of the movie industry* . . . Ibid., p. 438, *Los Angeles Times*, "Poor Immigrant became Mr. L.A."

31 *The year after Scott's death, his 18-year-old grandson* . . . "Most

Reverent G. Patrick Ziemann, Bishop of Santa Rosa, California."
www.santarosacatholic.org/Ziemann

Chapter 4

33 *When George Patrick Ziemann entered the seminary, he would have found himself in a world* . . . Sipe, A. W. Richard, *A Secret World: Sexuality and the Search for Celibacy,* pp. 51–54.

34 *Celibacy, it was assumed, freed a select number of men from intimate personal attachments* . . . Ibid., p. 62.

34 *The Church . . . confusedly adopted an uneasy coexistence . . .* Johnson, Paul *A History of Christianity,* p. 108.

34 *Peter . . . is believed to have had a wife and two children . . .* Sipe, *A Secret World,* p. 37, Schillebeeckx, *Celibacy.*

34 *And in fact, three later popes were the sons of previous popes . . .* Sipe, *A Secret World,* pp. 38–39.

35 *His thinking . . . maintained that all sexual activity except that within marriage . . .* Johnson, pp. 511–512.

35 *Saint Jerome . . . claimed to have been tempted by visions of dancing girls . . .* Sipe, *A Secret World,* pp. 206–207.

35 *Saint Paul . . . is believed to have been . . . a 40-year-old widower . . .* Ibid., pp. 36–37.

35 *By the late Middle Ages, the power and wealth accumulated by the Church had intensified the differences . . .* Ibid., p. 42.

36 *Finally, in 1139, the Second Lateran Council . . . declared all marriages of priests to be null and void . . .* Ibid., p. 44.

36 *More than a century later, the Synod of Bremen . . .* Ibid., pp. 44–45.

37 *Both . . . concerned sex . . . both tended to divide Catholics from other Christian Churches . . .* Johnson, p. 511.

38 *Introduced in 1960, the oral contraceptive pill was believed by its discoverer . . .* Sipe, *A Secret World,* p. 26.

38 *Between 1966 and 1984 . . . the number of diocesan priests in the United States dropped by 20 percent . . .* Unsworth, Tim, *The Last Priests in America,* p. xi.

Chapter Notes

39 *There was also, within Church tradition, the sensus fidelium . . .* Sipe, *A Secret World*, p. 289.

40 *As a priest, it was in some ways easier to enter into a relationship with a man . . .* Unsworth, p. 259.

41 *Successful celibacy, says Sipe, involves a dynamic . . .* Sipe, *A Secret World*, pp. 58–65.

41 *According to Sipe's estimate, half of ordained priests are practicing celibacy . . .* Sipe, *Sex, Priests and Power, The Anatomy of a Crisis*, pp. 68–69.

42 *In 1994, a former student at Our Lady Queen of the Angels Seminary . . .* "Catholic secrecy questioned as roll of priestly problems grows," *Santa Rosa Press Democrat*, August 22, 1999.

44 *Los Angeles Times, based on what must have been inside information . . .* Mike Gienella, *Santa Rosa Press Democrat*, interview, November 18, 1999.

45 *In late May of 1992, officers from the Los Angeles Police Department . . .* "A Church's Cross to Bear," *Los Angeles Times*, Ventura County Edition, August 9, 1992, p. B1.

46 *There was and still is concern among Ventura County and LAPD law enforcement investigators . . .* "Church refuses to press charges," *Los Angeles Times*, Ventura County Edition, July 8, 1992, p. B1; "Simi Valley Priest appears in court," *Los Angeles Times*, September 10, 1992, p. B3.

46 *The Cardinal, now Roger Mahony, stated how much Ziemann would be missed . . .* "Countywide: Ziemann named Santa Rosa Bishop," *Los Angeles Times*, July 15, 1992, p. B3.

Chapter 5

50 *The first bishop, Leo Maher, was a mogul . . .* Monsignor John O'Hare, interview.

51 *He did a Confirmation here in Boyes Springs one Sunday at eleven . . .* Ibid.

51 *He's the most accessible, hands-on bishop . . .* "Mass Appeal," *Santa Rosa Press Democrat,* October 12, 1997.

51 *He's a people's bishop.* Ibid.

52 *We have a weak bench, and here comes Jerry Rice . . .* Monsignor John O'Hare, interview.

52 *In 1992, Donald Hoard, a man in his thirties . . .* Interview, Don Hoard, Sr. May 5, 2000.

53 *His camp was a smorgasbord. The counselors did nothing to stop it. . . .* Ibid.

53 *In the course of the prosecution's case against Timmons, Judge Gallagher learned that the diocese's first bishop had destroyed . . .* "Timmons case leaves Judge feeling betrayed, haunted," *Santa Rosa Press Democrat,* September 8, 1996.

54 *Patrick McBride . . . too had a history of priestly sexual abuse . . .* Don Hoard, interview.

55 *This is a time of tremendous change, and I don't see the institutional Church helping the process too much . . .* "Depression, Fear Gripped Rev. Rogers; Church full for Eureka funeral." *Santa Rosa Press Democrat,* November 23, 1995.

55 *When I was ordained in 1959 . . .* A.W. Richard Sipe, *The Sipe Report,* #18, 19, www.thelinkup.com

56 *As early as 1949, the Catholic Church had opened a center . . . for the care of problem priests.* Ibid., #38, 48.

56 *Victims consistently report that they were seen as traitors and disloyal to their church . . .* Ibid., #57.

56 *An archbishop stated that . . .* Ibid., #58.

57 *In 1996, Timmons was convicted of felony child molestation . . .* "Catholics Ponder Impact of Timmons," *Santa Rosa Press Democrat,* September 8, 1996.

57 *As far as I can tell . . .* Ibid.

58 *Ziemann, in November of 1995, invited the men who had been molested . . . to a reconciliation ceremony . . .* "Mass Appeal," *Santa Rosa Press Democrat,* October 12, 1997.

59   *He spoke about reaching out, forgive and forget* . . . Ibid.

59   *I had a feeling of evil from this guy.* Don Hoard, Interview.

Chapter 6

62   *Originally conceived as a desperation measure for a struggling parish* . . . "Catholic Funding Arm Has Become a Big—and Controversial—Business" . . . *The Wall Street Journal/California*, March 17, 1999.

62   *Using $25,000 seed money supplied by the diocese* . . . Ibid.

62   *The way it works is that the Scrip Center buys scrip* . . . "SR Scrip Center Director Steps Aside" . . . *Santa Rosa Press Democrat*, Sept. 30, 1999.

63   *As of the end of 1999, the Scrip Center was doing $450 million worth of business a year* . . . Ibid.

63   *The most consistent leadership presence* . . . *in the diocese for more than 30 years.* "Once-visible Keys is now out of sight." . . . *Santa Rosa Press Democrat*, February 5, 2000.

63   *Recruited, following his ordination in Carlo, Ireland* . . . *The Wall Street Journal/California*, March 17, 1999.

64   *He became Bishop Hurley's secretary and returned with the bishop to Ireland* . . . Hurley, *Blood on the Shamrock*, p. 30.

64   *It was while Keys was a member of the USF MBA Program that he first learned of the Consolidated Account* . . . Santa Rosa Police Dept. *Crime/Case Report #99-19262*, p. 7.

64   *Each participant in the Consolidated Account would have checks printed* . . . Ibid., p. 7.

65   *When individual participants abused the Consolidated Account* . . . *it was Keys* . . . Ibid., p. 8.

67   *National Scrip Center* . . . *is my educational ministry,* . . . "Response from National Scrip Center," *The Wall Street Journal/California*, March 24, 1999, p.CA4.

68   *The Catholic Church* . . . *is much more episcopal than most people realize* . . . Monsignor John O'Hare, interview.

69 *Keys replied that in the course of his career, he had blessed* . . . "I'm a Shameless Homer, so What?" *Santa Rosa Press Democrat*, May 4, 1996.

69 *Keys* . . . *placed a hand on Cavonnier and intoned a prayer for the success and safety of the horse* . . . "A horse stops, and you think the worse." *Santa Rosa Press Democrat*, June 9, 1996.

70 *We got it!* "Oh, Soooooo Close: Cavonnier's Prayers Unanswered," Santa Rosa Press Democrat, May 5, 1996.

70 *And this is law, I will maintain/Unto my dying day, sir* . . . *I will be Vicar of Bray, sir!* . . . www.ingeb.org/songs/ingoodki

Chapter 7

71 *During 1997, Jorge Hume Salas made several return visits to his native Costa Rica* . . . Santa Rosa Police Dept. *Crime/Case Report #99-l0694*, p. 10.

71 *The bishop* . . . *would contact the priest and summon him to have sex with him* . . . Ibid., p. 11.

71 *Jorge Hume Salas was born on September 26, 1957* . . . "Hume's Road to Ordination: Booted by Three Seminaries," *Santa Rosa Press Democrat*, September 19, 1999

72 *It was during this time that I felt the call of God to the priesthood* . . . Ibid.

72 *According to Father Carlos Rojas* . . . Santa Rosa Police Dept. *Crime/Case Report #99-10694*, p. 11.

72 *Another Costa Rican priest, Father Ovidio Burgos Acuna, states* . . . Ibid.

73 *In 1983, he left Mexico for Honduras, where, despite his previous impostures* . . . "Hume's Road to Ordination . . . " *Santa Rosa Press Democrat*, September 19, 1999.

73 *After the seminary's director conducted his own investigation* . . . Hume Salas was expelled . . . Ibid.

73 *In a foretaste of Ziemann's covering-up for Hume, the Bishop of Comayagua* . . . Ibid.

74 *The official Universidad Intercontinental transcript . . . differs from a course list . . .* Ibid.

74 *On one of his visits to Costa Rica, Hume Salas identified himself as a Claretian priest . . .* Ibid.

74 *He was expelled after being caught acting as a priest . . .* Ibid.

74 *In 1992, Jorge Hume Salas was expelled yet again . . .* Ibid.

75 *A Santa Rosa police investigator compared Hume's situation with Ziemann . . .* Santa Rosa Police Dept. *Crime/Case Report #99-10694*, p. 14.

75 *In the spring of 1996 . . . Hume had been sent on a retreat to Spain . . .* Ibid., p. 4.

76 *He said that . . . he thought Hume might be intending to commit suicide . . .* Ibid., p. 5.

78 *Sexual maturity . . . is an elusive goal . . .* Sipe, *A Secret World*, p. 136.

78 *These men . . . have severe or at least moderate guilt feelings . . .* Ibid., pp. 136–137.

79 *In the spring of 1997, Ziemann assigned Salas to St. John's church in the city of Napa . . .* Santa Rosa Police Dept. *Crime/Case Report #99-10694*, p. 11.

80 *It was no wonder that this popular bishop . . . was routinely mentioned as a candidate for much larger jobs . . .* "Mass Appeal," *Santa Rosa Press Democrat*, October 12, 1997.

Chapter 8

81 *In at least one instance . . . Church authorities had withheld from the police information concerning his whereabouts . . .* Don Hoard, interview.

82 *The Church opposed it on grounds that it was an intrusion . . .* Ibid.

82 *During the 1980s, Pope John Paul II explicitly forbade them to talk about . . .* Sipe, *Sex, Priests and Power: the Anatomy of a Crisis*, pp. 44–45.

83 *I have to speak out what I feel in my heart* . . . Letter, Sister Jane Kelly to Bishop Ziemann, August 2, 1996.

84 *The issue you raise* . . . *has not come up explicitly* . . . Letter, Monsignor James Gaffey to Sister Kelly, March 29, 1997.

85 *I am utterly astonished* . . . *to hear that Jorge Hume has been assigned to a parish* . . . Sister Jane Kelly to Bishop Ziemann, April 8, 1997.

86 *Mendoza made a tape where the "teenagers talked to the guys."* . . . Santa Rosa Police Dept. *Crime/Case Report #99-10694*, p. 9.

86 *The news that Hume had been reassigned* . . . *left him "totally disgusted with the Catholic Church."* . . . Ibid. p 11.

86 *Kids sitting in his lap in a way that seemed strange* . . . Chief Fred Keplinger, interview.

87 *I had sent three letters to the bishop and made two phone calls to him, and I needed to hear from him* . . . Sister Jane Kelly, interview.

87 *Keys feigned interest. Said he was going to take care of it* . . . Ibid.

87 *The bishop would call the priest at the parish rectory or beep him on his pager* . . . Santa Rosa Police Dept. *Crime/Case Report #99-10694*, p. 11.

87 *I need to see you, Ziemann insisted* . . . Ibid.

87 *On August 22, 1998, Ziemann and Salas met at the Embassy Suites in the city of Napa* . . . Ibid.

88 *Ziemann told Salas that if he was unwilling to return to Costa Rica, then he would need to leave the priesthood* . . . Ibid.

88 *The next day* . . . *Jorge Hume Salas was depressed* . . . Ibid.

89 *According to Hume Salas, during the act of confession he disclosed to three different priests* . . . Ibid.

89 *A few days later, Ziemann summoned Hume Salas once again to his residence. This time Hume had his own agenda* . . . Ibid., p. 12.

90 *Salas* . . . *continued to try to talk Ziemann into allowing him to remain at St. John's* . . . Ibid., p. 13.

90 *Maybe I'll make it up to you, Ziemann said. "It's too late, Bishop," Salas repeated* . . . Ibid., p. 13.

Chapter 9

91 *It was a deliberate construct . . . justified, . . . by Augustine's defi-nition* Sipe, *Sex, Priests and Power*, pp. 112–13.

92 *One can trace . . . the progressive and massive idealization of the image of virgin/mother . . .* Ibid.

93 *It has long been recognized . . . that these verses are an intrusion . . .* Ibid pp. 191–192.

94 *An animal is in the sheepfold. It is attacking the lambs . . .* Sister Jane Kelly, interview.

94 *Every move I made was going nowhere . . .* Ibid.

94 *I'd known Sister Jane for years before she came to me with this . . .* Mike Gienella, interview.

94 *We were wary of opening Pandora's box . . .* Ibid.

95 *For this lady to do what she did . . . is mind-boggling . . .* "Hell-raiser." *Sonoma County Independent*, September 9–15, 1999

95 *Ramon called Mike, and agreed to let his name be used . . .* Sister Jane Kelly, interview.

96 *Ziemann, when I talked to him over the phone, said . . .* Mike Gienella, interview.

97 *As a policeman, . . . you look for patterns . . .* Chief Fred Keplinger, interview.

97 *Everything had to be forced . . .* Mike Gienella, interview.

97 *The fact is, their attorneys had been negotiating with Hume Salas' lawyer for months . . .* "Lawyer Says Priest Tried to Avoid Scandal." *Santa Rosa Press Democrat*, July 28, 1999.

97 *These were the people right under the bishop . . .* Ibid.

98 *The amount was chosen at random, but was deliberately big enough . . .* Ibid.

98 *Thank God Jorge sued for eight million . . .* Sister Jane Kelly, interview.

99 *The Mendocino County District Attorney's Office rejected the police case . . .* "Ex-Ukiah Priest Won't Face Charges," *Santa Rosa Press Democrat*, February 23, 1999.

99   *Ziemann is intelligent, polished, slick* . . . Mike Gienella, interview.

99   *A group of teenagers* . . . *opposed being confirmed by the bishop* . . . "Ukiah Parish, Bishop Begin Making Up," *Santa Rosa Press Democrat,* June 13, 1999.

100 *Secrecy and silence are the tools of corruption and dysfunction* . . . Monsignor John O'Hare, interview.

100 *There are* . . . *three elements to the system of secrecy* . . . Sipe, *Sex, Priests and Power,* pp. 141–142.

101 *Something is terribly wrong with the institution* . . . Unsworth, *The Last Priests in America,* p. 192.

102 *It's a male chauvinistic denial hierarchy* . . . Sister Jane Kelly, interview.

Chapter 10

103 *Santa Rosa Police Detectives Ruben Sanchez and Martha Supernor* . . . *reported to the law offices* . . . Santa Rosa Police Dept. *Crime/Case Report #99-10694,* p. 3.

104 *I noted that there are abusive characteristics found in this case* . . . Ibid., p. 14.

104 *Ziemann had secretly submitted his resignation to the Vatican in April* . . . "Lawyer Says Priest Tried to Avoid Scandal," *Santa Rosa Press Democrat,* July 28, 1999.

105 *On July 16, a lawsuit was filed* . . . *on behalf of Jorge Hume Salas* . . . Ibid

105 BISHOP ZIEMANN QUITS . . . *Santa Rosa Press Democrat,* July 22, 1999.

107 *On July 22, the same morning* . . . *six Santa Rosa Police detectives* . . . Santa Rosa Police Dept. *Crime/Case Report #99-10694.*

107 *The following morning Ziemann responded to the second warrant* . . . Ibid.

108 *Ziemann's personal lawyer released a statement admitting* . . . "Bishop admits sex with priest," *Santa Rosa Press Democrat,* July 23, 1999.

109 *He reminds me of Bill Clinton* . . . Ibid.

110 *Our dependence in the past on Roman Catholic judges and attorneys* . . . *Executive Summary, Part I, The Doyle-Mouton Report* p. 10. www.thelinkup.com

110 *When people call me now with complaints* . . . Chief Fred Keplinger, interview.

111 *These studies* . . . *validated my observation of the emotional health and development* . . . *The Sipe Report*, #23, 24.

111 *A subsequent study* . . . *by Eugene Kennedy* . . . Ibid., #25.

112 *At a crucial stage of his personal development* . . . .*the young seminarian* . . . *Biechler* . . . "A Question of Rights: Celibacy and Pedophilia" *ARCC Light*, http://astro.temple.edu/-arcc/rights7.htm

Chapter 11

113 *She is telling you things that happened in mediation* . . . "Lawyer Says Priest Tried to Avoid Scandal," *Santa Rosa Press Democrat*, July 28,1999.

114 *In Crescent City* . . . *it was recalled* . . . "Catholic Secrecy Questioned as Roll Of Priestly Problems Grows," *Santa Rosa Press Democrat*, August 22, 1999.

114 *In Eureka* . . . *the principal of St. Bernard's* . . . Ibid.

115 *Bishop Ziemann* . . . *is the eighth of his rank or higher* . . . Ibid.

115 *Priests take all these oaths to maintain secrecy* . . . Ibid.

115 *Many priests* . . . *make a complete psychic split* . . . Sipe, *Sex, Priests and Power*, pp. 153–155.

116 *There surely have been gay priests, gay bishops, gay Popes* . . . Rev. Andrew Greeley, interview, *Modern Maturity*, May–June, 1996.

117 *In July of 1999, Sister Jeanine Gramick and Father Robert Nugent* . . . *were permanently barred* . . . "Pair dealt a lifetime ban on ministry to homosexuals," *National Catholic Reporter Online*, July 30, 1999.

118 *In his first address to the people of the diocese* . . . "Archbishop

talks of faith, not misconduct," *Santa Rosa Press Democrat*, August 23, 1999.

118 *In the Greek . . . the word "faith" actually means "trust." . . .* Fox, *Original Blessing*, p. 83.

119 *He didn't really address the main issue of misconduct. Santa Rosa Press Democrat*, August 23, 1999.

119 *On August 25, the Archbishop's office announced Keys' resignation . . .* "Diocese's Finance Officer Out," *Santa Rosa Press Democrat*, August 26, 1999.

120 *When the Archbishop says he needs to see you . . .* Monsignor John Brenkle, interview, January 15, 2000.

121 *On Wednesday, October 13 . . . I met with Kathy Ryan, Principal . . .* Santa Rosa Police Dept. *Crime/Case Report #99-19262.*

122 *Keys directed the school to . . . move all of its funds to the Diocese's Consolidated Account . . .* Ibid.

122 *Thomas Beecher reported . . . that . . . he learned from Monsignor John Brenkle that the balance in both accounts was zero . . .* Ibid.

122 *Don't ask me. I don't know . . .* Ibid.

124 *Keys explained how the Consolidated Account, which he described as his "brainchild" . . .* Ibid.

124 *Keys told the investigators that he reported the bishop's misuse . . . to the Vatican . . .* Ibid.

125 *What recourse does a priest have under these circumstances? . . .* Monsignor John Brenkle, interview.

125 *Ziemann, Keys said, "was very generous with other people's money . . .* Santa Rosa Police Dept. *Crime/Case Report,#99-19262.*

125 *Brenkle remembers it differently . . .* Monsignor John Brenkle, interview.

125 *It was not operating by any system that got him into trouble . . .* Ibid.

Chapter 12

128 *On September 15, Archbishop Levada traveled to Ukiah for a . . .*

meeting . . . "Diocese Debt $15 Million" *Santa Rosa Press Democrat*, September 16, 1999

128   *The diocese . . . was more than $15 million in debt* . . . Ibid.

130   *In early December, a letter was sent to the archbishop* . . . Open *Letter to Archbishop Levada*, December 8, 1999.

131   *There's no means of upward communications* . . . Greeley interview, *Modern Maturity*.

132   *The private investigator turned this information over* . . . Santa Rosa Police Dept. *Crime/Case Report #99-10694.*

132   *In June of 1999 . . . Salas had officiated, as a priest* . . . Ibid.

133   *He is playing to an audience. He knows he is on tape* . . . "Hume captured Ziemann in taped conversation." *Santa Rosa Press Democrat*, October 1, 1999.

133   *It accused the Latino men . . . of conspiring with Ziemann* . . . "Ex-priest claims bishop conspiracy," *Santa Rosa Press Democrat*, October 29, 1999.

133   *How could I be working for the diocese, when nobody* . . . Sister Jane Kelly, interview.

134   *The former finance officer, Monsignor Keys, had resigned* . . . "SR Scrip Center director steps aside," *Santa Rosa Press Democrat*, September 30, 1999.

135   *There has been an intermingling of funds* . . . Monsignor John Brenkle, Town Meeting, Monsignor Becker Center, February 4, 2000.

135   *The Scrip Center . . . is a not-for-profit corporation that is basically owned by nobody* . . . Ibid.

135   *The Scrip Center is on the verge of becoming a cash cow* . . . Ibid.

136   *Traditionally . . . parish priests were supported by benefices* . . . Daly, The Laborer is Worthy of His Hire, A Survey of Priests' Compensation in the Roman Catholic Dioceses of the United States, 1999 ed. p. 1.

137   *The average monthly salary for a priest in the Diocese of Santa Rosa* . . . Ibid., p. 41.

137   *The monthly salary of an enlisted person, rank E-3 . . . Military Pay and Benefits, 2000, Office of the Secretary of Defense.*

138   *When an individual is not sufficiently rewarded . . . National Federation of Priests' Councils, Consultation on Priests' Morale,* 1994.

Chapter 13

139   *The presence of a lawyer always chills certain dialogue . . .* "D.A., Chief blame Bishop," *Santa Rosa Press Democrat,* November 11, 1999.

140   *In a meeting at the Chancery office . . . the detectives were told . . .* Santa Rosa Police Dept. *Crime/Case Report #99-19262* pp.11–13.

140   *A survey . . . confirmed the deep disconnect between the people . . . St. Leo's Diocesan Crisis Survey,* January 8–9, 2000.

141   *The overriding response . . . reveals a mature Catholic population . . .* "Santa Rosa Catholics speak on "crisis, not a crisis of faith." *National Catholic Reporter,* March 10, 2000.

141   *The Chief and the D.A. announced that no criminal charges would be filed against Bishop Ziemann . . .* "D.A., Chief blame Bishop," *Santa Rosa Press Democrat,* November 11, 1999.

142   *Investigators had produced evidence showing probable cause . . .* Ibid.

142   *It would have been a hotly contested issue . . .* Ibid.

142   *I'm convinced that neither party is credible . . .* Ibid.

142   *Let me state that at a minimum, Father Salas was a victim of sexual harassment . . .* Ibid.

143   *There were individuals in the hierarchy . . .* Ibid.

143   *He was warned . . . He ignored those warnings . . .* Ibid.

144   *Unless the Church is in a position to assume an active role . . .* Santa Rosa Police Dept. *Crime/Case Report #99-19262.*

147   *In December, it was revealed that Ziemann . . . had . . . spent some $561,000 . . .* "Bishop spent $561,000 to help victims," *Santa Rosa Press Democrat,* December 7, 1999.

CHAPTER NOTES

147 *In his police interview, Monsignor Keys had told* . . . Santa Rosa Police Dept. *Crime/Case Report #99-19262.*

148 *To help bail itself out of debt, the diocese was considering selling* . . . "Diocese Selling 14-acre Carrillo Site . . . ," *Santa Rosa Press Democrat,* February 17, 2000.

148 *It was revealed that, apparently as a desperation measure, Keys had invested five million dollars* . . . "Scheme costs SR diocese $5 million," *Santa Rosa Press Democrat,* February 2, 2000.

148 *Other dioceses have had financial disasters* . . . *But this one did the deepest damage* . . . Monsignor John Brenkle, interview.

150 *Nuns don't like priests* . . . Rev. Andrew Greeley, interview, *Modern Maturity.*

151 *Equality of women is the single most threatening factor* . . . Sipe, *Sex, Priests and Power,* pp. 101–102.

Chapter 14

153 *On a crisp, dark February evening* . . . Town Meeting, Monsignor Becker Center, St. Eugene's Church, Santa Rosa, February 4, 2000.

159 *The reason we haven't been more forthcoming with information is that we don't know ourselves where some of the money went* . . . Monsignor John Brenkle, interview.

Chapter 15

169 *His refusal was based* . . . "*upon his concern that there may be criminal charges* . . . " "Ziemann Takes Advice, Doesn't Testify," *Santa Rosa Press Democrat,* March 28, 2000.

170 *We weren't interested in apologizing for anti-Semitism or slavery* . . . Sister Barbara Flannery, interview, June 7, 2000.

171 *For our lack of facing the truth regarding abuse by clergy* . . . *The Catholic Voice,* official newspaper of the Oakland Diocese, April, 2000.

171 *Bishop Cummins . . . acknowledged the failure of the Church . . .* Ibid.

171 *Many dioceses in the United States took no decisive action . . .* Ibid.

171 *Some individuals . . . chose not to come to the front of the room to tell their stories . . .* Ibid.

172 *We protected our colleagues . . .* Ibid.

172 *We didn't worry about attorneys. What attorneys say didn't count . . .* Sister Barbara Flannery, interview.

172 *On April 9, 2000, Bishop Ziemann made his first public statement in nine months . . .* "Ziemann Asks for Forgiveness," *Santa Rosa Press Democrat,* April 9, 2000.

174 *The release of Ziemann's letter was timed to coincide with the naming of his successor. . . .* "Vegas Bishop to lead Santa Rosa Diocese," *Santa Rosa Press Democrat,* April 12, 2000.

176 *On April 25, the diocese announced that a settlement had been reached . . .* "Hume to get $535,000 in settlement with SR Diocese," *Santa Rosa Press Democrat,* April 25, 2000.

176 *This is outrageous . . .* Ibid.

176 *For the first time in my life, I am ashamed to be a Catholic . . .* e-mail, Mary Shea to author, April 26, 2000.

177 *None of his clients had received as much as Hume Salas had . . . Santa Rosa Press Democrat,* April 25, 2000.

178 *Amazing as it may seem, there is virtually little that can be done . . .* "Hume may always remain a priest, despite lay protests," *Santa Rosa Press Democrat,* April 27, 2000.

178 *According to the 1996 Report on Examination submitted to the State of Vermont . . .* Don Hoard, e-mail to *Santa Rosa Press Democrat* forum, July 11, 2000.

Chapter 16

180 *In recent months . . . Keys has been unavailable for comment . . .* "Once-visible Keys is now out of sight," *Santa Rosa Press Democrat,* February 5, 2000.

CHAPTER NOTES

181 *I first met Tom Keys in 1991* . . . Interview, Bob Coyle, Sr. and Bob Coyle, Jr., July 20, 2000.

182 *You guys are saviors* . . . Ibid.

182 *We were going to do a joint venture* . . . Ibid.

182 *My brother John and I decided the hell with them* . . . Ibid.

183 *I payrolled them for a few months* . . . *The Wall Street Journal/California,* March 17, 1999.

183 *We found out later* . . . *Keys had hired five guys* . . . Bob Coyle, interview.

183 *Tom Keys had a little group of people set up who didn't know one another* . . . Interview with Bob Curry, July 24, 2000.

184 *The way Keys worked, he was continually stalling* . . . Ibid.

184 *I said everybody should meet and discuss the whole problem* . . . Ibid.

184 *He sat on it, because Keys told him to* . . . Ibid.

184 *In the arbitration, Keys basically lied* . . . Ibid.

185 *When they bought the assets* . . . *Ziemann signed a promissory note* . . . Bob Coyle, interview.

185 *National Scrip rejected a $100,000 offer* . . . *The Wall Street Journal/California,* March 17, 2000.

185 *He walks into the building like an eighty-year-old priest* . . . Bob Coyle, interview.

185 *Keys lied his ass off. They threw what he said out* . . . Ibid.

186 *Where financial questions were concerned* . . . Interview with Father Ray Decker, August 28, 2000.

186 *Ziemann relied on Keys to do all his fiscal stuff* . . . Bob Coyle, interview.

187 *Ziemann told me,* . . . *"I don't know anything about finance."* . . . Bob Curry, interview.

187 *Normally* . . . *Zieman just sat there in a stupor* . . . Bob Coyle, interview.

187 *Ziemann was an immature man* . . . *He spent no time in the office,* Ray Decker, interview.

187 *Keys would have known everything about Ziemann's sexual practices* . . . Bob Coyle, interview.

Chapter 17

189 *I first met Tom Keys at a computer conference* . . . Interview, Carey Daly, November 16, 2000.

189 *It was like he was an ex-priest who was still wearing the uniform* . . . Ibid.

190 *I gave him a tool to do some things that I'm not so happy about* . . . Ibid.

190 *At this conference* . . . *He got up and explained to the audience how he had written the software* . . . Ibid.

190 *Keys challenged my copyright* . . . Ibid.

190 *I lost it. I got into a shouting match with Keys* . . . Ibid.

191 *I knew how bank clearing worked, how documents were processed* . . . Ibid.

191 *And Keys was the Diocese, financially* . . . Ibid.

192 *Keys said to me, "Tell me how I can use the overnight balances to leverage into the money market"* . . . Ibid.

192 *Instead we devised a concept of dialing in* . . . Ibid.

192 *Keys* . . . *calculated the interest he paid* . . . *on a monthly rate published in The Wall Street Journal,* . . . Ibid.

192 *He was investing at times in private companies, including mine* . . . Ibid.

193 *According to a petition, filed by the Coyle family* . . . *Tribunal of the Roman Rota, An Examination of Rights* . . . submitted by John Edward Coyle and Robert John Coyle, p. 7.

193 *This figure has been confirmed by its source* . . . e-mail to author, Alan R. Kershaw, October 24, 2000; Carey Daly, interview, November 16, 2000.

193 *It was* . . . *on Monday morning, let the fun begin* . . . Carey Daly, interview.

193 *It becomes a slush fund—self-propagating* . . . Ibid.

Chapter Notes

193 *Keys also grasped the concept of the "short month . . . " . . .* Ibid.

194 *He said, "I got a free loan, got it from the Consolidated Account . . . "* Ibid.

194 *Keys hatched it. He was active in it . . .* Ibid.

195 *Self-insurance means you pay it back . . .* Don Hoard, interview.

195 *For a diocese . . . the money will come from parishioners . . .* Ibid.

195 *He is . . . "on a retainer of twelve thousand dollars a month from the Diocese . . . "* Carey Daly, interview.

195 *Keys was bringing folks over from Ireland . . . and paying them under the table . . .* Bob Curry, interview.

195 *I had hired one of Keys' nephews . . . He had no papers . . .* Carey Daly, interview.

196 *A Derry-born priest . . . who has been described as one of the most dynamic and famous . . .* Derry Journal, August 9, 1996.

196 *Tony Culley-Foster went around asking political figures for letters . . .* Carey Daly, interview.

197 *Keys is a sort of Rodney Dangerfield figure . . .* Ibid.

197 *It was always a question of creative accounting . . .* Ibid.

197 *We had an office geared to do card processing and fulfillment . . .* Ibid.

197 *I was involved with it . . . I knew it was not nonprofit . . .* Ibid.

198 *I told Keys I didn't want to be part of something that violated tax laws . . .* Ibid.

198 *You sign it.* Ibid.

198 *I never saw any place as totally locked down . . . The atmosphere was totally paranoid . . .* Ibid.

199 *He stood up and lied to them all . . .* Bob Curry, interview.

199 *Right up to the last moment, they were hoping for a bailout . . .* Monsignor John Brenkle, interview.

200 *Authorities in the Church . . . did not investigate thoroughly . . .* Father Ray Decker, interview.

200 *Keys made people indebted to him. That's why there is not a lot of criticism . . .* Ibid.

200 *They keep saying it's not that big a deal . . .* Bob Curry, interview.

200 *The simple fact is that the diocese failed to cooperate fully.* "Police say inquiry ended when Diocese failed to cooperate . . . " *Santa Rosa Press Democrat*, February 5, 2000.

201 *What Ziemann did was out of human weakness. What Keys did was calculating and premeditated . . .* Father Ray Decker, interview.

201 *Basically, they threw Ziemann under the bus . . .* Carey Daly, interview.

Chapter 18

204 *A number of priests . . . are just disgusted with Keys . . .* Bob Curry, interview.

204 *I believe that a deal was cut . . .* Carey Daly, interview.

204 *I would like your readers to know . . . that Monsignor Keys was immensely helpful . . .* Keyes' [sic] Strength" Letter, *Santa Rosa Press Democrat*, March 10, 2000.

205 *He had the power, under canon law, to stop it . . .* Bob Curry, interview.

205 *These tragedies . . . have undermined the credibility . . .* "New SR bishop installed," *Santa Rosa Press Democrat*, May 23, 2000.

205 *There can be no code of silence or cloak of secrecy . . .* Ibid.

206 *This stuff, unexamined, happens again and again . . .* Father Ray Decker, interview.

206 *Let us speak of this, you who are wisest, even if it is bad . . .* Sipe, *Sex, Priests and Power*, p. 108.

209 *By the third anniversary of Ziemann's resignation . . . the aftermath of financial violence, were everywhere . . .* "Rebuilding Finances and Faith," *Santa Rosa Press Democrat*, July 23, 2000.

Chapter Notes

210 *If the Consolidated Account had been operated honestly* . . . Carey Daly, interview.

210 *George Patrick Ziemann . . . was . . . at a monastery . . .* Santa *Rosa Press Democrat,* July 23, 2000.

210 *The Reverend Jorge Hume Salas . . . was in his native Costa Rica,* Ibid.

210 *On July 1, 2001, the diocese of Santa Rosa ceased all involvement . . .* Santa Rosa Press Democrat, July 22, 2001.

211 *Who truly knew Christ's gospel and would preach it . . .* Chaucer, *Geoffrey, The Canterbury Tales,* Penguin Classics Edition, Prologue, pp. 16–17.

Chapter 19

214 *We are convinced . . . Who We Are,* www.cta@cta-usa.org

215 *The issues that are our major concerns are almost nonexistent in the gospels.* Anthony Padovano, address to CTA Conference, Plenary session, August 12, 2000.

216 *There are other organizations . . . who maintain . . . that they are following the legitimate dictates . . . What is Opus Dei?,* Opus Dei *Awareness Network,* www.odan.org

216 *They got it wrong . . .* Padovano, CTA Conference address.

222 *In 1999, the People's Republic of China appointed five Roman Catholic bishops . . .* "China's ordinations may be traditional after all," *National Catholic Reporter,* June 8, 2000.

222 *Celibacy . . . shouldn't have been linked to order . . .* Padovano, CTA Conference address.

Chapter 20

226 *Pope John Paul II . . . delivered . . . a denunciation of "materialist consumerism . . .* "Pope blasts consumerism as human rights threat," *National Catholic Reporter,* NCR Online archives, www.natcath.com

227 *Before our eyes we have the results of ideologies . . .* Ibid.

229   *In a series of surveys of American Catholic laity* . . . "Special Report: American Catholics," *National Catholic Reporter, NCR Online Archives,* www.natcath.com

229   *It's not that they are increasingly angry at the Church* . . . Ibid.

231   *I'd return to the priesthood in a minute if the Pope ever came to his senses* . . . Interview, Joe Skillin, August 7, 2000.

231   *Tod, Teufel, Sund und Holle* . . . . . *Death, devil, sin and hell* . . . No. 64, J.S. Bach, *Christmas Oratorio.*

Bibliography

Ackroyd, Peter. *The Life of Thomas More*. New York: Anchor Books/Random House, 1998.

Bach, J.S. *Christmas Oratorio*, libretto. Calif.: Sonoma County Bach Society, 1999.

Berry, Jason. *Lead Us Not Into Temptation, Catholic Priests and the Sexual Abuse of Children*. New York: Image Books/Doubleday, 1994.

Chaucer, Geoffrey. *The Canterbury Tales*, Penguin Classics Edition. London: Penguin Books, Ltd., 1951.

Cornwell, John. *Hitler's Pope, The Secret History of Pius XII*. New York: Viking, 1999.

Daly, William P. *The Laborer is Worthy of His Hire, A Survey of Priests' Compensation in the Roman Catholic Diocese of the United States*, 1999 edition. Chicago: The National Federation of Priests' Councils.

Dourley, John P. *The Illness That We Are, A Jungian Critique of Christianity*. Toronto: Inner City Books, 1984.

Dulles, Avery. *Models of the Church*. New York: Image Books/Doubleday, 1978.

BIBLIOGRAPHY

Fox, Matthew. *Original Blessing*. Santa Fe: Bear & Co., 1983.

Hurley, Mark J. *Blood on the Shamrock, An American Ponders Northern Ireland*. New York: Peter Lang, 1990.

Johnson, Paul. *A History of Christianity*. New York: Simon & Schuster, 1976.

Lacouture, Jean. *The Jesuits, A Multibiography*. Washington, D.C.: Counterpoint, 1995.

Lynn, Kenneth S. *Charlie Chaplin and His Times*. New York: Simon & Schuster, 1997.

National Federation of Priests' Councils, *Consultation on Priests' Morale, a review of research*, funded by The Lilly Endowment. Chicago: National Federation of Priests' Councils, 1994.

Powers, J.F. *Morte D'Urban*, New York Review Classics edition. New York: 2000.

Price, Reynolds. *Three Gospels*. New York: Simon & Schuster, 1996.

St. Leo's Diocesan Crisis Survey. Boyes Springs, Calif.: St. Leo's Church, January 8–9, 2000.

Santa Rosa Police Department. *Crime/Case Report #99-10694, Sexual Battery, Oral Copulation*.

Santa Rosa Police Department. *Crime/Case Report #99-19262, Suspicious Cirumstances*.

Sipe, A.W. Richard. *The Sipe Report, a preliminary expert report*. www.thelinkup.com

Sipe, A.W. Richard. *A Secret World, Sexuality and the Search for Celibacy*. New York: Brunner/Mazel, 1990.

Sipe, A.W. Richard. *Sex, Priests and Power, Anatomy of a Crisis*. New York: Brunner/Mazel, 1995.

Unsworth, Tim. *The Last Priests in America, Conversations with Remarkable Men*. New York: Crossroad, 1993.

Wilhelm, Anthony. *Christ Among Us, A Modern Presentation of The Catholic Faith for Adults*. San Francisco: Harper/San Francisco, 1996.

Wilkes, Paul. *The Good Enough Catholic, A Guide for the Perplexed.* New York: Ballantine Books, 1996.

Wills, Garry. *Papal Sins, Structures of Deceit.* New York: Doubleday, 2000.

Wilson, A.N. *Jesus, A Life.* New York: Fawcett/Columbine, 1992.

Index

INDEX

INDEX

INDEX

civil suit settlement and, 98,
177-78
in Costa Rica, 210
immoral behavior of, 3-4, 14,
72-74, 86, 132, 142
investigation of, 131-32
Mendoza and, 85-86
ordination of, 7, 8
parishioner complaints about,
13-14, 76, 86, 97, 104
St. John's Church assign-
ment, 79
youth soccer team supporter, 6
Ziemann
cover-up of theft by, 4-5,
83-85, 86, 95-96, 139
meetings with, 76-77, 87-90,
228
relationship with, 75, 78-
79, 103
sex with, 14-15, 16-17,
17-19, 71, 77, 87, 142
Hume Salas' suit against Ziemann
See also Hume Salas; Ziemann, Most Reverend
Bishop
attorney rhetoric, 132-33
consequences of, in Diocese,
199
criminal charges dropped,
141-44
Hume Salas background
leaked, 132
investigation and filing of,
103-10

semen sample and tape of
Ziemann, 77-78, 97-98,
103, 142
settlement of civil suit,
175-78
Hurley, Bishop Mark J., 63-64,
67, 196

Ineffabilis Deus, 146

Jerome, Saint, 35
Jesus, xii, 51, 67, 167-68, 179,
207
See also Bible quotes
Johnson, Paul, 34
Jones, Mark, 51
Judin, Jay, 19-20, 104

Kazantzakis, Nikos, 43
Keillor, Garrison, 66
Kelly, Sister Jane
accused of working for Ziemann, 133
berates Levada in public,
153-54
biographical information,
12-13
conscience-governed, 6, 93-94,
126
on Hume Salas, 5, 8, 98,
176-77
on Keys, 87, 208
on male chauvinistic denial
hierarchy, 102
silent protest at Chancery
Office, 148-52

INDEX

INDEX